THE EVOLVING MIND

Robin Cooper (Ratnaprabha)

The Evolving Mind

Buddhism, Biology, and Consciousness

Windhorse Publications

Published by Windhorse Publications
Unit 1-316 The Custard Factory
Gibb Street
Birmingham
B9 4AA

Printed by Biddles Ltd, Walnut Tree House,
Woodbridge Park, Guildford, Surrey, GU1 1DA

Design   Lisa Dedman
Cover design   Dhammarati
Illustrations   Andy Gammon
Cover illustration   Swayambhunath Stupa, Kathmandu
Photo by Gavin Hellier, ASPECT

We quote by permission of the Pali Text Society
which owns the copyright in the following works:
I.B. Horner (trans), *Middle Length Sayings*, vols I & II, Luzac 1954 and 1957
C.R. Davids, *Psalms of the Sisters*, Luzac 1980 (1st edn 1909)

British Library Cataloguing in Publication Data
A catalogue record for this book is available from the British Library

ISBN 0 904766 74 8

CONTENTS

About the Author

Born in London in 1954, Robin Cooper developed an early fascination for natural history. After obtaining a First in physics at Sussex University, he went on to study the history and sociology of science. On leaving university, he joined the physics department of the Open University to teach and produce the science courses pursuing research in environmental physics.

At this time Robin Cooper became more and more drawn to Buddhism and Buddhist practices. In 1982, while living as part of a Buddhist community in Norfolk, he was accepted into the Western Buddhist Order, being given the ordination name Ratnaprabha. Since then he has been teaching Buddhism and meditation, and lecturing on Buddhism and related topics in Scandinavia, Spain, and Singapore, as well as in Britain. In 1986 he moved to Cambridge to write, and to help found the Cambridge Buddhist Centre where he is now chairman.

INTRODUCTION

The strongest principle of growth lies in human choice.
George Eliot, *Daniel Deronda*, 489

A PERSONAL PREAMBLE

The giant panda; the Cuban solenodon; the spectral aye-aye of the
Madagascan forests; the vast blue whale in the vaster ocean deeps: as
a seven year-old child, I watched these creatures emerging from their
hiding places. They were hiding in packets of tea.

When the kind dinner lady had finished her chores, she would find
me standing shyly by the door to the school kitchen. Then she would
give me another two or three of those little oblong picture cards that
came with Brooke Bond tea. Other cards – the ones which came with
bubble gum or Weetabix – I would happily gamble away in games of
card-flicking on the tarmac of the school playground. But not these.
These were somehow precious, wonderful: a first introduction to
knowledge of the world's strange animals; a first stirring of empathy
with living things, and of indignation at the exploitation of their
helplessness.

I took the tea cards home, and reverently stuck them in a picture book. Series on tropical birds, African animals, and others followed. But it is those first fifty pictures with their poignant captions that are most vivid in my memory. Even now, the aroma of a new packet of PG Tips brings back the images. The series was on Animals in Danger: in danger, of course, from man's depredations. I was a child, and my heart was open; indignation fountained from it at the plight of threatened creatures. And a child's natural but evanescent solidarity with the living world was embossed on my mind by a new understanding, present even now.

Those picture cards were the source of a stream of choices which fed my fascination with animals and their evolution. Another stream, weaker at first, flowed among fields of the human mind, as I tried to comprehend my own consciousness and its slow and painful maturing. The two streams of interest remained quite separate until I came across Buddhism, with its dedication to the seemingly conflicting aims of expressing active compassion for all that lives, and cultivating the individual mind without limit. I began to see that, for me at least, Buddhism shared an underlying rationale with biology and the study of consciousness. That rationale is the evolving mind.

During my teens, the combination of empathy and indignation on animals' behalf gradually transferred itself to people: fervent discussions, written political tirades, huge marches from Hyde Park Corner to Trafalgar Square. I felt shocked at the injustice that the less powerful individuals faced from powerful groups; in Vietnam, in Ireland, in South Africa. Was it real empathy? Was it the personal solidarity that a kind person feels for another in trouble? I think it wasn't, or not wholly. The oppressed groups were distant. I did not know it, but they symbolized the imprisonment I felt as a boy sullenly struggling through adolescence, wrestling with my divorced mother's reasonable restrictions. For a time I reserved my love for a menagerie of pets, and for the zoo animals that I visited again and again, enchanted. Human beings were still marked for me with the guilt of betraying those animals, so trusting, beautiful, defenceless.

Yet a sense of justice was gradually focusing itself in discussion and thought on left-wing politics, so that an idea of a wise and kind essence of 'humanity' was distilled in my imagination into an ideal to feel passionately for. And as I entered the world of academic science, the animals returned. I studied Darwin and the ferment his ideas gave rise to. I tried to fathom evolution.

Meanwhile, something else had been happening, something far more difficult to articulate from wordless memories, although it doubtless occurs in everybody. In fits and starts, I had become more self-aware. I discovered vantages from which I could survey my inner world, my continuation through time, and I developed a small ability to choose what I would experience. A vivid memory is there (I was eight, perhaps) of looking back at the terraced houses, a sunlit green gate to a garage drive, my dog running joyfully and obliviously ahead, and telling myself: 'This is now, take it all in, it will never happen again!' Or, eager to be free from school and all restriction, admonishing my future self: 'Remember, O remember! These are not the happy and carefree days of adult myth.'

Now I feel gratitude, even a sense of reverence, for the boy who struggled so for a higher degree of awareness. It is my impression that very many people have magically vivid experiences during adolescence or before. They hear an imploring voice, as it were, from their brightest possible future, intuiting an intensification of awareness. It may become anchored (I would say prematurely) in religious piety, but usually it is forgotten, fading for the lack of a language in which to affirm its reality. It seems a great loss to settle into the routine responsibilities of human maturity without some lingering sense of the wider dimensions of consciousness. Herman Melville glued a note to the desk where he wrote *Moby Dick*: 'Keep true to the dreams of thy youth.'[1]

BUDDHISM AND EVOLUTION

Another deeply charged memory that remains with me is of lying in bed as a teenager and feeling that I ought to meditate. (Why? It seems eerie now.) So I shut my eyes and tried. However, I had no idea what meditation was, and got nowhere. The notion remained dormant until years later when I found a meditation teacher. My university finals were about to start, yet I tried to practise meditation every day. Half a year later I was writing on Darwin and on world-views as part of postgraduate work. At the meditation centre in a crumbling little terraced house in Brighton, the title of a taped lecture caught my eye: 'Evolution, Lower and Higher'. It was by the English Buddhist teacher, Sangharakshita. Later I met him; later still he agreed to ordain me into the Western Buddhist Order.

Sangharakshita tried to present a grand vision of evolution, from the organic development of species right up to the self-selected evolution of an individual bent on enlightenment. Herbert Spencer attempted something vaguely similar in Darwin's time, and many have widened the connotation of the word 'evolution' since. The difference here was that Sangharakshita put evolution – all evolution – in a Buddhist context. And Buddhism, as he presented it, seemed so intrinsically evolutionary yet so much more far-reaching than Western scientific and religious views that a great excitement gripped me as I listened to the tape. That excitement led me, nearly ten years later, to start work on this book.

Religion had baffled me in my period of teenage idealism. I was rudely dismissive of the God notion, yet people seemed to need to worship, to need an image of perfection that filled a yearning sky. I too felt an immanent sense of reverence. Perhaps, I mused, evolving humanity could provide the transcendent image? Yes! And a sort of vision of some future perfected man had coalesced in my mind, fused from science fiction stories and ideas of biological evolution. This would be the being to worship: an imagined paragon, freed by the evolutionary process of all flaws of body and spirit.

There was something similar about Sangharakshita's Buddhist view of further evolution, and something radically different. He claimed that one did not need to wait for some hoped-for evolutionary future, but that all the further evolution that really mattered (the evolution of consciousness) could be telescoped into each person's individual life. This further evolution was the deliberate process of refining one's mind and its responses; Sangharakshita termed it the path of higher evolution. He said that the enlightened sages of the past and present are, if genuine, people who have traversed the path, and they try to indicate its twists and turns to others.[2]

Meditation had already had a tangible effect upon my degree of awareness, so I had an inkling of the value of refining the mind, and I felt very excited to have encountered a 'religious' system which was so immediate and human-centred. In any case, studying Darwinism was undermining my faith in a future being, perfected by biological evolution. What was there to guarantee this continued evolution? Current New Age thinking has a major blind spot here, I believe. There are very good reasons for supposing that we are born no kinder or wiser now than were our ancestors twenty and more centuries ago: nothing automatic and collective can take the human mind any further, whatever hopeful New Age believers may read in the stars.

LOWER AND HIGHER EVOLUTION

If Sangharakshita's 'higher evolution' was not something happening to the whole human species, or to any race or grouping within it, then why call it evolution? Surely the biological evolution of living forms was the real thing, other uses of the word being loose or confusing? However, reading some of the eighteenth- and nineteenth-century sources, I realized that the word evolution has narrowed in its meaning as it has been defined more and more tightly in biological terms. What usually happens when something evolves is that it changes gradually into a more complex or advanced form, whether it is a lineage of horses, of jet engines, of library systems, or of human minds. Indeed, when it was first used in connection with living things in the eighteenth century, 'evolution' was applied to the development of an embryo in the womb or egg.

An expansion of awareness and sensitivity in someone following a spiritual path can, then, reasonably be called an evolution. Applying evolution to the mind in this way prompts us to look back on biological evolution in similar terms. And, yes, as life has evolved, there has been a continuous improvement in the best mental abilities of each successive period. The brightest animals have got brighter and brighter, culminating in mankind. There may have been other increases over evolutionary time, but the only increase that has intrinsic value is the rising level of consciousness, that is, of the scope of the mind's awareness. So we can be unashamedly human-centred! It seems obvious to me that if we want to see evolution as an evolution in some quality that living forms possess, mind is the one to select. Sangharakshita took that for granted in the taped lecture I heard, and so he saw a continuity between the lower (biological) evolution that culminated in self-aware human beings, and the higher (spiritual) evolution that a self-aware person can follow.

He also stressed the differences between the two: lower evolution is unconscious and collective, higher is conscious and individual. (By unconscious, he did not mean without consciousness in the sense in which I use the term here, but without self-consciousness.) Lacking a close knowledge of developments in evolutionary biology, Sangharakshita missed something here, I think, that would have strengthened his argument: even in lower evolution, the choices of the individual animal can play a significant role. Lower and higher evolution are distinct, yet there are striking continuities between them.

Consciousness evolves, but not as a powerless plaything of biological forces. Consciousness in animals and humans contributes to its own evolutionary future; it nurtures the seeds of its own expansion, and so gives a direction to evolution.

This morning, two young starlings were bickering on the roof outside, splendid in their flecked winter jackets. They were alert and angry, inquisitive and quick: full to bursting with vitality. In my life too, a rush of energy, like my excitement over hearing the Buddhist lecture, feels of a very similar nature – a vitality that characterizes all living creatures, and drives evolution. I cannot believe in the mysterious 'life force' of the vitalist philosophers; in a way there is nothing mysterious about the adventurous energy of life itself. The philosopher of biology T.A. Goudge put it very neatly: 'The overall direction of evolution is towards the enlargement and amplification of life.'[3]

I started to appreciate that evolution is a framework or vision which comprehends life and the world, and, as Buddhism demonstrates, it can include an effective spiritual dimension, a programme for raising one's consciousness beyond the average human level. No being or consciousness is required outside the evolutionary process; a god claiming to fashion and command the world thus turns out (I was relieved to hear) to be unnecessary. And human beings are within nature. Those victimized animals on the tea cards still call to me; we cannot disown them. They are our cousins, myopic perhaps, but the life pulsing in them is the same life that shines behind our own eyes.

EVOLUTION'S FOUR DIMENSIONS

The life of any animal is composed of a string of sensations, followed by responses. The blue whale hears the booming songs of its fellows, and swims half an ocean to rejoin them. Finding a clump of tender bamboos, a panda ambles over and grabs the choicest shoots to eat. How does an animal respond appropriately to its sensations? By using its mind. That is what mind is for; that is why mind evolved.

We are going to consider evolution primarily as a development of mind, of consciousness. You will be able to follow the account most clearly if you recognize that there are four strands or dimensions of evolution: three relate to lower evolution, and higher evolution is the fourth. As well as the lower evolution of minds, there has been, of course, a biological evolution of the physical form of animals. The third dimension of lower evolution is culture – a gradual advance in the

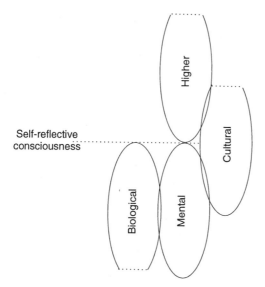

Fig.1 The four dimensions of evolution[4]

sophistication of social traditions, patterns of behaviour learnt and passed on down the generations.

Culture is not unique to human beings. Many social animals develop cultures. The learnt local song dialects in some species of birds, for instance, and cultural forms in animals and humans, evolve over time. Animals had to evolve a certain mental sophistication before they could create cultures; they had to be able to learn patterns of traditional behaviour. So cultural evolution depends on how far consciousness has evolved. In turn, some cultural contexts can stimulate the further evolution of consciousness; for example, as soon as early humans learnt to speak (a cultural form), they had a new tool, language, for exploring their own experience, and self-awareness became more of a possibility.

The mental and cultural are not the only strands of evolution to interact. Most obvious is the way biological evolution influences all the other three dimensions. For example, you cannot speak unless you can control sounds with structures like a voice box, tongue, and lips. You cannot think very well without a large and complex brain.

At first sight, one might not expect there to be any influences on biological evolution from the other dimensions, but, remarkably, there are. We shall see that animal behaviours that become long-lasting traditions can completely alter the course of evolution. They can create quite new environments, in which new varieties of animal will tend to evolve; in these cases, it is a matter of a culture guiding the genes to produce a new species. And where do behaviours come from? The mind. A rabbit bolts when someone comes near because the complex of sensations that enter its mind 'means' danger to it, and its pattern of responses, inborn and learnt, culminate in flight. It can learn, again via its mind, to become tamer. Occasionally, its evolving mind might come up with a new response, subtly altering the options available to rabbits.

When I started work on this book, I was not aware of the surprising connections between the evolution of new species and the behaviours of evolving animals. Then I came across the books of Alister Hardy, a marine biologist who set up the Religious Experiences Research Unit in Oxford in his later years. In his enthusiasm to champion the centrality of consciousness in evolution, Hardy lays great stress on behavioural selection (I shall call it behaviour-led selection), an idea originating before the turn of the century, but forgotten for fifty years in the excitement over the rediscovery of Gregor Mendel's work on biological inheritance.

Hardy's favourite example is the hypothetical transformation of birds' beaks by the evolution of their feeding behaviour. Birds which developed a tradition of probing in bark crevices for insects would, over the generations, tend to develop a beak increasingly suitable for their new feeding ability, since birds born with slightly better beaks would feed, and therefore breed, more successfully.[5]

The significance of behaviour-led selection has not been challenged, but neither has it been investigated closely by today's researchers. Nevertheless, Hardy finds very distinguished supporters among the great biologists of this century including Julian Huxley and Ernst Mayr, and C.H. Waddington, who concluded that 'we have considerable grounds for believing that mentality in the broad sense, or at least behaviour (biologists tend to be very timid about mentioning the mind), is a factor in evolution'.[6] As early as 1900, H.W. Conn was insisting that 'this conception of the action of selection evidently makes consciousness a factor in evolution'.[7] I shall suggest how consciousness is probably *the* factor in opening up new possibilities in animal evolution, particularly in reaching for further advances in consciousness itself.

So it is not only cultural and mental evolution that interact, but also biological and mental evolution; consequently, all three strands of lower evolution form an interconnected system. I shall not discuss any possible interactions between higher evolution and biological form. But I will be looking in some detail at how higher evolution fits into the overall development of consciousness, and at how it interacts with culture.

The Evolving Mind

We human beings are eager to understand ourselves and our world. Understanding is the business both of science and of Buddhism, and this book follows evolving consciousness through the domains of both these great traditions. Our consciousness receives the discoveries of the senses as they reach out for knowledge of the world. It takes in ideas and memories too, and attempts to find significance in their labyrinthine interrelationships. The phenomena in the world which are, like us, alive, are the most complex of all.

I would say that consciousness itself is the Ariadne's thread that indicates a path of intelligibility through the labyrinth of the living world. It does not reach into every chamber: plants are without mind, and mental capacities have stagnated in some lineages of animals. However, each one of us holds that shining thread in our hand; do we wish to follow it back?

In lower evolution, mind, that is, consciousness, has evolved. It has evolved in two vehicles: in physical bodies, which have developed through biological evolution, and in the collective traditions of animal and human behaviour, evolving through cultural evolution. Its evolution can continue in any self-aware person through higher evolution. The evolution of consciousness, then, that Ariadne's thread, is the string upon which the successive chapters of this book are strung.

Chapter 1 shows how evolution can be seen as continual self-transcendence, and stresses the importance of this concept. Charles Darwin, we shall see, demonstrated the reality of evolution and discovered its mechanism. Chapter 2 explains this mechanism – natural selection – and gives an account of the biological evolution of the lineages of living forms that gave rise to human beings. Chapter 3 looks at how animals' minds appeared, and at the stages the mind traversed as it evolved. Chapter 4 describes how mental factors, via animal behaviour, have influenced the biological process of evolution. Is there also a unique spiral process, intrinsic to consciousness, by which any mind has a tendency to stimulate the production of more sophisticated minds in future generations? Chapter 4 goes on to consider the evolution of culture in animals.

A great turning point in the evolution of consciousness was reached with the first appearance of people who could be aware of their own awareness. This self-reflective consciousness is the topic of chapter 5.

The history of the evolving mind is a chronicle of the successive attainment of new, less limited levels of consciousness. Different species of animals achieve different degrees of mental capacity. Any individual person fluctuates greatly in the scope of his or her awareness. I spend time each night in a deep and dreamless sleep in which awareness is all but extinguished, but at times I can feel quite bright and alert, fully self-conscious. And exceptional people seem to have attained to states of mind in which the boundaries of awareness are stretched and attenuated to an unimaginable extent.

Our brains have been big enough for self-reflective consciousness for a very long time: they have not significantly changed in size for a hundred millennia. Occasionally, during those thousands of generations, the right kind of mind has found itself in the right kind of cultural environment for self-knowledge to dawn. This seems to be as far as collective forms of mental evolution can take us – to an illuminated awareness of standing at the gateway to unexplored domains of human experience.

Every person, perhaps many times in their life, is like an amphibian washed up on a beach: the beach of self-awareness. Behind is the fertile ocean of lower evolution, teeming with living forms. Ahead is the unknown continent, invisible behind a ridge of shingle. It is so tempting to return to the supportive and nurturing billows of relative unconsciousness, and let them bear one dimly through a life like a million other lives. The alternative, the landward journey, must be undertaken by an individual decision, an individual effort. In other words self-reflective consciousness is the prerequisite for higher evolution, and higher evolution is not an automatic product of a particular stage in the evolution of bodily form, of mental capacity or of human culture. It is a personal choice, repeatedly available to each man and woman.

The first records of attempts at exploring consciousness from the base of self-reflection turn up in the 'axial age', considered in chapter 6. The period of a few centuries around 500BCE* is axial in that innovative individuals in several parts of the world initiated – independently, and

---

*   Buddhists and other non-Christians do not use the terms AD – 'Year of our Lord' – and BC. They refer to years under this accepted dating convention as either CE (Common Era) or BCE (Before Common Era)

at the same time – many fateful new movements in history. All the great world religions can trace their origins to this period, even those whose founders lived much later, and virtually all the possible major standpoints in human thought seem to have been discovered then. Chapter 7 concentrates on these axial age pioneers, and the universal religions that some of them inaugurated.

It was bound to happen sooner or later that self-aware people swimming along in the stream of cultural evolution should raise their heads high enough above the swirling currents to perceive the whole stream itself, to conceive of an evolutionary world view. The idea was present in some circles in Ancient Greece, and perhaps in China too (see Appendix). As far as I can tell, though, and this seems rather strange, only one of those axial sages who founded a great tradition of thought and religion also had a profoundly evolutionary vision. That was the Buddha. Consequently, only Buddhism among the major spiritual traditions seems to be intrinsically evolutionary (although similar notions can be traced in Chinese thought).

To simplify drastically, Judaism and its daughter religions, including Christianity, see humanity as enacting a grand historical drama, initiated and concluded by a non-natural, divine intervention. Before, the theatre is in an eternity of darkness; after, the actors are consigned to an indefinite period of 'resting': in passive bliss if heroes, in cruel torment if villains. In mainstream Hinduism, on the other hand, the cosmos is cyclic. Life and humanity perpetually renew a dance of emergence from and return to a ground of Being.

This is not to dismiss the heroic efforts of sincere thinkers from many backgrounds, especially Christians, to reconcile an evolutionary view with bounded myths such as the Christian one of creation, fall, redemption, and judgement. Yet still I maintain that Buddhism is the most evolutionary of traditions, by far. When I began to explore Buddhist ideas, that evolutionary perspective seemed one of its most attractive features.

Its chief concern is with the higher evolution of the individual. It also has several myths of the origins of humanity, all being evolution stories. But these are given very little prominence in Buddhism, and I feel that much of their usefulness has been superseded by the beautiful and accurate origin-accounts of Darwinian evolution. (These myths are not a part of the argument of this book, but some have been included for interest in the Appendix. I have never encountered a Buddhist who takes them literally, though doubtless such do exist.)

Chapter 8 covers the process by which the founder of Buddhism traversed the path of higher evolution, and the terms that he and his followers used to describe the evolutionary foundations of that path. Chapter 9 shows how full self-reflective consciousness is equivalent to the Buddhist term 'mindfulness', and describes the progressive sequence of states of consciousness that can be cultivated from a basis of mindfulness, according to the Buddhist tradition. We shall see that the most expanded and blissful meditative states are valuable, but are quite different from the kind of consciousness which is Buddhism's objective.

There is a characteristic – self-transcendence – that marks the history of consciousness as an evolution in the full sense, and not just a meandering process of change. Individual animals that pioneered new behaviours and thus opened the way for new species to evolve were transcending their inherited habits of life. The axial sages who had the courage to use their self-awareness to explore hidden potentials of consciousness were also transcending themselves. Chapter 10 looks at the Buddhist methods for completing the process of self-transcendence.

In chapter 10 we investigate the faculty of unlimited awareness that does not recognize the time-honoured boundaries between internal and external experience, and which culminates in enlightenment. Its effect on life is compassion – the final achievement of higher evolution. Compassion is the disowning of any vestiges of self-other boundaries which might distinguish one's own interests from another's. Compassion is the overwhelming impulse to dedicate one's life to the happiness and fulfilment of every being that plays and suffers in those oceans and on those beaches of evolution.

Chapter One

THE SCOPE OF THE EVOLUTIONARY VISION

*We must take the best and most indisputable of human doctrines and
embark on that, as if it were a raft on which to risk the voyage of life.*
Plato, quoted Eiseley, *The Unexpected Universe*, 26

BEYOND THE STATUS QUO

Walking innocently through a park in East London, a friend of mine
was confronted by a group of skinheads, who taunted him because he
looked a little bohemian. Then one of them hit him in the face; and they
all seemed ready to pitch in and give him a nasty beating. My friend's
reaction was unusual. He told me he felt neither frightened nor angry,
only rather surprised. 'Why did you do that?' he asked. They were at
a loss; if he'd fled in terror, or if he had fought back, they would have
happily continued their assault, but in the face of his calmness they just
walked on past him, muttering a few more imprecations in farewell.

It wasn't an extraordinary incident, but I mention it because my
friend was taken aback by his own response. Not so long before, he
said, he would have had no other choices than fight or flight, and he
would probably have been beaten up. But something in him had

moved on (he is a Buddhist, and the change may have been due to his meditation practice), so that he could face the attack without descending into the skinheads' world of ill-will and fear.

In developing a new equanimity, he had changed. He had gone beyond the limitations of his former self, in an act of self-transcendence. The friend I knew had been impulsive, even a bit aggressive at times, so his calm response to the attack surprised me as much as him. I knew his old self quite well, and the small changes I saw taking place in him were of great interest to me. He was demonstrating the ability of living beings to behave in unexpected ways.

In this chapter I shall discuss self-transcendence as a fundamental property of mind or consciousness at all levels, a property which gives minds a greater role in evolution than biologists generally recognize. In adopting the term 'self-transcendence', I am referring not to any concept from European philosophy, but to the potential that every mind seems to have to generate unprecedented responses, a potential that may be important in the evolution of the higher animals. From the point of view of self-transcendence, evolution is much more than a biological theory. It provides the most fruitful and realistic framework for viewing existence as a whole, as well as for appreciating fully the value of a person.

Is it possible to describe a person fully as they are now? All observers of life, from scientists to novelists, choose a subject and then try to depict its *status quo*. A snapshot of the present state of affairs is not sufficient. To understand someone, you need to see them in their different moods, engaged in various tasks. You need to be with them and watch the play of expressions on their face. More than watching, you need to listen to what their voice conveys, even to feel with them in their crises and triumphs, as well as in the boring routines of life. And then, maybe, you've captured the state of affairs that is that person. You've caught them as a dynamic personality, sometimes adaptable, sometimes habit-bound. But have you really caught them? Someone asks: 'What sort of a person are they?' and you try to sum them up. However, the next time you meet them, they might surprise you, because they may decide *not* to act within the character you have delineated so exhaustively.

It seems to me that this unpredictability is a mark of any evolving being, any evolving system, especially one with a mind. It exhibits a state of affairs that you can come to know in ever greater detail. It also retains a capacity to surprise you, to take a quite new direction. No matter how hard you try to tag all the new things it might become, eventually it will become something quite different: it will transcend itself.

For me, self-transcendence is what makes evolving systems so fascinating. One day we (or our grandchildren) may arrive on a youthful planet where life is just beginning to appear in the soupy oceans. But even if the new world is much like the early earth, we will not be able to picture accurately what sort of creatures will be sporting in the same oceans in the planet's future. Life is stick-in-the-mud, yes, and successful forms can follow their limited life-styles for millions of generations pretty much unchanged. But life also extricates itself from the sticky mud and finds ways of being that go beyond the old ones in unpredictable ways.

Choice, self-transcendence, and Buddhism

In animal or lower evolution, new ways of being arise through a number of mechanisms, as we shall see in the next three chapters. With human beings, a quite different method of self-transcendence becomes possible: conscious choice. Every human life has its habitual routines which express the *status quo*, and every human personality provides standard responses to familiar experiences. So my friend believed that if he did not fight, he would have to run away. Yet, as he did then, one often faces opportunities for rising above the routine.

The chance to open a quite new direction for one's character, such as responding to provocation with equanimity, may come infrequently. But tiny opportunities for conscious self-transcendence arise all the time, hard though it is to recognize them. In such moments, a new, creative response is accessible. If one only has the confidence, one is presented with a genuine choice.

I think that this power of conscious choice is a vital human endowment. It allows meaning to enter one's life, since one can decide on the course one's life should best take. It ensures one is not impelled down instinctual roads of action, but can search out and adopt a new solution to any dilemma. It permits artistic creativity and the opening up of new styles of life, and it even permits progress to human enlightenment in the Buddhist sense, by means which we shall explore later.

A significant image of self-transcendence in the Buddhist tradition is the 'going forth', in which an individual is seen leaving behind all that is familiar and secure to strike out into the unknown in search of freedom. The classic picture is of the founder of Buddhism galloping away from his sleeping wife and child, letting go of wealth and power, to don the rags of a hunter and live as a wandering ascetic. For an aspiring Buddhist, the going forth might be a process of disentangling himself or herself from inner emotional attachments, but it also usually involves a radical change of life-style, with a drastic reduction in worldly responsibilities.

However, the heart of the Buddhist system is an unending 'inner' self-transcendence. Human life is not satisfactory; the human world is obsolete in some respects and needs making anew. As well as having the means to make the same old mistakes in updated ways, people have a potential for creativity. With sufficient awareness, the existing state of affairs can always be the basis for a better one: a wiser man, say, or a more compassionate government. According to Buddhism, one can learn self-transcendence. In particular, the Buddhist teachings show how awareness can be enhanced progressively by conscious choices, so that one's actions become more effective and more realistic. Each type of consciousness is transcended, yielding a higher type which encompasses more of reality.

SELF-TRANSCENDENCE IN ANIMAL EVOLUTION

A Sussex writer describes watching a fox, hard pressed by a pursuing pack of foxhounds. Out of sight for a moment, it leapt up to the branch of a tree, and watched the frantic hounds pelting by within feet of its perch. Then it calmly jumped down and trotted back along the trail of the pack, so that the hounds would not pick up its scent again.

You probably have your own anecdotes of animal genius.[8] Animal innovators are not making self-conscious choices, but they are, in a sense, 'choosing' new behavioural possibilities. Animals are extremely habit-bound, trammelled both by their mental limitations and by the imperatives of their genes. So even a small innovation in behaviour is of great interest, especially if it spreads through a whole population.

More often the routine behaviour rules, as it must most of the time, since traditions and instincts appeared because they helped survival and reproduction; routine is valuable in its own sphere. To understand self-transcendence it is necessary to see that habits sometimes need breaking, in animals as well as in people. Every animal in its own environment is a marvel of adaptation: the hedgehog rolling into a prickly ball, and so discomfiting even a large and powerful dog; ants that can follow their scouts' scent trails for miles to a source of food, and then eagerly rush back to feed the colony, carrying huge burdens; the monkey that can detect a predator's approach by the slightest of signs or noises.

Yet confronted by a roaring car, the average hedgehog still rolls into a ball, as thousands of flattened corpses on English country lanes testify. There is a famous dirty trick to play on ants: give them a circular scent trail, and they will all relentlessly march round and round in the circle until they drop and die of exhaustion. The South African writer Eugene Marais dug a trench across the habitual track of road-making ants, and filled it with water so that they could not cross. He provided a narrow bridge, but their aversion to water was such that they still would not cross. Carried over the trench by Marais, they would continue on the trail as if nothing had happened, collect food, and return with it across the bridge! This anomalous behaviour never changes, even if one ant has repeated the trip over the water many times. They brave the bridge on the homeward journey, claims Marais, because of the strength of their homing instinct. But they simply cannot learn that a bridge that is safe one way is also safe the other way.[9]

There is a story that some species of monkey can be trapped by baiting a narrow-necked jar with food, and fixing it to the spot. Reaching in and grasping the bait, the monkey cannot withdraw its hand. Yet even the terrifying arrival of the hunter does not induce the self-trapped monkey to let go of the food and thus free its hand! I did not believe this well-known tale until a friend told me he had seen it used successfully in India. It serves well as an epitome of self-defeating greed, as if the victim knows it could escape by relinquishing the food, but cannot bear to let it go. More likely it does not occur to the monkey that holding the food is in any way connected with its hand being trapped.

So animals are extraordinarily habit-bound. But not completely so. There is some variation in what they do from individual to individual, and some flexibility in behaviour, especially if certain habits have to be learnt afresh by each young animal instead of being inborn. If it were not for variations and flexibility, behaviour could not have evolved into the extraordinary variety of ways of life that we see now in the living world.

A group of forest-dwelling monkeys (Japanese macaques, *Macaca fuscata*) were eventually persuaded to frequent the nearby beach, when sweet potatoes were regularly scattered there by experimenters. Major changes of habitat of this kind show that Japanese macaques are not completely habit-bound. Not only that. The animals were able to adapt their behaviour to the new habitat in ingenious ways. First they took to washing the sand off food by carrying it to the sea. The researchers observed how an individual monkey (they named her Ima) invented two separate techniques for washing sweet potatoes and grain and how the less conservative members of the troop learnt from her. Then the monkeys learnt to swim in the sea, a few even diving for seaweed.[10]

Examples of exploration and innovation show that animals have some ability to transcend their existing ways of life – to transcend themselves as they are, and to become something slightly different. Many such self-transcendences seem to add together to yield an evolutionary advance in consciousness, by methods to be considered in chapter 4. Individual animal consciousnesses are the source of innovations, and in the long run the consciousnesses of the innovator's descendants get the advantage of resulting mental advances. Why is the exceptional animal prepared to abandon an ingrained, comfortable habit and transcend its inherited self? Indeed, why do *we* sometimes transcend our time-honoured habits? I don't really know. I do not think it is just by chance. There seems to be something intrinsic to mental functioning that gives any being with a mind the ability to perceive novel possibilities in life, and the courage to explore them if circumstances allow. The self-transcending faculty is present in creatures with the first glimmerings of sentience (whose self-transcending evolution can only proceed in the minutest steps) as well as in the most advanced human meditators. There is a lust for living and for producing descendants which sharply distinguishes living from non-living things. This vitality is usually taken up with the demands of day-to-day life on its own level, living as one's forefathers have and as one's impulses dictate. Yet sometimes the vitality finds a chink in the opaque cycle of life, and beams out as a transcendence. When this happens in oneself, the same principle seems to be operating as when it happens in a Japanese macaque or a magpie.

If such transcendences really are important in animal evolution, as I shall suggest they are, then they demonstrate that mind or consciousness, through its occasional openness to transcendence, is as crucial as the environment in the arising of new forms of animal life. And if self-transcending minds can open up new areas for natural selection to work in, in which animals with greater mental abilities can develop, capable of new forms of self-transcendence, then we have found a progressive process in evolution, culminating in the self-reflective type of consciousness of human beings.

SELF-TRANSCENDENCE IN HUMAN BEINGS

People too can 'evolve', but now through conscious effort, and within their own lifetimes. An animal's options for self-transcendence are very limited. Even if it is intelligent enough to possess learnt traditions, all it can do is to innovate new behaviours that might in turn promote further mental evolution. People, however, are sometimes self-aware, and each time they are self-aware there is an opportunity for further self-transcendence.

Like animals we can transcend our own selves in finding new responses to unfamiliar situations. As a child matures, it transcends itself in a sense over and over again; however, growing up generally follows a pattern well set by biology and cultural tradition. In good conditions, the emerging adult is well adapted (well adjusted, as we say) to his or her milieu, and can go on and raise a similarly well-adapted family, as every other kind of animal attempts to do. So growing up is a self-transcendence only in a very limited sense. It is not really something one chooses to do.

When one is old enough to make choices, each moment of self-reflective consciousness presents one with two or more options, options which can be classified in various ways, and which we shall look at in chapters 8 and 9. For present purposes, the options which transcend the limited self are those which take one at least a little bit beyond one's current boundaries, beyond the sum total of one's cyclic habits, whether learnt or innate. Selecting the transcending options again and again is what is meant by higher evolution.

Few people, very few, are capable of choosing the self-transcending option every time. Yet transcending oneself is not a weird and mystical discipline, it is a matter of common experience. One cannot state for certain which actions do manifest this higher evolutionary principle and which do not. Under some circumstances, buying somebody a bunch of flowers, say, might be a noble, generous, and exuberant act; under others it might be motivated by cynical self-interest. But one usually knows which it is: feelings of guileless happiness, emotional release, or increased insight and understanding tend to follow self-transcending behaviour, and it also, typically, has beneficent consequences. Here are some examples:

- Overcoming an initial resistance and speaking in a friendly way to someone who is lonely
- Persisting with bold integrity in a train of thought, and so coming to original conclusions, truly one's own
- Taking a stand against received opinion when it conflicts with one's principles: for instance, standing back from the general slide into bleary confusion at a party, or helping a scapegoat to overcome general derision
- Breaking free of conditionings to achieve something that someone in one's 'category' would not expect to be capable of, maybe as a woman or a black person, or as someone, say, who is foreign, timid, old, or unemotional.

All these hypothetical transcendences are creative impulses in a self-aware consciousness, which have been firmed and reinforced by being carried through into action. As soon as consciousness becomes self-reflective (on earth this has only happened in the human species as far as we know), such actions can start, that is, higher evolution can start. It seems that everyone intuits this possibility deep down, and feels its urgings: Buddhists would call it an urge for enlightenment. 'The urge for Enlightenment is immanent in all forms and spheres of life, from the humblest to the highest,' writes Sangharakshita, 'and manifests whenever a kind and intelligent action is performed.'[11]

It is because an evolutionary principle can be felt working in one's own life that one easily recognizes a similar principle operating among forms of life that are not self-aware. So it is not that the biological theory of evolution suddenly planted the possibility of spiritual evolution into people's minds. On the contrary, spiritual or higher evolution has been an accessible part of experience for thousands of years, and not just in Buddhism. The uncovering of biological evolution in the last 150 years has simply added a row of pieces to the bottom edge of the evolutionary jigsaw puzzle.

So it is creative responses, emerging from the space of self-reflection, that drive higher evolution, the self-aware kind of evolution. Self-transcendence is what makes evolution a true 'spinning out', a meaning of the Latin root. As it seems to in animals, self-transcendence in people allows consciousness to discover routes to more, or higher, consciousness. Possibilities for self-transcendence are inherent in consciousness, and so consciousness can always sooner or later beget *more* consciousness. Hence self-transcendence provides the pressure that ensures an evolutionary direction of increasing consciousness; it is the key of evolution.

The Evolutionary Vision

Responding creatively to life is not a luxury, reserved for a few artists. Everyone, I think, is more or less trapped in cycles of frustration, struggling to cope with the trials of life, and barred from its richest successes. This is true in every society as well as in the individual. Finding creative responses, which means transcending oneself, is a necessity.

To be creative, you need to believe that creative responses are possible. Ideally, you need a belief system that takes notice of change, one that incorporates an excitement in processes of development and innovation. Consequently, an evolutionary world-view is 'the best ... of human doctrines ... on which to risk the voyage of life'.[12] Our minds seem to need a system or framework for understanding life, at least until we can apprehend reality directly and without the mediation of concepts.

An evolutionary viewpoint is, I would suggest, the most productive framework, as well as the one which seems to accord best with reality. If one sees chiefly the cruelty and confusion of humanity's evolutionary legacy, that can be a spur to create a more fully human self and world. If one has visions of a wonderful evolutionary future, then let them inspire one to bring it into being.

The biologist Julian Huxley (1887–1975) coined the term 'evolutionary vision' in advocating such an outlook, suggesting that 'unlike most theologies, it accepts the inevitability and, indeed, the desirability of change, and it advances by welcoming new discovery, even when this conflicts with the old way of thinking', and 'it shows us mind enthroned above matter, quantity subordinate to quality'.[13] Elsewhere, Huxley went even further, and claimed:

> The different branches of science combine to demonstrate that the universe in its entirety can be regarded as one gigantic process, a process of becoming, of attaining new levels of existence and organization, which can properly be called a genesis or an evolution.[14]

The idea of evolution has emerged repeatedly in diverse cultures since the axial age. Sometimes it has arisen from observing the processes of

physical development or from spiritual ideas of expanding consciousness (this notion of the spiritual path appears at times in just about
all the great religions). Sometimes reflections on the unity of life have
led to evolutionary theories of a diversified descent from common
ancestors.

Long ago, philosophers speculated that animals and humans were
kin in the sense of being included in a network of living species which
all evolved from simpler forms that lived in the past. Yet it was all
speculation until Darwin. Because of Charles Darwin's work, evolution
is now the dominant world-view of the West. Darwin (1809–82) provided the first systematic account of how a causal and continuous
process of evolution could have given rise to the living world of today,
an account supported by twenty-five years of his careful observations
and research.

In biology, at least, evolution was no longer only a philosophical
option; it had become the only tenable scientific theory. It is true that
the mechanisms by which life evolved were only partially understood
(they are better understood now, but still not completely), but the fact
that life *has* evolved has, since Darwin's time, been disputed by reasonable people only very rarely.[15] He established the fact of biological
evolution, and he also provided the first tenable theory of how it works.
After some important modifications, the overwhelming majority of
biologists working today still adhere to a version of Darwin's theory,
which is described in chapter 2.

The chief tenets of the theory were reasonable almost to the point of
self-evidence, once they had been proposed. Many of nature's mysteries were explained, and a number of intriguing avenues to further
research were opened up. This was the main reason why evolution was
greeted so enthusiastically, though certain subsidiary ideological reasons were of great importance. Evolution contributed ammunition
against the biblical fundamentalists, and for some it seemed to provide
excuses for the cut-throat competition and social inequalities of the
capitalist economic system. The success of the biological theory fed
new life into the more all-embracing evolutionary philosophies, too. In
biology, evolution was virtually indisputable. Was it so far-fetched to
suggest that it provided the appropriate viewpoint in other areas of life
and experience as well?

Today, then, 'evolution' is a term that is not restricted to biology. Ideas
are said to evolve, as well as nations, technologies, indeed anything
that changes. When used in a considered way and not merely as a

cliché, however, the idea of evolution connotes more than change. It implies a process which, as in biology, is uninterrupted and causal, and which appears to follow an overall trend.

The sociologist P.A. Sorokin noted that: 'The stand-point of "origin and development and evolution" is our main stand-point in studying anything, from religion to the stock-market. It has rooted itself in our mind so deeply that many of us cannot even conceive of any other – non-historical, or non-evolutionary, or non-developmental – approach to the study of phenomena.'[16] The validity of evolution may seem self-evident, but alternative viewpoints have been taken seriously, and still are by some. Perhaps change is illusory, and things have always been as they are; or perhaps this state of affairs is the outcome of a divine decree. The evolutionary view is surely preferable for most thinking people; even the extreme mechanist who claims that all has come into being by the purely fortuitous jostling of atoms does not get a very sympathetic hearing.

The evolutionary view can accommodate a scale of values without losing its fluidity, and it can envisage ceaseless change without losing meaning and harmony. It maintains that the present situation came about through an orderly process, not contradicted by the discovery of radical and unpredestined changes within that process. With a vision of the evolving mind, future possibilities can be anticipated and pursued without an insistence on predetermined fate; the future is not predictable, but it can be the creation of each human being. I said that self-transcendence is the key to evolution. Conversely, evolution is the viewpoint that best supports the pursuit of self-transcendence.

Buddhism and Evolution

Biology has an evolutionary vision, and so does Buddhism, perhaps alone among the world religions. Biology concentrates on lower evolution, while the main concern of Buddhism is higher evolution. It suggests methods and viewpoints designed to open one to self-transcendence, methods consolidating the self-reflective level of consciousness, particularly by mindfulness practice and ethical awareness. It also offers approaches for establishing types of awareness that are in a sense super-human, using meditation, contact with the wise, and the purging of selfish biases from one's mind so that one can contemplate deeply the significance of one's experience of life. Chapters 8–10 explain some of these methods.

Buddhism is evolutionary in the sense that it promotes a spiritual evolution of consciousness. One builds on one's existing resources and present experience, seeking not just to understand them but to go beyond them. The identifying factors of evolution are all there: changes and developments which are continuous and causal, and which follow an overall trend. The causal factor is the basis of Buddhism as a system of personal development; one tries to find out what mental adjustments and practical disciplines actually achieve the evolutionary changes which are possible at one's current stage of development.

The trend followed is often described as 'towards the goal of enlightenment'. But really, Buddhism has no fixed goal; its aim, its highest value, is continual self-transcendence. Similarly, there is no end to the creative exuberance of a great composer. His final symphony is not the goal of his work. In Buddhism, enlightenment seems not to be a definable state, but endless self-transcendence itself, liberated from all restrictions.

All this may sound very fine, but the possibilities described in Buddhist texts need to be manifested in real people's lives if they are worth anything in practice. Indeed the Buddha asked his followers not to take what he said on trust, but to test it against their personal experience, as a goldsmith tests the purity of a piece of gold. With a book such as this, a reader can do little more than assess the cogency of its arguments and the reasonableness of its evidences. It is too easy to imbibe vast quantities of second-hand experience from the written word, rather than choose a suggested course of action that appears reasonable, and test it thoroughly for oneself.

EVOLUTION AND THE WHEEL OF LIFE

Buddhism, then, is a vast set of principles and practical guidelines designed to be applied in real life. Its literature is of secondary importance. Yet the written word is not *un*important, because it contains a sort of cultural legacy, enabling one to learn from accounts of the experience of others, as well as learning from one's own experience. This fact explains a puzzling image in a well-known Buddhist symbol, the Tibetan Wheel of Life.[17]

The Wheel of Life (*bhavachakra*) depicts the ever-rolling cycles of existence – life-cycles, perhaps – that make up lower evolution. It shows human and non-human beings, including the whole of animal existence, continuously recycling their lives in an endless round from birth to death and on to rebirth. (Rebirth is explained in the appendix.) Driven by vital urges of yearning and aversion, and limited by ignorance, beings seek food, evade danger, acquire skills, find mates, pursue status and material security, and raise their families. Though essential for survival, these activities are repetitive and predictable, and hence the symbol is in the form of a turning wheel. As well as illustrating the circular nature of lower evolution, the Wheel of Life incorporates emblems of the universal possibility of self-transcendence. One segment depicts the animal world, and among the deer and wolves, the fish and geese, there is a solitary human figure, clearly a Buddha. (A Buddha – 'awakened one' – is someone who has fully traversed the path of higher evolution.) He is offering the animals a means of transcending the endless round of animal existence, and what he offers, I think, reveals the secret of the transition from lower to higher evolution. He is shown presenting them with a book.

Fairly obviously, the book represents culture, which involves an evolution – a transcendence – from animal-type to human-type existence. A book is a store of ideas and information. It transmits what it contains from person to person, even from age to age. It is learning, it is culture. Charles Darwin, to take an example, discovered how evolution works, and painstakingly recorded scores of examples in *The Origin of Species*. He is dead, but his book survives, and today we can share it, learn it, and move on from it.

In general animals have little culture, and their consciousness is 'collective' consciousness. Each human has a distinct personality, shaped by unique background, education, choices, personal reflection and so on. In the case of animals, only small chance variations generally distinguish the mind of one animal from the minds of all the other members of its species. There is very little that is personal or individual about one mackerel in a shoal of mackerel; in the same situation, each one would respond in just the same way. Evolution's legacy of inherited ways of responding to the world is a legacy shared to a very large degree by the whole species. Sometimes inborn behaviours are even used to define a particular species. The eighteenth-century parson-naturalist Gilbert White discovered that the willow warbler was not a chiff-chaff when he noticed its consistently different song, although the two look almost identical.

Animals only become distinct individuals through *learning*. This is because no two animals encounter the same circumstances, so that if one creature learns something, that modification of consciousness will be unique to the individual.[18] Learning and the development of culture are, then, the first steps towards individual self-awareness. Being aware of oneself as a separate being who can take independent decisions is the crucial breakthrough in the evolution of consciousness, both in a single life as one matures and also in the history of humanity. I call this stage self-reflective consciousness, and agree with the general view that it is the one essential ability that makes us human. That is why the animals on the Wheel of Life are offered the book: culture and cultural evolution is their self-transcendence, their approach to the self-awareness characteristic of the human world.

Self-reflective consciousness was the next evolutionary step for the animals that evolved into human beings. Self-reflection has its own limitations, however. An intense sense of self leads to separateness. And so egotism and anxiety, with all their appalling consequences, are prominent at the human level.

The next evolutionary step for a self-aware human is to leave behind the tight and isolated ego for more expanded types of consciousness. As I have said, methods for achieving this can be partially conveyed in books, and that is one of the aims of the present work. But in the human world on the Tibetan Wheel of Life, the image of further transcendence is not a Buddha offering a book as it is in the animal world. There is a Buddha, but he offers the staff and bowl of a wandering monk. They signify the renunciation of defensive ego, letting go of one's very attachment to the wheel, always choosing options that take one a little bit beyond the sum total of one's cyclic habits. Carrying a bowl, a symbol of one's basic needs, one walks, mindfully but with a light step, into the unknown, excitedly grasping the wanderer's staff.

THE THREAD OF CONSCIOUSNESS

The unknown is not the *terra incognita* of the old explorers' maps. Rather, it is the unexplored terrain of the mind's potentials, in which further evolutions of consciousness are always accessible.

Truly satisfying meanings for human life can only be found, I think, through the evolution of consciousness. A consciousness is precisely what one is. Its past and its possible futures must surely be urgent matters, supremely urgent, to any thinking person. If one is inclined to accept some form of directed change as the preferred future for one's own consciousness, then a process of similarly evolving consciousness makes best sense of one's past. In this way, the thread of mind, evolving out of the past and into the future, makes sense of the universe, and especially of life.

I hope to show that the thread of developing consciousness runs unbroken from lower evolution into higher evolution. They are continuous, the higher emerging out of the lower, as a waterspout emerges from the ocean. However, higher evolution is applying lower evolution's vitality in a completely new dimension. It requires full self-awareness; it is a creative process, not dominated by circular, repetitive, and habit-bound patterns.

Because we are conscious of ourselves, we can come to understand the past and project ourselves into the future. As I have said, we hold consciousness in our hands like Ariadne's thread. Not only can we follow it back to explore the genesis of our minds, but it can also take us ahead into regions of the labyrinth we have never visited.

When I was a child and recognized a connection with animals, one could say that I was following the thread of consciousness back, though I did not know it at the time. Because powerful remnants of animal perceptions and animal emotions lingered in my experience, I could *feel with* my dog as she raced across Hampstead Heath, I could recognize the languor of a lion yawning in London Zoo. The study of biological evolution is another way of following the thread back. It shows that one is a growing bud on a great tree – a family tree – and all the other buds eventually connect in ancestral relationships. In this way, evolution reveals the unity of life.

If it is true that all life is united, it is particularly true of humanity. Just as a thread of consciousness connects an individual's past and future, so threads of consciousness connect each person with all others. One does not empathize with others just because all have ancestors in common. Empathy also springs from reeling the thread back in memory in one's own life, seeing that everyone grows through similar stages, everyone encounters similar challenges, possibilities, and insecurities. If in his place, yes, one might well behave in the same way as the next man.

An awareness of connections with others is a natural discovery made in some way by every child. Its extension to the whole of humanity, even the whole of life, comes more slowly and is much more difficult to keep in mind. I think it was also slow to dawn in human history. And the same is true of discovering where the thread of consciousness runs in the forward direction. The possibility of affecting the future course of consciousness by deliberately changing oneself and the world is a fresh discovery, both in the growing person and in the human race. Every time one feels a passive victim of circumstances and of one's inborn traits, one has lost knowledge of the thread that gleams into the future.

TWO DISCOVERIES

Following the thread back to reveal connections, following it forward to reveal potentials – one's understanding of both perspectives is fitful. And it faces another obstacle. There is a peculiar thing about considering either the past of consciousness or its future in oneself, which is that it is very difficult to hold both perspectives in mind at once, just as a thread can only be followed in one direction. It may be that people are disposed to specialize in one or the other, the two combining only in exceptional men and women. Perhaps this explains why someone with an enquiring mind usually chooses science *or* art and religion, academic *or* humanistic psychology, history *or* fiction, politics *or* personal growth, the objective *or* the subjective.[19]

Some look for meaning in the unity of life or humanity, some in paths and disciplines of mind-expansion and self-transformation. Under a conviction of hidden unities, people have sought the laws of harmony which underlie both the objective universe and social life. In contrast, an aspiration for the fruits of conscious development has motivated mystics, contemplatives, and visionaries down the ages, as well as the founders of the great universal religions.

Both discoveries can be routes to self-transcendence, since both leap over one's ego boundaries. The unity discovery does so by opening links with others, the self-transformation discovery does so by creating ever new and fluid selves, so that each discovery alone is revolutionary and liberating in its potential consequences. Further, without an awareness of each discovery, how the world suffers! Scan history, and one sees that solidarity with all humanity (let alone with nature) has rarely motivated the acts of the powerful. Nor have they often recognized the human potential for growth and awakening.

Making one of the discoveries is so exciting that one easily gets obsessed, and the other discovery never dawns because it requires such a different mental set. If somebody else excitedly champions the other discovery, one is drawn into an attitude of at least incomprehension and perhaps hostility. So, for example, a Nietzschean individualist, who falls on the self-transformation side of the fence, is highly suspicious of a utopian socialist who struggles for equality and the rights of all.

Each discovery is out of balance without the other. An unbalanced obsession with unity can blind one to the possibility of further evolution. (The connections between consciousnesses do not prevent some of them from being more limited than others.) And if proponents of conscious transformation lack in fellow-feeling, they are tempted to promote unjust and fixed hierarchies of power, with sections of the community becoming despised and oppressed.

There is hope of reconciliation, however. Follow each precarious discovery through, and where does it lead? As we have seen, exploring the past of consciousness can yield a sense of empathy and unity. Does this not produce transcendent love and compassion if one nurtures it and gives it full expression? Pursuing the potential future of one's consciousness reveals possibilities of directed self-transformation, which open to view the secret workings of human experience, and ultimately wisdom. According to Buddhism at least, the highest compassion and the highest wisdom are two sides of the same coin. We shall see in chapter 10 that they are respectively the emotional and perceptual reflexes of an outlook that has dissolved the boundaries between subject and object. The two tendencies are united in an ultimate self-transcendence.

ORIGINS OF THE TWO DISCOVERIES

I call them discoveries because there was a time when *no one seemed to know anything about either of them.* It is almost unbelievable, but there was a time when people knew neither true disinterested sympathy for strangers, nor the possibility of taking responsibility for one's own future.

This is what the silence of the early records conveys, but as I write it, I rebel against the conclusion. There comes into my mind an image of some lake village before the age of metal, and a weary traveller from distant parts being kindly taken into the smoky warmth of a turf hut, fed and comforted. Is that not empathy? Or the starry-eyed son of the same family disobeying his father's prohibition and leaving for the shaman's cave to be his apprentice. Did he not consciously embark upon a spiritual quest? Yet I have to say again: nothing we know of early thought reveals any of the insights that must follow if the discoveries had already been made.

Look at Homer's *Iliad*, *Genesis*, Hammurabi's code of law, *Gilgamesh*, the early Vedas. One can find traditions of hospitality and fair treatment, stories of quests and initiations. But never the conclusion 'it is as wrong to kill your enemy as to kill your uncle', or 'my life is in my own hands; no lore or god can pre-empt my independent discovery of myself, or my moulding of whatever of the future world I can reach'. Homer's epics, for example (around 900BCE), do not know of genuine personal decisions, says one scholar, nor do they display any universal standards of value.[20]

The two breakthroughs in human thought enter recorded culture as discoveries of the first individuals, the first men and women who could stand somewhat aloof from their conditioning, and assess what they knew in objective ways. These pioneers first appear in the axial age, the prolific centuries centring on about 500BCE. Some were statesmen, some were prophets, some were poets, and their very names and personalities come down to us in ghostly echoes.

For evidence of a sense of common humanity, consider the Greek playwright Euripides (480–406BCE), who elicits real sympathy for Medea, though she is a mere barbarian. In China, the philosopher Mo Tzu (flourished 479–438BCE) said:

At present feudal lords know only to love their own states and not those of others. Therefore they do not hesitate to mobilize their states to attack others. Heads of families know only to love their own families and not those of others. Therefore they do not hesitate to mobilize their families to usurp others. And individuals know only to love their own persons and not those of others. Therefore they do not hesitate to mobilize their own persons to injure others.... [This] should be replaced by the way of universal love and mutual benefit ... [which] is to regard other people's countries ... families ... [and] person as one's own.[21]

Similar quotations displaying true fellow-feeling are fairly easy to find in the works of the early sages of Judea, India, China, and Greece.

The possibility of autonomous personal growth seems to dawn more gradually, though it is implicit in frequent exhortations to choose righteous action and reject the unrighteous. It is most explicit in Buddhism, and many quotes could be given. This is from the *Dhammapada*, by the Buddha (about 560–480BCE):[22]

By you must the zealous effort be made. The Tathagatas [Buddhas] are only proclaimers (of the Way). Those who are absorbed in super-conscious states eventually win release from the bondage of [death].... One who does not make use of his (spiritual) opportunities, who, though young and strong, is lazy, weak in aspiration, and inactive, such a lazy person does not find the way to understanding.[23]

Personal growth can be one's evolutionary future. Conscious growth is difficult, but it is easier if one is aware of one's starting point, the nature of the being that one is now. This being is a product of lower evolution, constituted largely of urges and physical characteristics adapted to serve the needs of the animal one has evolved from. So now we shall look at the past of evolution, the transformations of being and mind that led us to the human state.

Chapter Two

NATURAL SELECTION
AND THE EVOLUTION OF LIFE

Every production of nature [is] one which has had a history....
From so simple a beginning endless forms most beautiful and most
wonderful have been, and are being, evolved.
Charles Darwin, *Origin of Species*, 456 and 460

THE UNITY OF NATURE AND NATURAL SELECTION

How did we get here? Here we find ourselves, a diverse community of
two-legged beings, who can see and speak and reflect, filling the globe
with our busy fabrications. In perceiving our unity – humans have far
fewer differences than they have features in common – we naturally
wonder what common process gave rise to us. Searching for our
origins, we notice that we share graded sets of similarities with other
living animals. For instance, chimpanzees are sufficiently like us to
share our curiosity, and a certain slapstick sense of humour. Rabbits
have the same general arrangement of limbs and sense organs. Everything living, from a germ to a tree, uses almost exactly the same set of
complex chemicals as we do to fuel the processes of life.

Charles Darwin and other biologists of the nineteenth century could not help noticing that the array of kinds of organisms now living seemed like one generation of a vast family tree. Humans are like brothers and sisters, chimpanzees like our cousins, and others like our distant relatives. If this similarity reflects a real ancestral relationship, how did the differences we see between the various kinds of animals and plants originate?

Darwin started to answer this question with his theory of natural selection. He wrote in *The Origin of Species*:

> If variations useful to any organic being do occur, assuredly individuals thus characterized will have the best chance of being preserved in the struggle for life; and from the strong principle of inheritance they will tend to produce offspring similarly characterized. This principle of preservation, I have called for the sake of brevity, Natural Selection.[24]

Darwin did not know about genes, how they are transmitted from generation to generation, acting as 'recipes' for the development of new organisms, and how the recipes can get a little modified if the genes mix up or mutate. But he loved the living world, and observed it closely and tirelessly. He noticed that animal and plant breeders can change the appearance of a particular variety by choosing to breed only from certain individuals. They can select only sheep with white wool, dogs with strong jaws, or horses with quiet temperaments. Darwin's own favourites were pigeon fanciers.[25] He surmised that natural pressures could also select in a similar way. Here, nature's preference was not the whim of a pigeon-fancier, but was for efficiency at surviving and raising young.

The fan-tailed pigeon was Darwin's example of artificial selection by breeders. A pigeon-fancier had liked the appearance of a few of his birds, which had wide tails. He had only bred from those with the widest tails in each generation, and eventually he produced a distinct breed, the fan-tail. Similarly, in the wild, nature will 'prefer' a pigeon which, say, flies faster than its contemporaries when chased by a falcon, since it is more likely to survive and raise a brood each year. If its chicks also turn out to be faster than average, then falcons will gradually weed out the slow birds, until the speed characteristic spreads throughout the population. This is natural selection.

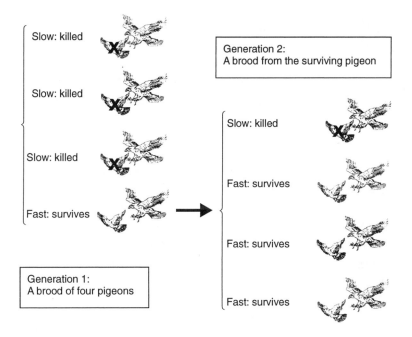

Fig.2 Natural selection of pigeons

Each of the four chief elements that Darwin's process of natural selection requires in order to work has been repeatedly demonstrated as occurring in living organisms. Natural selection must occur if:

- Animals and plants sometimes differ from their parents
- They sometimes pass on these variations to their offspring
- Such inherited variations sometimes help organisms possessing them to leave more offspring than those without them. To use the technical term, the variations can increase an organism's 'fitness'
- A significant proportion of the individuals in each generation – the less fit ones – will not leave descendants.[26]

Darwin saw no reason why the selecting power of nature should stop modifying populations as the generations go by. Eventually, an interbreeding group of organisms (a population) will differ so drastically from its ancestors as to constitute a new species. A particularly streamlined species of wild pigeon, for example, might evolve in a region where falcons were common. Elsewhere, other factors might favour the original plumper but slower type of pigeon.

On occasion, a species will be unable to replace deaths by births, perhaps due to competition from a rival species, pressure from predators or disease organisms, or a hostile environment. Such a species will become extinct. Extinction and the arising of new species are said to explain the succession of different kinds of animals and plants found as fossils in successive layers of sedimentary rocks. Thus every kind of organism now living is thought to be descended from ancestors which are different to an increasing degree from it as one goes further back in time.

Darwin himself could only guess how parents' characteristics are passed on to their offspring, and why they should sometimes vary. Today we have the advantage over Darwin of having a detailed and well-verified theory of genetics. Genetics provides a mechanism for the transmission of the characteristics of plants and animals to their offspring, and it also explains how variations arise between generations.

It is important to realize that genetics provides for no direct causal connection whatever between benefits to the organism and the source of variation.[27] Pigeons may need to improve their speed because of the depredations of falcons. But that need does not itself lead to more pigeons with 'speed mutations' being born. It just ensures that any speedy pigeons that do happen to be born will have a strong selective advantage over their contemporaries, and their speediness genes will become more frequent in the population. So all the inborn ways in which animals differ from their parents are, as far as we know, no more likely to be advantageous than disadvantageous. Mutation, and the gene shufflings that are a part of sexual reproduction, are essentially random. (There are possible exceptions to this in very simple organisms.) Any progression in evolution has to be sought in changes in what is advantageous, not in changes in the genes.

Modern genetics together with Darwin's theory of natural selection is called neo-Darwinism, and is the orthodoxy of modern evolutionary theory. Most biologists believe that neo-Darwinism can provide a full and adequate explanation of the whole process of biological evolution. There are dissenting voices, however. (Mark Ridley lists a number of objections, and answers them from the neo-Darwinist viewpoint, in his well-argued book, *The Problems of Evolution*.) There are also those, and I would agree with them, who accept neo-Darwinism, but feel that the sources of environmental change need greater attention. Changing environments force natural selection to act, if a species is to adapt successfully. One important source of environmental change is an organism's innovatory behaviour, and this is where consciousness (the animal's mind as the initiator of its actions) influences the direction of evolution, as we shall see in chapter 4.

NATURAL SELECTION IN ACTION

The adaptation of rabbits in Australia to the disease myxomatosis is a fascinating example of natural selection at work.[28] By 1950, ninety years after the introduction of two dozen from England, hundreds of millions of rabbits were swarming over the huge Australian sheep-stations and competing with the sheep for grass. So Australian farmers deliberately started an epidemic of a rather nasty disease called myxomatosis. It is a virus disease, spread in Australia in mosquito bites, and nearly all (95 per cent) of the infected rabbits died of it. Within a few years, 99 per cent of all the rabbits in Australia were dead. However, many of those that survived were found to be immune to myxomatosis, and it was shown that their resistance was genetically inherited.

Another factor improved life for the rabbits still further: evolution did not only select resistant rabbits, it also selected less virulent strains of the virus. This was because mosquitoes only bite live rabbits, so forms of the virus which do not kill the rabbit will spread far more quickly than fatal forms. So Australian rabbits, with the help of natural selection, have outwitted their sheep-farmer rivals.

Myxomatosis was also used to control rabbits in Britain, but it is interesting that they defended themselves with a strategy that was behavioural rather than genetic. Since in Britain the agent spreading the virus is a flea, which lives in the communal rabbit burrows, it was rabbits which chose (or happened) to abandon their burrows and sleep and breed above ground that survived. We shall see in chapter 4 that new selective forces acting on animals which have altered their life-styles by adopting new behaviours may account for many evolutionary advances.

ORGANISMS EVOLVING

Darwin's account of the natural selection of beneficial characteristics helps to explain how animals and plants have altered their forms over the ages. As the implications of Darwin's discovery sank in, man 'reluctantly gave up his dreams and found his own footprints wandering backwards until on some far hillside they were transmuted into the footprints of a beast'.[29] What, then, were the transformations in form, the slowly changing footprints, that led up to us, human beings?

A complete account of 'how we got here' would include theories on the big bang, the early universe, and the formation of the galaxy. It would describe the consolidation of the solar system, including our sun and earth, perhaps out of a swirling disc of dust and gas. In order not to take up too much space, I shall skip those millions of millennia of cosmological and stellar 'evolution', and provide a sketch of what is suspected about the course of biological evolution on earth.

Our planet is thought to have formed some 4,500 million years ago (mya). By 1,000 million years later, temperatures were not far from today's, and the earth had oceans, continents of shapes quite unrecognizable to us, and a poisonous (to us) atmosphere. There was no oxygen in the primeval air, which meant no ozone layer keeping out the sun's ultraviolet radiation. Ultraviolet, together with lightning storms and volcanic activity (which may have been more intense than nowadays) could have provided the energy to manufacture a thin 'soup' of chemicals in the oceans, chemicals now associated with life, and therefore called 'organic'. Some scientists believe that this witch's brew could have given rise to complex molecules capable of self-replication and evolution, possibly on clay particles, in drying-up pools, or in hot volcanic springs. These molecules would have been the first genes. Others suggest that a microbe spore might have somehow arrived from a distant planet or other body, where it had evolved by means too remote to be discovered, inoculating the earth's ocean with primitive life.

Whatever the case, perhaps as early as 3,800mya, life there was. It was of a kind similar to the simplest of today's organisms, bacteria and blue-green algae, and a study of the rocks formed by sedimentation in oceans reveals evidence of such micro-organisms in the very oldest of them.

For 2,000 million years, these micro-organisms drifted unchallenged in the oceans, evolving a multitude of chemical and genetic systems, but hardly altering in outward form. In fact, all the chemical and genetic systems in present-day organisms appear to share a common basic structure, suggesting a single ancestral type for all the living things now surviving.

The teeming cells were not passive inhabitants of a purely physical environment. They had profound effects on the earth, evolving ways of making use of the many chemicals dissolved in the oceans. Eventually, they started using the energy of sunlight to help them grow and multiply. This technique is called photosynthesis. Later versions of photosynthesis produced oxygen as a by-product, as does photosynthesis in modern green plants. So much oxygen was produced that the air gradually changed from having no oxygen when the process started, over 2,000mya, to having one part in five today. Organisms had to learn to cope with what was to them a deadly poison gas, and some even started using oxygen to break down the chemicals in the bodies of other organisms (or their own stored food chemicals), by a process called respiration. Respiration, usually using oxygen, is still the energy source of all animals, including us.

The next major evolutionary advance occurred about 1,400mya, when a new kind of organism appeared. It was still tiny and single-celled, but was far more complex than the bacteria and blue-green algae. It is thought that several primitive organisms may have clubbed together to make up the new cells, in what is called a symbiotic partnership. The outer covering and the nucleus of genetic material were provided by one partner, which permitted other organisms to shelter within its outer covering in return for their services. One specialized in respiration, one, present only in plants and some single-celled organisms, specialized in photosynthesis, one helped in cell-division, and one, not always present, helped the cell to get about (the flagellum or cilium).

It was these new kinds of cells that first reproduced sexually, instead of by simple splitting, their predecessors' only recourse. Sexual repro-duction can be wasteful, as two individuals are required, and usually only one of them can bear young. Some animals and plants rarely or never bother with sex, but most do. Presumably this is because each plant or animal born through sexual reproduction gets a new mix of genes, half from one parent, half from the other. The remixing of genes in each generation allows evolution to proceed at a much faster rate than does waiting for single mutations.[30] A bacterium (bacteria do not reproduce sexually) has only one great-grandparent, say, to inherit a beneficial mutation from. You and I, however, have eight great-grand-parents: eight chances of getting the advantage of that mutation.

Some of the new, complex cells extended the habit of symbiotic partnership into the formation of co-operating colonies, and the first many-celled organisms came into being. The cells in many-celled or-ganisms did not each have to carry a complete survival pack of all they needed to stay alive. They could rely on other cells for some functions, and themselves specialize. This breakthrough signalled an explosion in the rate of evolution, at least according to the evidence of the fossil record.

The new larger organisms adopted, very broadly, two life-styles. Some lived by trapping the energy of sunlight, using photosynthesis to raise their unstirring structures. These were plants. Others, the animals, were busy and hungry, seeking food and mates, and fleeing organisms which preyed upon them. Only the animal life-style demanded skills of alertness and discrimination, and only the animals evolved minds.

By the beginning of the Cambrian period, 570mya, nearly all the main groups of invertebrate animals (animals without backbones) were present in the oceans. Vertebrates (animals with backbones) appeared by 500mya. At first, there were just various kinds of fish, but about 350mya, large, newt-like amphibians followed primitive plants on to the dry land of the continents. (Insects, spiders, millipedes and such like had independently braved the land even earlier.) Reptiles later evolved from the amphibians.

Human ancestors

From now on, let us just follow the line culminating in human beings, concentrating mainly on the evolution of physical form, and leaving the development of mental abilities until the next chapter.

Before the extremely successful dinosaurs arose some 200mya, certain primitive reptiles – therapsids – started to walk with their legs turned under, with their bodies well clear of the ground, like mammals (modern reptiles can't generally do this). These therapsids had certain other mammal-like features, and by the time the dinosaurs were dominant, true mammals had also probably evolved. However, the primitive mammals were no match for dinosaurs, and seem to have survived only in the form of small, shrew-like creatures that could hide in the undergrowth and feed by night.

There is no evidence that the early mammals contributed to the extinction of the dinosaurs, which occurred around 65mya, but they soon took advantage of the habitats the dinosaurs left vacant. Thus the main orders of mammals evolved. Some of the shrew-like early mammals seem to have taken to the trees, possibly a behaviour-led form of evolution, as suggested in chapter 4. It is from this line that the earliest primates developed, the first members of the mammalian order which now includes mankind. Primate-like fossils 80 million years old have been found, from well before the dinosaurs vanished. These creatures grew long tails for improved agility, and eyesight took over from smell

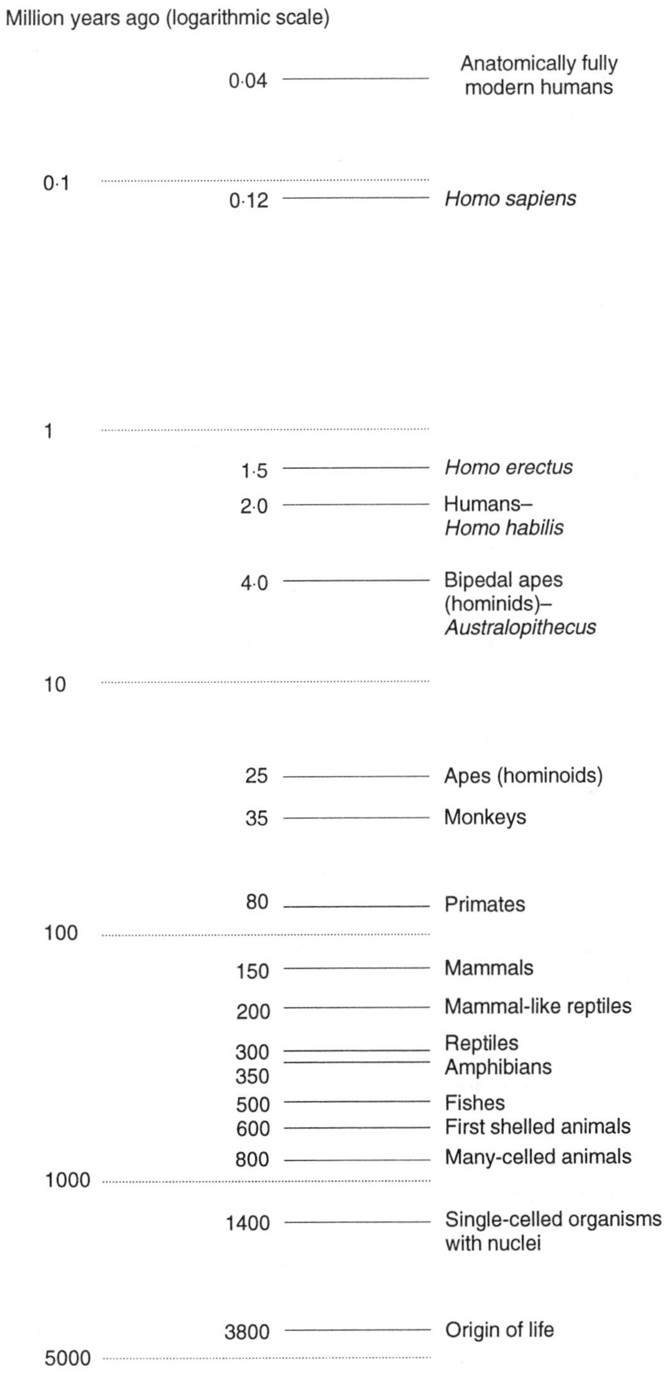

Million years ago (logarithmic scale)

0·04 ————————	Anatomically fully modern humans
0·1	
0·12 ————————	*Homo sapiens*
1	
1·5 ————————	*Homo erectus*
2·0 ————————	Humans– *Homo habilis*
4·0 ————————	Bipedal apes (hominids)– *Australopithecus*
10	
25 ————————	Apes (hominoids)
35 ————————	Monkeys
80 ————————	Primates
100	
150 ————————	Mammals
200 ————————	Mammal-like reptiles
300 ————————	Reptiles
350	Amphibians
500 ————————	Fishes
600 ————————	First shelled animals
800 ————————	Many-celled animals
1000	
1400 ————————	Single-celled organisms with nuclei
3800 ————————	Origin of life
5000	

Fig.3 Important events in biological evolution

as the dominant sense, since sharp eyes are vital for movement, feeding, and social behaviour in the treetops. These creatures must have looked something like the modern tree shrews.

In the widespread tropical forests of 50–40mya there were abundant primates much like modern lemurs and tarsiers, with brains already significantly larger than their ancestors'. It was presumably from them that the first monkeys evolved, and monkey fossils appear from 35mya onwards. Monkeys typically are tree-dwellers active by day, a life-style that gave a strong selective advantage to grasping and dexterous hands, good co-ordination and intelligence, and acute stereoscopic vision. What is more, the higher primates are the only mammals able to see colour. All these abilities are likely to have been significant for the development of the human level of consciousness. From the Old World monkeys, the group known as the hominoids evolved about 20–30mya. The hominoids include ourselves and our closest living relatives: the gibbons, orang-utan, gorilla, and chimpanzee.

THE APPEARANCE OF HUMANS

The next step in the biological evolution of human beings is the most intriguing: the arising of ape-like men (hominids) from man-like apes (hominoids). It is intriguing partly because virtually no relevant fossils have so far been found for the period from 8–4mya in which the common ancestor of human beings and certain other apes is generally thought to have diverged into two lineages.

The study of how hominids evolved after their divergence from apes is at present one of the most exciting of the frontiers of science. More and more new fossils are being found, often upsetting old theories. In addition, the analysis of the genetic differences between humans and their living relations is a further independent source of information. This genetic research, incidentally, indicates that hominids and apes diverged at least 5mya. What follows is the consensus at the time of writing, so far as there is one, on hominid evolution.[31]

The first hominids, to judge from brain size, were probably no cleverer than other hominoids, but their significant advance was upright walking. Our earliest evidence for upright walking is twofold. First, the wonderful fossil footprints of two adults and a child, discovered by Mary Leakey in Laetoli, Tanzania, and dated at 3·75mya. Secondly the young female nicknamed Lucy, and associated finds, from Hadar in Ethiopia, which are from 3·3–3·0mya. These finds represent a very early hominid, given the generic name *Australopithecus*, and they suggest that the human line comes from Africa.

Unlike their ape ancestors, which lived up trees in dense forests, the australopithecines lived in wooded savannah. It has been suggested that this bizarre habit of walking erect on two legs arose as the old African forests shrank into small islands of woodland, with open ground in between. If apes were not to be stuck in these little woods, they would have to descend from the trees and cross the open ground. Now, bringing home food, watching over the tall grass for predators, and perhaps using tools while on the move, all militate for upright walking, with the hands free.

Having warily ventured, out of necessity, on to the open savannah, our apes seem to have taken full advantage of the new habitat, and spent more and more time in the open and less time in the trees. Thus bipedal hominids came into being. Tooth-wear studies suggest that they started eating roots, and they probably also foraged for carrion and did some hunting. In any case, the upright gait was not a minor adaptation, but, according to the palaeontologist Owen Lovejoy, 'one of the most striking shifts in anatomy you can see in evolutionary biology.'[32] So it must have conferred some major advantages.

As the australopithecines evolved, they diversified, and gave rise to several new but fairly similar species. In addition to these, by 2mya, a more advanced hominid was present in Africa, possibly also evolved from the early australopithecines. It had a much larger brain and is placed in a new genus – our own genus – the first *Homo*. There is evidence from both East and South Africa that *Homo* and *Australopithecus* lived at the same time in the same environment: two kinds of early 'humans'. One was to change extremely rapidly into modern-type people; the other was to stagnate and eventually become extinct.

A clue to the reason for the difference in success between the two types has been found in South African caves near which both kinds of hominid were apparently living. Hyenas and leopards killed and dragged in a large number of australopithecines over the years, and left their bones scattered about. But few if any *Homo* individuals were killed. The inference is that the relatively stupid australopithecines returned to the caves as the weather got cold, year after year. But *Homo* soon learnt how to avoid the danger, and intelligence combined with social learning spread the tradition through the whole local population.

There were great pioneers in the earliest *Homo* populations. With them are associated the first stone tools, dated to as much as 2·2mya.

Tools probably permitted much more meat to be consumed, since carcases of thick-skinned herbivores could be cut up. The meat may not have been hunted game: it may have been from animals already dead from natural causes or killed by predators such as lions. It has been suggested that the new food-source not only promoted a population increase, but also encouraged true food-sharing and other social behaviours unknown in other primates.

Skulls of early *Homo* show that the speech areas of the brain had enlarged, and also that the voice-box had dropped down in the neck. The descent of the voice-box is a very risky departure since it permits choking (most animals have throats built so that food cannot go down the wrong way), so the reason for the change must have been highly adaptive. The reason, it is inferred, was the development of primitive speech. We shall return to dexterity, tool-use, speech, and social behaviour in chapter 5.

The earliest *Homo* finds are assigned to the species *Homo habilis* or 'handy man', but within a mere few hundred thousand years, a distinctly new species – *Homo erectus* – appeared, still more like modern humans. *H. erectus* fossils go back to before 1·5mya. This very successful hominid was the first, on present evidence, to spread out of Africa into Europe and Asia. The well-known 'Java Man' and 'Peking Man' were *H. erectus*, as well as the people of the Acheulian culture in Europe including Britain. All these definitely hunted systematically, learnt to use fire (cooking makes meat and starch more digestible), and refined the manufacture of stone tools; and they may have developed rituals. By 400,000 years ago, they were building shelters.

Gradually, with no clear dividing line, their anatomy changed until, by 120,000 years ago or earlier, they were sufficiently like us to be labelled *Homo sapiens*, our own species. According to the best supported theory, one line of *H. sapiens*, the stocky, powerful neanderthals, became extinct; but another line gave rise to people virtually indistinguishable from the modern races of mankind. These modern human beings had appeared by 40,000 years ago. Since then, we have hardly changed at all in appearance and structure. Evolution seems to have transferred its impetus to the increasing sophistication of our cultures and the abilities of our minds.

A DIRECTION TO BIOLOGICAL EVOLUTION?

Evolution is a word that has a sense of advancement embedded in it. This is true both of its original meaning, and of its modern colloquial use. For most biologists, however, it is anathema to bracket evolution with progress; they chalk up in big letters on their blackboards: NEVER USE THE WORDS HIGHER AND LOWER. The phrase is Darwin's: he wrote it as a little memorandum to himself in the 1840s, but often ignored it in later life.[33] He certainly thought of humans as being higher than all their animal relatives.

This book is concerned with what is surely the most conspicuous trend in life's history from the human point of view – the progressive development of consciousness. Nevertheless, 'mind', 'consciousness', even 'behaviour', have only recently started appearing in the indexes of evolutionary biology texts, and that taboo on 'lower' and 'higher' still obscures an understanding of the evolving mind.

Before we concentrate on advancing consciousness, can we discern any other directions in biological evolution? To establish whether any trends exist, we need to decide on what it is that is evolving. The obvious choice is the living organism. Then we can look at each of its characteristics, and judge whether there is any overall tendency of increase or decrease in the prevalence or importance of that feature over evolutionary time.

Broadly, there are two kinds of trends observed in evolution: increases and improvements. In principle, at least, an *increase* in some characteristic of organisms should be objectively measurable – it is a quantitative change – while an *improvement* requires one to make a retrospective value-judgement, since it is a qualitative change. If one wishes to exclude all considerations of human values from evolution, then only quantitative trends could be considered.

For example, the prehistorian Gordon Childe measured evolutionary progress in terms of population increase.[34] Using population size as the ordering principle for an evolutionary framework for existence yields an interesting hierarchy of forms, with rats, sparrows, and earthworms well ahead of people, insects doing better still (a million million or so by a 1960 estimate) and of course micro-organisms at the top. Alternatively, we could be a little more sophisticated, and acknowledge an overall evolutionary progress because the total number of living organisms has increased, together with their total bulk, their gross turnover of matter and energy, and their diversity of form.[35]

A quantitative criterion more acceptable to biologists is *fitness* – success in life.[36] Fitness can only be measured relatively: one organism would be twice as fit as another if twice as many of its descendants have survived after a certain period. But increasing fitness turns out not to provide an overall trend for evolution, since fitness is measured not only relative to specific competitors, but also within a specific environment. Natural selection works to adapt organisms to survive and breed more and more successfully in their existing circumstances. However, circumstances – environments – change, and the long-term changes in evolution involve the discovery of entirely new circumstances, throwing up entirely new problems in life. A trout is superbly adapted to life in the river, a hedgehog is ideally suited for hunting for slugs on the river bank, and a toad is not terribly good at either life-style. Yet the river may dry up or the land may flood, and only the toad will survive both emergencies. Which of the three is furthest on in the process of evolution?

Julian Huxley's answer to this question is to notice a sequence in the 'dominance' of groups of animals. We read of the Age of Trilobites, the Age of Fishes, of Reptiles, of Mammals; these are the groups regarded as dominant in each epoch, and we might infer that each supplanted its predecessor owing to some superiority, and so is more advanced, perhaps more 'fit'.[37] However, the story is probably not so simple. It now seems likely, for example, that the mammals replaced the dinosaurs not by out-competing them in any sense, but because they happened to be small enough to survive an environmental catastrophe that wiped out the majority of animal species then living, including the dinosaurs. In any case, several groups are often dominant at any one time, each in its own sphere: are we now in an age of mammals, of birds, or of insects – or of humans? There must be several lineages of dominance. (Where different types are competing, the prize probably goes to the one that can be most active. This means the type with the highest metabolic rate, which might therefore be used as a measure of progress.)

The enlargement of life

Perhaps an increasing ability to adapt to a wider range of circumstances represents a real trend. Have organisms become more adaptable over evolutionary time? The answer is yes and no: in every epoch, there have been some highly successful specialists, and some adaptable generalist species. It is usually said that the specialists enjoy a heady period of success until time deprives them of the special conditions they exploit so well. Then they die out, unable to adapt, and the new world is colonized by descendants of the generalists, many of which evolve into new specialists in new environments. The mammals perhaps survived the dinosaurs in this way.

If we look only at the best generalists in each period, we may be justified in saying that adaptability does indeed increase in each succeeding period. (The point about choosing the best in each period – the leading edge of evolution – seems to apply to any potential trend. There appears to be no trend in evolution which draws all organisms in its wake. Some species are highly conservative; they found a cosy role in the living world millions of years ago, and there is nothing to impel them to risk advancement. Blue-green algae scums on modern estuary muds, for example, are almost indistinguishable from fossils 2,500 million years old. We can only seek directional changes at a leading edge of evolution.)

In discerning a growing adaptiveness, we are infringing the provisional ban on human judgement, since the adaptability of two creatures living in different periods cannot be compared objectively. The same goes for a similar criterion suggested by many biologists, namely how independent an organism is of its environment. Nevertheless, both adaptability and independence do definitely seem to have increased at the leading edge of evolution, and human beings, with the benefit of technology, can adapt to more environments and remain more independent of them than any previous species.

A characteristic that not only seems to have, but definitely has, increased is complexity. In the first phase of life's evolution, each major new group of organisms to evolve was more sophisticated than the older groups, with a more complex structure, new internal organs and physiological mechanisms, and being capable of a greater range of subtle responses to needs and threats. But already by Cambrian times (570–500mya), organisms were very complex, and it is not clear how one could demonstrate an increase in complexity since then. Is a human being really more structurally complex than a 400 million-year-old fish? Sometimes, indeed, a progressive simplification may accompany what we would regard as progress.

However, it is true that the nervous system has become more complex and centralized, with the maximum brain size showing a continuous increase. Increasing complexity is reflected in an increasing amount of information that needs to be passed down the generations to bring an animal and its way of life to maturity. Until cultural traditions became possible, much of this information was encoded in the genes. Consequently, a bacterium has about five million information-carrying molecules in its genes (equivalent to ten 250-page books full of printed data); a mammal has nearly a thousand times as many.

'The realization of possibilities: that is perhaps the best way of viewing biological advancement.'[38] I think this conclusion by Julian Huxley sums up the trends I have mentioned so far. In a way, they are all quite straightforward, and to be expected. If, as is thought, life arose from a non-living matrix by gradual, causal processes, one would expect that its earliest forms would be very simple, uniform, fairly inflexible, and very susceptible to environmental injury. Some changes essayed by evolution were bound to lead to greater complexity, adaptability, and so on.[39]

The last biological trend to be considered brings us full circle, back to the evolution of consciousness. G.G. Simpson defines it as an 'increased awareness and perception of the environment and increased ability to react accordingly.'[40] We have considered some more or less objective trends, increases rather than improvements. But is the discovery that things are getting more complicated and diverse really sufficient for us to make sense of our world? Is it a trend that we would necessarily wish to co-operate with, to extend further? Even greater adaptability, desirable though it may be, is not necessarily the one aim and direction that can best define our attitude to shaping the future as well as unifying our understanding of the past.[41]

A survey of the mental precursors of human consciousness shows a very definite trend over evolutionary time, a trend of gradually improving mental capacities in each era's most advanced species, and of successively higher degrees of awareness. This is a trend that underlies independence from and control over the environment, as well as much adaptability. It is reflected in an increased individualization as animals, through the mental processing of their unique experiences, became more and more distinguishable from their fellows. It is not in fact human-centred in the sense of being arbitrarily chosen to give humans pre-eminence, yet it unequivocally places mankind at the summit of evolutionary progress. Developing mind or consciousness would seem to be the ideal unifying principle to seek in all parts of an evolutionary framework for existence. This is the topic of the next chapter.

Chapter Three

MENTAL EVOLUTION

The greatest thoughts are accessible to the least of men.
Why do we have to struggle so? Because understanding is a function
not of ratiocination but of the psyche's stage of growth.
Lawrence Durrell, *Clea*, 138

'INSIDE', 'OUTSIDE', AND BEHAVIOUR

The most fundamental and striking characteristic of experience is that we split our perception into an 'inside' world and an 'outside' world. The inside is called the subject and is identified with 'I', 'me', and to some extent 'mine'. It is apprehended more or less directly. The outside world is called the objective universe and is distinctly 'other', only apprehended indirectly, through the five senses. (One's body sometimes seems part of the inside, sometimes part of the outside.) As subject, my inside seems absolutely unique: only I can experience it as such. Yet everybody else apparently experiences an exactly parallel split, but with a quite different inside to mine.

As self-reflective human beings, we have the ability to observe the workings of our own 'inside', by introspection or self-awareness. What of those entities in the universe without the capacity for self-aware-ness? Do they use an 'inside' distinguishable from an 'outside'? One can infer that at least some of them do.

A.N. Whitehead's philosophy of purpose provided an 'inside' or 'mental' dimension for all phenomena without exception. Non-living natural objects, however, show no signs of any mentality! Living things have been distinguished from non-living by their ability to *perceive* their environment and act on the basis of their perceptions.[42] When we watch other living things, we just see their actions and the environment in which they act. We don't see any mental activities. But we surely notice that actions are usually suited in some way to an organism's changing environment. We can also see the efforts organisms make to find out about what's going on, using their senses.

What lies between sensation and behaviour? There must be internal processes which connect the two. In plants and very simple animals, these processes are very highly constrained so that only a few responses are possible, and the link between a stimulus and a response is imme-diate and very predictable. Often scientists can even discover chemical and physical processes connecting the stimulus (or sensation) and response. For example, growing plants respond to light and gravity, employing chemical and mechanical processes which are thoroughly understood.

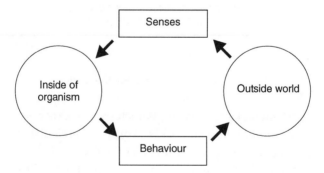

Fig.4 Outside and inside

In most animals, behaviour is much more flexible. A similar stimulus can produce various responses in different situations. Goal-directed behaviour – hunting for prey, for example – is influenced by sensation but does not result directly from an external stimulus. The internal processes occurring between sensation and action must be very complicated.

ANIMAL MINDS

The connection between sensation and action is often ascribed entirely to physical and chemical processes occurring in the body, especially the nervous system, although the precise nature of such processes is not known. Without, in many cases, having thought very much about it, biologists and psychologists tend to hold to this mechanist/reductionist view, and transmit it to their students.

As I shall argue later, the evidence is indeed of a very strong correlation between animals' mental capacity and the size and structure of their brains; however, the mechanist/reductionist view goes much further than merely recognizing such a correlation. It asserts that mental processes *are* certain physical processes, and nothing more. Such a view seems very remote from the nature of one's own mental processes as actually experienced. It is true that interpretations of subjective experience vary wildly, and workable criteria for choosing between interpretations are not available to most people; yet before the arguments start, there it is, that uninterpreted life of experience that is all anybody knows directly. (We shall be exploring rational accounts of internal experience later.) But whether or not one is a reductionist, it is clearly meaningful to speak of animals having an 'inside' similar in some respects to ours, consisting of processes connecting sense-inputs and behaviour. In some cases the 'inside' also includes processes originating or terminating internally, such as dreaming. In more complex animals, at least, it seems reasonable to call all these internal processes 'mind'.

Different kinds of animals differ greatly in both their senses and their behaviour, and so they presumably differ in their minds too. Some animals would seem to have much more sophisticated minds than others, and as the structures and life-styles of animals have evolved, so have their minds.

In the past, biologists have tended to see minds as evolving in the same way as bodily organs: passively through natural selection in changing environments. Biologists are increasingly recognizing, however, that the mind is qualitatively different from all other evolving systems, in part because of its role in governing behaviour. We shall see in chapter 4 that animal behaviours can influence the course of evolution by effectively altering the selection pressures that an animal is subject to.

Consequently, animal minds play a potentially active role in evolution by initiating behaviour: they are not just the passive playthings of natural selection.

In understanding ourselves as humans, we see our minds, arguably, as by far the most important aspect of ourselves to be considered. They are our immediate source for values, feelings, insights, and indeed the sense-based experience which permits knowledge of every aspect of the material universe. Thus Buddhism takes the human mind as its starting point: how it works and how it can be developed. Although Buddhism has an evolutionary viewpoint, the ancient Buddhist masters did not have the knowledge of biological evolution that we have now, and if we are fully to understand our minds, we need to discover how they evolved. The sense organs, the nervous system, and, more recently, animal behaviour, have been considered carefully by evolutionary biologists, but the evolving mind itself has been rather neglected. It is true that the study of its evolution presents practical difficulties. But it is perhaps also the case that some conventional scientists feel rather embarrassed to display an interest in the subjective pole of existence; it is so difficult to analyse dispassionately.

The practical problems in coming to understand the minds of others, even of other species, are not completely intractable, as some of the great psychologists and ethologists of this century have shown, and work has been done on the evolution of mind in animals.[43] Nevertheless, any discussion of the way minds have evolved is bound to be fairly speculative in that nothing is known directly about the minds of other species. It is only possible to get to know their behaviour and structure and infer things about their minds by comparison with human experience. It is also speculative because fossils of extinct animals cannot tell us nearly as much about their minds as about their structure.

Fortunately, nearly all the major groups of animals that appeared in the distant past have left living descendants which are quite similar in their appearance and way of life. So in the accounts that follow, I shall assume that the minds of the successive varieties of organisms that came into being during biological evolution were similar to those of the nearest living representatives of their type.

The evolution of minds: simple organisms

Very broadly, living things can be divided into four categories according to their mental capacity: simple organisms, organisms with centralized nervous systems, birds and mammals, and human beings.

In the category of simple organisms I include single-celled organisms, plants, and animals without a centralized nervous system.

Plants are a special case: they have evolved very sophisticated structures, but being fixed to the spot, and never pursuing moving food, they have not required complex processes to mediate sensation and reaction. As far as we know, there is no real reason to call their internal processes 'mental'. In principle, their responses, such as seeking the light, involve no higher a level of 'consciousness' than the central heating thermostat, which turns the heating on when it gets cold. Like a thermostat, they have rudimentary 'senses', but with very coarse discriminating powers. A clover plant, for example, can 'see' whether it is day or night, and so open its folded leaves in the morning, but it cannot see the difference between a bee and a sheep.

Before the plants evolved, the oceans were teeming with living forms. It is reasonable to assume that the earliest organisms had minds like those of modern species with no nervous system or with just a network of nerve connections: single-celled organisms, sponges, starfish, jellyfish and corals, and some worms.[44] In such organisms, responses to stimuli from outside and responses to processes such as developmental changes happening in the body are highly predictable and inflexible. Larger animals in this category and even some single-celled ones have rudimentary sense-organs.

The internal or 'mental' processes connecting stimulus and response seem to be quite direct. They are probably straightforward chemical and physical mechanisms, as in the case of plants, though how nerve cells in primitive animals influence each other in appropriate ways is not fully understood.

The early evolution of mind is a development of one ability in particular: recognition. Primitive animals have inbuilt, inborn mechanisms which distinguish between the messages that different sensations convey. Are they neutral, are they to be approached, or are they to be escaped? Detection of food or a potential mate induces approach, while the recognition of a predator, or some environmental danger, gives rise to avoidance behaviour. This is recognition in the sense that the animal responds appropriately to the 'recognized' stimulus, but there is no internal, remembered image to which the stimulus is compared, as there is when we recognize someone's face.

These basic reactions are fairly inflexible, but can be modified to some extent on the basis of experience, by a combination of habituation and sensitization. In habituation, the organism gradually ceases to respond if a slightly attractive or slightly frightening experience is repeated often, without leading to any real reward or damage. Tap a sea anemone, and it withdraws its tentacles, but tap repeatedly and it eventually ignores you. Sensitization counteracts habituation: if an animal finds food or is attacked, then for a while it is very sensitive to any slight stimulus. In the first case the stimulus might represent more food, and there is an approach response. In the second case the sensitized animal is not taking any chances, and hides at the slightest unfamiliar sensation.

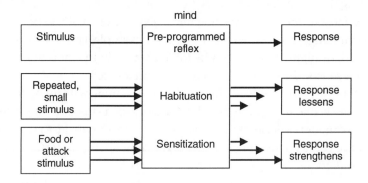

Fig.5 Habituation and sensitization

ANIMALS WITH A CENTRAL NERVOUS SYSTEM: PERCEPTION

After nerve networks, the next important structural advance in the development of mental abilities was a centralized nervous system. This had probably evolved by the beginning of the Cambrian period, 570mya, and today it is found in animals such as most worms, snails, squids, most shellfish, crustaceans (crabs etc), spiders, insects, and many other invertebrates. Vertebrates all possess central nervous systems, and the fish, amphibians, and reptiles will be considered here; birds and mammals wait until the following section since they show certain profound mental advances.

Animals with a central nervous system are still capable of pre-programmed reflex responses, habituation, and sensitization; indeed, all animals with 'higher' mental functions continue to be capable of all the 'lower' ones, in appropriate circumstances. But their recognition capabilities have expanded greatly. Much recognition remains innate, but now quite small differences between objects can be recognized. Female fish, for example, can recognize males of their own species from other very similar fish by a complex pattern of visual and behavioural cues. Such animals do not need to wait passively for a stimulus to respond to. They are capable of sophisticated patterns of behaviour continually modified by sensations, for example, migration and nest building.

To see both how impressive and how limited the behaviour of such animals is, imagine a butterfly looking for food. Hungry, it first moves restlessly about in what is called appetitive behaviour. Sight of a suitable flower then stimulates a purposive flight to the flower; and sight, smell, touch, and taste provide further stimuli as it lands on the flower and starts sipping the nectar.

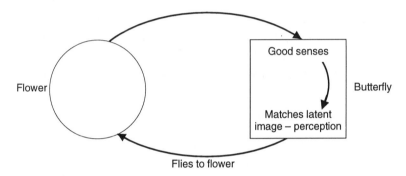

Fig.6 Butterfly perception

The butterfly has not learnt anything, it has not planned or remembered anything, yet at each stage a sort of mental recognition has occurred.[45] A certain sensation of shape, colour, and brightness produces a mental counterpart in the butterfly, a pattern of mental processes which we could call an 'image' of a flower.[46] Latent in the butterfly mind is another image, an inborn mental pattern, and recognition of a flower is simply the matching of the sensed image and the latent one. Such a matching is not a conscious process, of course: the matching leads directly to the appropriate act. The two are inextricably linked.

The butterfly's latent image fails on several counts to rival a human, remembered image. It is nowhere near as detailed or well defined, and there is no question of its being contemplated at leisure when the flower stimulus is absent. A latent image, incidentally, is not necessarily connected only with sensations that are visual; it could link with smells, noises, or other sensations.

So these lower animals can recognize certain things. They are capable of perception as well as sensation. Goldfish, for instance, have been found to be able to recognize abstract shapes. However, the images that can be recognized by lower animals are often only broadly defined. Butterflies are attracted to coloured discs as if they were flowers, and frogs will treat any small object that moves across their line of sight as if it were a fly.[47]

As the mental ability to recognize significant events improved, it is not surprising that animals' sensory abilities improved too. Animals evolved eyes which can form images and see colour, very delicate senses of smell, receptors for hearing and for vibration, balance organs, receptors that detect temperature, organs of touch such as the 'whiskers' of catfish, receptors for body position and internal body states, and so on. The sense organs are often grouped at the front end of the body and have a concentration of nerve tissue near them: the brain.

The senses filter a chaotic jumble of messages about the world, and pick out relevant sections for the mind's attention. The mind recognizes what is important, and chooses the best response it has in its repertoire.

Animals with a Central Nervous System: Association

A mind which can only pick out a single stereotyped and inborn behaviour for each experience is not a very interesting mind. But even primitive animals are capable of changing their responses by habituation and sensitization, as we have seen. Some can do much more: they can learn by association.

Certain experiences are followed by significant events: association means simply learning a connection between the two. If the shadow of a predator is followed by attack by that predator, an animal will quickly learn (if it survives) to associate the two, and flee at the shadow without waiting for the attack. This kind of association is the basis of the classical conditioning experiments of Pavlov, in which dogs learnt to associate bells or lights with their feeding time, as proved by their carefully measured drooling. Animals more primitive than dogs are capable of the same kind of associations; they can learn to recognize that an experience has a certain significance, without having any inborn knowledge of what the experience tells them.

Even more impressive is the association of a particular behaviour with a particular result: learning to do something special in order to gain a reward or avoid a punishment. This is the basis of all training of

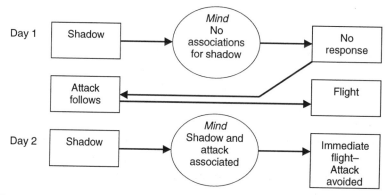

Fig.7 Association of an experience with its consequences

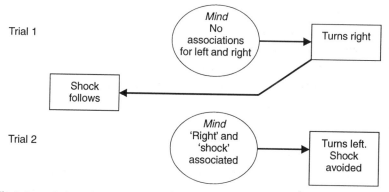

Fig.8 Association of a behaviour with its consequences

animals, and of innumerable experiments with hapless rats and pi-geons in boxes; but even worms can mentally associate actions with certain consequences. They will soon learn to turn left in a maze if a right turn leads to an electric shock.

The lower animals are not very clever. But their associative abilities show that they can generate a mental image from a sensation. They can detect the meaning, for them, of an image by acting on the basis of any match between it and images latent in their minds; to a butterfly, a flower 'means' food. And they can somehow remember important images, later to be checked against their future experience, and even learn and remember associations between images, and between images and behaviours. For a trained worm, the right arm of the maze 'means' danger, though of course it does not use concepts or words. Increas-ingly subtle kinds of associations between different mental processes, and the fixing in memory of those associations, became more and more important to animals as they evolved.

MAMMALS AND BIRDS

In most mammals and some birds, innate patterns of behaviour are both more intricate and more flexible than in lower animals. Their ways of life vary more and are less predictable. They can exploit their environments more effectively because their behaviour is less stereotyped.[48]

The improvement is not only in degree; mammals and birds evolved quite new mental abilities, and we shall investigate these abilities in the rest of the chapter. In summary, mammals and birds:

- can associate very well
- have offspring which can learn from their parents
- can learn from fellows in their group
- can learn by experience
- can postpone response – caution
- have minds which can learn generalized 'ideas'
- have minds which can construct mental representations
- have a drive to explore
- make innovations in behaviour.

Higher animals have impressive learning abilities. They can learn to associate their experiences and actions with the events that follow with far greater speed and subtlety than the animals we met in the previous sections. Birds and mammals look after their young, and so offspring can learn from their parents. Many of them are gregarious, and they can learn a great range of social and other behaviours from their fellows, both by reward and punishment, and by imitation. They also learn by experience, and often seem keen to explore their surroundings, to try out different foods and so on. They can even invent completely new forms of behaviour, as we shall see in chapter 4.

Since birds and mammals are not confined to automatic or highly stereotyped responses, they can postpone a response in order to allow time to find out more about a situation.[49] A cat does this briefly when it pauses before jumping up on to a wall, as does a rat when it thoroughly explores a new environment before taking any steps to build a nest or eat. Postponement may even give space for completely new actions to be invented.

Birds and mammals do not have radically different or better senses than some lower animals. So to account for their new improved behavioural capabilities, we need to look behind the senses, to their mental processes.

Captive pigeons can learn to distinguish pictures showing trees from pictures without trees, despite there being many other differences between all the pictures.[50] This implies that the latent images in pigeon brains are no longer either inborn, as in the butterfly's image of a flower, nor just the remembered images of significant things they have seen in the past. The images have been generalized or abstracted to some extent from many observations. All the images of particular trees seen by the birds have gone into the construction, one presumes, of a single image of 'tree', which includes what all the experienced images have in common.

Being careful not to assume all the human, language-based associations with the word, we can follow the psychologist Stephen Walker in calling the composite, abstracted image an 'idea'.[51] The pigeon has an 'idea' of what a tree is. Birds and mammals can build up very subtle ideas from their sensations, discriminating between similar things, and picking things out from confusing backgrounds of irrelevant information. They can also learn a number of networks of associations between many images; they can accurately remember such associations, and modify them efficiently according to new experiences. These networks of associations are mental representations of the external world.

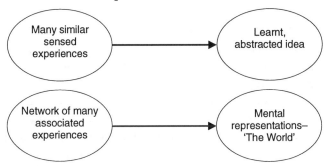

Fig.9 Ideas and mental representations

MENTAL REPRESENTATIONS

Mental representations[52] include 'mental maps' of an animal's environment, by which it can find its way around and locate relevant objects very fast. Shrews, for example, seem to learn mental maps. A shrew in the wild races along its familiar runs at breakneck speed, and will tend to collide with any new obstacle, such as a stick placed across its path. Then it backs off and explores very cautiously until it has found a new route around the stick. Each time it encounters the stick again, it becomes more confident, until it has become just another familiar bend on the racetrack.

The metaphor of a 'map' could be misleading. It is very unlikely that animals have a fixed mental picture of an aerial view of their territory, which they stop and consult every few paces. What presumably happens is that the sequence of images being generated from their sense experience as they move around is being continually compared to an associated network of remembered images, and they control their movements accordingly.

Human beings also have mental representations, and they are major components of our inner world. What is more, we experience a very definite frontier between the inside and outside poles of experience – an outside world quite separate from the inner realm of thoughts, images, and feelings.

Knowing about mental representations, however, does not really suggest that the inside–outside frontier is ultimately valid. In fact, all we truly apprehend is a border between two mental representations, one of the 'outside' and one of the 'inside'. By definition, we have no observation point in the 'outside' half. We learn nothing of the reality or otherwise of the subject–object duality through contemplating mental representations.

In any case, in discussing representations I am simply offering a useful model of a particular level of mentality. We should not conclude that there is literally a structure 'in' the mind that corresponds to a subset of a literal outside world. An animal and its perceived world evolve together, combining the perceptions of one lifetime with the results of long-term evolutionary developments. (And because our own history is different, our perceived world is quite dissimilar to any animal's.) Thus there are inevitable symmetries between an animal's collection of mental processes and the 'world' it inhabits.

We have seen that primitive minds functioned to ensure that particular sensations always gave rise to certain actions, behaviour that was likely to be beneficial to the animal. Minds carrying internal representations of the sensed world are capable of much more than this.

They are capable of so much more that it appears that the potential performance of vertebrate minds has tended to be well in advance of the animals' present needs, a phenomenon called pre-adaptation.[53] Growing mental powers seem to have their own momentum, as if the possession of a certain amount of intelligence can itself lead on to greater intelligence still in future generations, even if there is no immediate use for it. Minds introduce, it would appear, a self-transcending tendency in evolution over and above the processes of natural selection, which demand that changes in structure are beneficial. How can this be? I shall consider in chapter 4 how minds may cause better minds to evolve. For the present, here is Stephen Walker's suggestion. It refers to primates, but may also apply to other intelligent species. He proposes that, far from being promoted by natural selection,

> the *lack* of selection pressure allowed the emergence of primate intelligence as a luxury not available to species more hard pressed. Cogitation may, like other civilized pursuits, be a product of surplus, leisure, and excess, and not a consequence of struggle, deprivation, and need.[54]

INTELLIGENT MINDS

What are these new abilities that mental representations permit? Animals with internal representations can, to some extent, anticipate the future, plan their actions, and avoid risks. They can do these things by running through various sequences of associated ideas in their minds, without having to try out all the related behaviours. As a result, intelligently directed behaviour becomes possible. For example, captive chimpanzees have been observed to look at a miniature maze given to them as a test and ponder about it for some time before choosing the correct path, without any trial and error being necessary.[55] Anticipation also permits an animal to feel and then act upon mental urges directed towards particular results, results perceived in the form of images or ideas.

The degree of intelligence possessed by an animal seems to be closely associated, as we have seen, with its preparedness to postpone habitual behaviours. Before acting, it can improve its internal representation of the situation it is in, and then mentally manipulate that representation. As a result, intelligence also correlates with how good a memory the animal has. The better the memory, the greater the size and complexity of the representation it can store.

Some psychologists even suggest that certain animals include images of themselves in their mental representations,[56] which would be the beginning of self-reflective consciousness. What is more likely is that the presence of a coherent mental world in which the animal's imaging can move gives rise to what could be called a 'centred experience'.

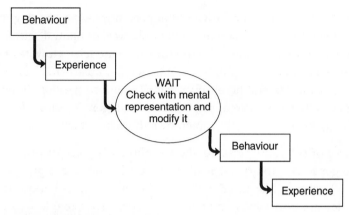

Fig.10 Using mental representations

An animal which makes continual use of mental maps will experi-ence a centre and a periphery to its awareness, and thus start to distinguish itself from its surroundings. The centred experience there-fore starts to split the undivided consciousness typical of animals. The completely undivided consciousness is actually 'unconscious', less aware than we are when we are dreaming, a fact which illustrates the difficulty of extending rather vague words like 'consciousness' down to the animal level. An animal consciousness which is equivalent to our consciousness during dreaming first emerges when experience has a centre, and it has been termed the level of 'simple consciousness'.[57] The centred experience, and how simple consciousness leads into self-reflective consciousness, will be considered in chapter 5.

As mental life became richer, the immediate feelings of appetite and aversion experienced by lower animals must have started to colour the images and ideas that were growing in animal minds, so that emotions and distinct volitions enter the drama of mental evolution. And it is suggested, especially by those who know animals well, that the lan-guage of affect (that is feelings, or simple emotions) is appropriate for some mental processes in mammals and birds. For example, 'pleasure' when eating, 'anger' when fighting a rival, 'fear' when fleeing a preda-tor.[58] An individual animal can develop tastes as it grows: some foods or experiences or companions it likes, some it dislikes.

ANIMAL CONSCIOUSNESS

To summarize, it seems that images, ideas, and mental representations can exist in an animal's mind. Images are the simplest: each one is the mental equivalent of a particular sensory experience. An image can be inborn: the butterfly recognizes a flower without having to learn to. Or an image can be memorized, so that if the same sensory experience recurs, it can be recognized.

Sometimes, perceived images stimulate the animal to do something: it has recognized a sensory experience as being relevant to its life. Again, the behaviour may be innate or learnt. Then animals may learn to associate a lot of images together, taking out the common factors to form a general 'idea'. The idea of a tree for a pigeon allows it to behave quite flexibly. It knows that oak trees, say, may be suitable for nesting in, even though it was raised in a sycamore. When a complicated network of ideas and images is associated together, the animal has a mental representation of part of its world, a representation which can be adjusted according to experience.

The table sums up the succession of levels of animal consciousness, all that the evolving mind achieved until human beings arrived.

Level of consciousness	Characteristics	Animals possessing it
5. Centred experience	Simple consciousness. Dream experience. Associative 'thinking' with non-verbal concepts. Planning, problem solving, complex communication. Flexible cultural traditions.	The most intelligent mammals
4. Representation	Images combined in ideas and mental representations; memory, anticipation, likes and dislikes. Communication and imitation learning, exploratory and innovative behaviour. Beginnings of cultural transmission.	Birds and mammals
3. Perception and association	Recognition of complex stimuli by comparison with innate 'images', goal-directed behaviour, association learning, training.	Animals with central nervous systems
2. Recognition	Recognition of simple classes of sensations, fully stereotyped responses. Sensitization and habituation 'learning'.	Animals with nerve-nets
1. No consciousness		Non-living matter, living things without nervous systems

Table 1: Levels in the evolution of pre-human consciousness

CONCEPTS AND THINKING

We can come to some understanding of the workings of the minds of simple animals by regarding them in rather mechanical terms. We can understand mental processes in other people because we know they think much like us, using concepts and words. But bridging the gap between simple, predictable animals and humans like ourselves is difficult: how do intelligent animals think when they have no words?

They do not have words, but they do have ideas, generalizations from many images of their sensed world, like the pigeon's 'tree'. The most intelligent animals, such as monkeys and apes, seem to have a huge repertoire of ideas, and their ideas may be more abstract (further from actual perceived images) than those of lower animals. They are apparently able to associate ideas together in a chain or array, so that they draw a 'conclusion' from a particular experience (or even perhaps from a memory or a spontaneous mental image), and act on that conclusion. Connecting ideas together like this is surely 'thinking', and to match common usage, we can call the ideas that are connected 'concepts'. If the train of thought reaches a conclusion, that is another concept.

O. Koehler trained mice to learn to run a maze, and then tried to confuse them by putting them in similar but altered mazes. Some were doubled in size, others used different angles of corners or rounded off the corners, and others were mirror images of the original maze. 'In every case where a mouse was presented with one of these modified maze forms, it hesitated at the first point that looked different, then ran back to the starting point, making a few other similar errors. But then suddenly it understood: without further training, each mouse would run the changed path to the end almost without mistakes.'[59] Blind mice could adapt just as quickly, but if the primary visual centres of their brains were destroyed, though they could learn, they could no longer adapt to the modified mazes. Koehler concludes that the mouse has a 'figurative image of the path', which it can manipulate mentally – in other words, a mental map.

Concepts are likely to derive from memories of sensed images, so they are presumably experienced as similar to sensed experiences, except that their source is internal. In the case of highly visually oriented animals such as apes and hominids, a concept is likely to be a composite mental picture. In our case, the bare concept is translated into a verbal thought so rapidly that many people, especially academics, cannot imagine such a thing as a non-verbal concept. The experience of intelligent animals without self-reflective consciousness is probably rather like our dream experience – a stream of fluid images with a centre of awareness, as just suggested. Actual sensory perception may well seem to animals just like a stronger form of mental experience. Of course, my account here is an informed piece of imagination.

With the presence of concepts in animal minds, we come to the borders of human-type experience in mental evolution, and so I have used the term 'thinking' for the first time. However, there are no strict dividing lines in mental evolution, and some might like to call simpler processes which manipulate images 'thinking', just as others prefer to restrict the terms 'mind' and 'consciousness' only to human-type mental processes.

We human beings can consciously direct our thinking, so that the concepts connect together in logical ways; alternatively, our thinking can be associative. Presumably, other animals are only capable of associative thought: the sequence of concepts is determined by the emotional associations of each concept in turn, and the overall direction is provided by volitional factors.

For example, the chimpanzee studying the maze would appear to be 'thinking' about the problem; but, since it almost certainly lacks the ability to attend to its own mental processes, it cannot consciously direct its thinking. It is more likely that it is somehow visualizing a series of possible movements through the maze, its concentration motivated by a desire to solve the problem and receive a reward.

THE HUMAN MIND AND LANGUAGE

The pioneer psychologist William James suggested that thoughts in animals tend usually to evoke only certain specific follow-on thoughts, which are determined by habit. So animal trains of thought tend to go down habitual ruts. One concept or thought, says James, can give rise to another by association, but the association is one of contiguity. That is, the second thought is always adjacent to the first, like two dominoes stood on end and ready to knock one another over. James concludes that animals are enslaved by habitual thinking; groups of concepts cannot break across in unaccustomed places.[60]

In human beings, however, and occasionally in intelligent animals, thoughts can evoke other thoughts by their similarity, even if the two have never been associated before. By this process of associative thinking based on similarity, humans can create new patterns of thinking, new ideas, new conclusions, and can form highly generalized, abstract concepts and classes of concepts, such as 'life' or 'the future'. Associative thinking is not consciously directed. Consciously directed thought, using abstractions, which I shall deal with later, adds yet another potential level.

The development of speech led to a vast improvement in the scope of thinking. The advent of true verbal language is the evolutionary step that is sometimes used to distinguish human beings from animals.[61] Fossil evidence points to primitive speech arising together with the first *Homo* populations, up to 2mya (see chapter 2).

One can guess that hunting, food-sharing, and other social behaviours among those early people called for accurate and versatile communication by voice and gesture. Gradually, more and more different types of cries were used, with more and more different meanings. At the same time, conceptual thinking was constantly improving. However, it may have been a long time before utterances and concepts were brought together, and most authors believe that speech in the full, modern sense had to await the evolution of modern types of human beings, some 120,000 years ago at most. Early *Homo* probably had utterances – 'words', if you like – only for commands and warnings, and for fairly simple ideas such as 'leopard', 'water', and so on.

True language involves the bringing together of mental concepts and vocal utterances. Mental hearing is added to mental visualizing in the mental map. When this started to happen, it may well be that thinking ability and speaking ability evolved together, each improvement in one prompting an improvement in the other. Both in turn would have affected, and would have been strongly influenced by, the new ecological ways of life people were opening up as they spread over the world and discovered new behaviours.

The different requirements of thinking and communicating would have contributed different elements to language. Conceptual thought demands words for generalized abstract concepts, which were derived from sense experience only at several removes: 'food', 'winter'. It demands forms of words referring to past and future, and the provision of words to link other words so that they can be strung together to make meaningful sentences: 'died', 'and', 'so'....

The primitive utterances by which people communicated also added something to language. This was the possibility of an uttered name standing for an object, that is, for a specific image. Once naming was extended to whole concepts, not just simple images, it allowed an

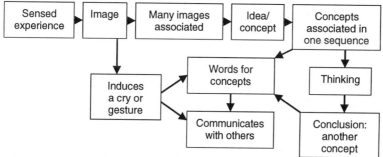

Fig.11 Language, thinking, and communicating

increase in the efficiency of thinking. Instead of manipulating concepts – each an unwieldy flock of many images – it became possible to conduct an internal verbal 'argument' using words, and come to a quicker conclusion. 'Uncle died when we left them alone last winter, so we shall take aunt into our hut and give her food.'

We can think verbally, but there is a price to pay for the efficiency this offers. The associations between words are derived from associations between concepts, which in turn are composite mental images. We easily forget this, if we ever noticed it, and behave and think as if the words themselves had inherent realities, and as if words can only be associated as we have always associated them. Through mistakes in the ways we associate words together, often habitual or even traditional mistakes, and the tendency for words to drift away from the concepts and experiences they were founded on, language and thought become more and more divorced from reality. We shall return to this in chapter 10, when we consider the Buddhist insistence on transcending verbal descriptions in coming to a direct and complete apprehension of reality.

Sensory experience and the emotional states this evokes: this is the world that animals live in. Language is rooted in this world, and the names we use, even abstract ones, seem to be derived from words referring to sense experience. Look at the abstract or generalized words in the last sentence: *language* (from a word for the tongue), *rooted*, *abstract* (drawn away from), *derived* (flowing from), *referring* (carrying back). All associations between concepts and therefore all associations between words were also originally validated by reference to the sense-based world. Mental experience as a part of life genuinely distinguishable from sense experience does not come into play until self-reflective consciousness arises. Even when people have a distinct mental life, the language used in attempting to convey its contents to others still has to be the language of the sense-based world.

Before people started trying to communicate conceptual thinking, they were using language for its original purpose: to communicate on the level of the senses and basic emotions. Such communication gave enormous advantages to the groups that had acquired the ability to speak. What it also did was allow people to share with others, for the first time, the deductions and plans they had made in their own minds. A chimpanzee can solve a maze, but it is almost certain that a chimpanzee, without true language, could not pass on the solution to others, except by demonstration.[62] Humans can pass on what they discover, and this is the basis of human cultural traditions, discussed in chapter 5.

THE NERVOUS SYSTEM

So far in this chapter, I have confined myself to analysing mental processes, without reference to the brain activities associated with them. The standard account of animal behaviour and animal mental processes tends to start with the nervous system, usually taking it for granted that 'mind' is a word for certain electro-chemical processes and structures located in nerve tissue. Whether or not this is so, surely nerve tissue is not the *logical* starting point for such a discussion. We could start with the actual observed behaviour of animals (including their sensory abilities). Alternatively, we could start with what is in our own consciousness, introspected and compared with others' descriptions. William James adopted this point of view, and opened his classic *Principles of Psychology* with an account of what we directly experience.

Once we are clear about how internal, mental, processes manifest themselves, we are in a good position to investigate how much we can ascribe such processes to the 'mechanics' of the nervous system. The evidence is of a very strong correlation between mental capacity in animals and the size and structure of their brains,[63] although it is interesting that S. Brenner of the University of Cambridge, who succeeded in completely mapping every cell and connection in the nervous system of a tiny nematode worm, was still unable to predict its behaviour.[64] There is not space in this book to go into detail on the evolution of the brain and how each stage corresponds to mental capacity. The general conclusion is that higher levels of sense-based mental ability require brains with more cells, more connections between the cells, and more specialized brain regions. It seems reasonable to conclude that the bigger the brain, the better an animal is in manipulating and associating images and, eventually, concepts.

H.J. Jerison has studied the brain sizes of evolving groups of vertebrates by measuring and studying casts of the insides of their fossil skulls. In virtually all groups, brain size, relative to body weight, grew rapidly while the group was yet young, and subsequently remained steady for very long periods of time, until the present or until extinction.[65] Jerison's figures imply that true evolutionary advances are correlated with a rapid increase in brain size. This is particularly so for advances associated with a new group adapting quickly to occupy many newly accessible environments (adaptive radiation). However, animals that are not evolving rapidly tend to make do with a brain no better than that of their ancestors.

It may well be the case that each image, remembered or resulting from sensations, corresponds to a pattern of electro-chemical impulses in brain tissue. As for how mental processes are manipulated, that is a question to which several philosophical answers are available, under the heading of the 'mind–body problem'.[66] Some Buddhist attitudes to consciousness are considered in chapters 8 and 9. They have not yet entered the Western mind–body debate in an effective way. The almost unquestioned assumption in the scientific community is that consciousness is an effect of which the body (brain) is the cause. In Buddhism, while body and mind mutually condition one another, it is consciousness that is said to be primary. The world as we perceive it is largely a product of evolving consciousness. Ultimately, Buddhism questions the whole basis of the mind–body problem: the very distinction between 'inner' and 'outer'.

MIND IN EVOLUTION

We can be very confident that our earth has supported a continuous process of the evolution of the structure of living organisms. More tentatively, we can also trace how the 'internal' dimensions of animals – their minds – have evolved. It is fairly clear that the capacity of animals' minds has been limited by the size, complexity, and degree of centralization of their nervous systems, so that the evolution of physical form has constrained the evolution of mind. But has the feedback worked in the other direction too? Did mind play an active role in evolution, or was the human mind just 'an accidental afterthought in a quirky evolutionary play', as the biologist S.J. Gould puts it?[67]

Natural selection leads to increasing adaptation to a specific environment; it tends to promote specialization. In the mind, specialization is served by very specific inborn habits and instincts, which evolve by natural selection. But mind has an element which works in the opposite direction, particularly if individual learning and cultural traditions are possible: mind can be flexible. It can adapt an animal by coming up with behaviours that suit unexpected circumstances.

Because of its great adaptability, it turns out that mind has indeed been active in evolution. In particular, through behaviour, it can influence the process of natural selection itself. Apparently, behaviour can direct selection. To understand how this may be possible, we need to appreciate that changing environments, or more precisely ecological niches, are at least as important as natural selection in influencing the course of evolution.

Chapter Four

BEHAVIOUR, ANIMAL CULTURE, AND EVOLUTION

All progress is based upon a universal innate desire
on the part of every organism to live beyond its income.
Samuel Butler, *Notebooks*, Life, xvi

ADAPTING TO NICHES

Looking around at the natural world, it is obvious that it is made up of a huge variety of plants and animals, each kind very good at following a particular way of life. It has already been explained in chapter 2 how natural selection maximizes the fitness of a population of organisms by weeding out those that are less well adapted to their environment. Why, then, is there not just one 'super species', ideally perfected by natural selection, which has covered the whole earth and eliminated all competitors? The main reason is that so many different environments and ways of life are possible on this planet.

What I have called a way of life is technically called an *ecological niche*, or just a niche. R.C. Lewontin defines a niche as a multidimensional description of the total environment and way of life of an organism. Its description includes physical factors, such as temperature and moisture; biological factors such as the nature and quality of food sources and predators, and factors of the behaviour of the organism itself, such as its social organization, its pattern of movement and its daily and seasonal activity cycles.[68]

For example, the puffin's niche includes the rocky coasts it inhabits (in particular climatic zones), specific types of cliff top with burrows suitable for nesting, and a place in the food web, feeding on certain fish (varying with the time of year). Predators on adults and eggs contribute to the niche, as do the interactions with other puffins in colonies.

Natural selection adapts organisms to their own, special niches, which leads to the crucial observation that natural selection is normally a *conservative* mechanism, preventing, not promoting, change. The *status quo* that we study is of the array of organisms already very well adapted to their niches. If a mutation occurs in one individual, it is almost certain to be harmful. That is, mutations nearly always reduce reproductive success or fitness, they rarely increase it. The needs of organisms do not seem to influence which mutations arise. For example, adaptations to life on land, such as the beginnings of lungs and legs, are likely to be impediments to the life of a fish in its underwater niche. They are only useful, so the argument runs, in a niche quite unfamiliar to the fish: dry land. Tiny mutations, however, will occasionally offer the animal a small advantage, and so they will persist.

The natural selection of genetic variations, then, provides a full and clear mechanism for small-scale evolution. It explains the small adjustments that may continually improve the adaptation of a species to its special niche. But what of the major changes that have occurred in evolution? The greatest changes seem to have been relatively rapid, implying that they did not take place by gradual processes in a stable niche.[69] Can natural selection account for these changes? The answer is that it probably can, if another factor is brought in.

This second factor, obvious but often played down, is *changes in niche*.[70] If a population somehow finds itself in a niche different in some way from the one its species is adapted to, its normal members will no longer be so well adapted, and unusual individuals may respond better to the selection pressures, and leave more offspring. The unusual types will become commoner and commoner until a different kind of stable organism, well adapted to the new niche, has arisen. Thus evolution proceeds.

So if we explain evolution as being a process of adaptation to an environment and way of life by natural selection, we have only given half the answer, the half that describes how an organism changes over the generations in a fixed niche. The other half of the answer must account for how the niche itself can alter, and a full explanation of evolution must describe the interaction of the two processes.[71]

NICHE CHANGE

Lewontin's definition shows that niches are not just the physical surroundings that organisms live in. A niche is itself an interaction between organism and environment, so changes in niche can originate from the organism itself, the environment, or a combination of both. Here are four processes leading to niche change.

(1) *Chance niche change after mutation.* For example, a species of bacterium might develop, by mutation, an enzyme that digests plastics. Then, bacterial spores landing by chance on plastic (a new niche) can survive and multiply instead of dying of starvation. Some new diseases probably start in this way, but it is unlikely that it plays much role in the evolution of higher organisms. They tend to be able to maintain themselves rigorously in the niche they are adapted for, and so would be unlikely to find by chance a *different* niche for which a chance mutation just happened to be adaptive. For example, imagine a land-living otter-type animal that mutated webbed feet. It is surely unreasonable to imagine that the mutant would discover the value of its webbed feet in swimming if its niche never included life in water. A more plausible suggestion is given below. What is more, for a sexually reproducing population to become established in the new niche, the mutation and chance change of niche would have to occur in several individuals in the same generation.

(2) *Niche change by environment change.* Imagine a change in one of the following aspects of the environment (not an exhaustive list):
- Climate: e.g. the winters get colder
- Physical geography: e.g. an island becomes joined to the mainland
- Habitat: e.g. the forests where an animal lives are destroyed
- Food: e.g. prey animals start running faster
- Parasites or predators: e.g. a new predator arrives on the scene

• Competing species: e.g. competitors become better at exploiting a shared food-source.

There is very strong evidence that such environmental changes have induced the evolution of new species.

(3) *Niche change by migration and distribution.* Organisms tend to range into new areas in search of food and other resources, and sometimes in search of mates. Larger animals do this under their own steam, at various stages of their lives. Plants usually disperse only as seeds or spores. On occasion, some individuals may stumble upon a new niche, most often one opened up by a geographical change.

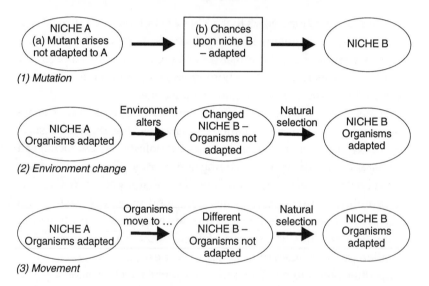

Fig.12 Niche-change mechanisms

All these changes are known to occur, and all are likely to change the selection pressures on a population, which will lead to evolutionary change if the organisms can cope, or extinction if they can't.[72]

(4) *Niche change by behavioural change.* The biologist Ernst Mayr claims that 'A shift into a new niche or adaptive zone is, almost without exception, initiated by a change of behaviour. The other adaptations to a new niche, particularly the structural ones, are acquired secondarily.'[73] The opening up or creation of a new niche by the adoption of new behaviours is the most interesting source of evolution from the point of view of this book. It is interesting because it may be described as 'mind-led', and it is discussed later in this chapter.

THE ORIGINS OF NEW SPECIES

If the entire population of a species is subjected to an environmental change ((2) above) then extinction or successful adaptation of the whole species will follow. The new, adapted type may be significantly different from the former type, in which case it is regarded as a new species, completely replacing the old one. The same can be true if the whole population is exposed to one of the other methods of niche change. As long as the individuals which successfully exploit the new niche remain in competition, and breed, with the rest of the population, the new niche is assimilated into the way of life of the population, which may thus evolve into a new species.

However, it is thought that new species often arise by the splitting of a parent species, not by its wholesale replacement. For this to occur, the population must be separated into two or more populations, reproductively isolated from each other. Reproductively isolated populations are ones which do not interbreed with each other, so that any new genes which arise in one cannot get mixed up with the old genes in the other population. Imagine that one of these populations starts exploiting a new niche: over the generations, as it adapts, it will become more and more different from the old populations. The parent species still remains in the old niche, but a new species has come into being as well. Splitting is important because new variations in a large population are easily swamped by the mass of genes which have not changed. Evolution can happen much faster in a small, isolated group.

I wonder what might happen to the sheep of the desolate island of Barra, in the Outer Hebrides, as an instance. At present, these sheep live largely on seaweed. If left to their own devices, as their hooves adapt to slippery rocks, their teeth to soft food, and their digestive tracts to a salty diet, they could suffer a sea-change – a new species of marine sheep?

There are various mechanisms which can permit reproductive isolation to occur,[74] the most obvious being geographical. People introduced the Barra sheep to their island, but a flock of birds might be blown on to a previously uninhabited island and successfully breed in the new habitat. The 'islands' of forests in an encroaching 'sea' of savannah probably encountered by human ancestors could have isolated small populations of hominoids, encouraging the rapid evolution of mankind.

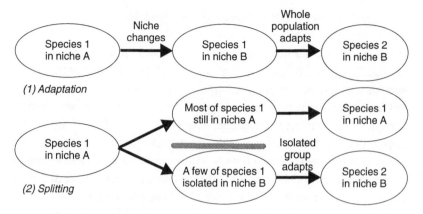

Fig.13 Speciation mechanisms

There have been occasions in evolutionary history when a grand new collection of niches has been opened up by a pioneering species, for example, during the first colonization of the land by higher animals. In such cases, the ancestral species very rapidly, in evolutionary terms, gives rise to a large number of new species, each exploiting one of the new niches. The process is called adaptive radiation. A classic example of adaptive radiation, first noted by Darwin, is provided by the closely related but highly diverse group of 'Darwin's Finches' on the Galapagos Islands.

Natural selection, then, combines with niche-change to permit the evolution of new species of organisms. Two almost independent causal processes continually intersect to determine what future generations are like: the replication of the genes with its occasional errors and variations, and the changing niche. It may well be that it was the fourth source of niche-change, behavioural changes, which had the profoundest effect on evolution; profoundest from the human viewpoint at least.

BEHAVIOUR-LED SELECTION: AN EXAMPLE

Here is a plausible example of how animals' behaviour can direct the evolutionary line their species follows.[75] As always in biological evolution, change is very slow, or if there are fast changes, they are very rare. This means that complete examples of behaviour-led selection have not been observed occurring in nature. In addition, fossil evidence for behaviour as opposed to structure is very hard to come by. So my example is of what may have happened, not of something that definitely did happen.

The only mammals that survived the dominance of the dinosaurs were little shrew-like creatures, probably living in the undergrowth of woods and forests, and feeding by night on small animals such as insects. They had smallish brains and used their noses rather than their eyes to sense their surroundings. By 80mya, some of these insectivores had taken to the trees, giving rise to the order of primates, mammals such as monkeys, apes, and humans. Some of the earliest fossil primates were rather like bushbabies with buck-teeth, having big, forward-facing eyes, and large brains. How did the change in habitat and structure come about?

Imagine a particularly fearless early mammal running up a low branch one night. Perhaps it is being pursued by a predator; perhaps it is in pursuit of a large and juicy beetle; or perhaps it feels a vague stirring of curiosity. It finds up the branch a snug hole, and spends the dangerous daylight hours asleep there. It is safer from predators, flooding, and other dangers than its relatives, who still hide by day in burrows, under rocks, or in piles of leaves. So it teaches its own young to sleep a little above ground level. Perhaps other members of the same species imitate it, or discover the new behaviour for themselves.

Because of the extra safety, individuals with the new behaviour survive better and leave more offspring (which follow the new tradition) than conservative individuals, and scrambling into low branches every morning becomes the norm throughout the population, probably within a few dozen generations. What is more, the pioneering behaviour has opened up a new ecological niche for the species – the trees. Trees offer safer nesting holes, and also a new range of insect foods; perhaps berries and fruits, too. Our pioneering insectivore may be tempted to spend the whole time in the new habitat.

A change of environment, a new ecological niche, means new selection pressures, and this is where the conventional evolutionary mechanisms come into play. The animals are spending time in trees. However, they are not adapted for climbing but for scampering about in the leaf litter. Any mutations will be strongly selected for if they tend to develop hands that can grasp the branches, a bushy tail for balance when jumping, good binocular vision for safe climbing and finding food, and so on. So first we had a behavioural change which introduced the animal into a new environment, and then naturally selected inherited variations changed the animal's structure. Even before the change of structure, incidentally, the new climbing behaviour could become an innate, inherited behaviour rather than one that has to be learnt afresh

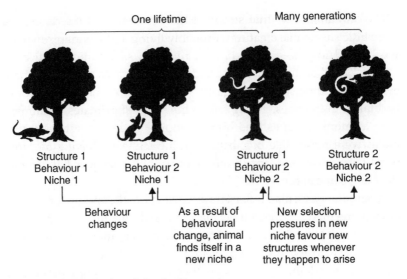

One lifetime   Many generations

Structure 1   Structure 1   Structure 1   Structure 2
Behaviour 1   Behaviour 2   Behaviour 2   Behaviour 2
Niche 1   Niche 1   Niche 2   Niche 2

Behaviour   As a result of   New selection
changes   behavioural   pressures in new
                  change, animal   niche favour new
                  finds itself in a structures whenever
                  new niche   they happen to arise

Fig.14 General behaviour-led selection process

by each baby mammal. Natural selection sometimes 'prefers' instinctive to learnt behaviours, because they can be carried out more quickly and automatically, freeing the attention for other tasks.[76,77]

BEHAVIOUR AND NICHE-CHANGE

The example of ancient insectivores discovering life in the trees showed how innovations in behaviour can open up a new environmental niche. The finding of new niches has been a vital part of animal evolution. I said that evolution requires not just natural selection but also a change in niche, and behaviour-led selection can be involved in all the types of niche change that I listed earlier in this chapter. If the environment alters, or if some individuals stray into a new environment, behavioural changes are very likely to play a role in helping them to survive. For example, if our primitive insectivores were plunged into a series of severe winters, behavioural innovations in making cosier nests might well prevent the extinction of the population for long enough for thicker and thicker fur to arise by the natural selection of inherited variations in fur length.

The potential for new behaviours is also, presumably, often important when an animal is faced with changes in local habitat and geography, food supply, predators, or competitors. If the insectivore lives mainly on slugs but the slugs die out, it must turn to another food or starve to death. (We must not forget here an even more direct way in which animal choice influences evolution. That is the selection of a preferred mate, whose genes will mix with the suitor's genes to contribute to the next generation.)

I mentioned earlier that new species are thought to arise usually by the splitting of an existing species, so we need some mechanism which isolates the population from any remaining members of the species still following the old life-style, so that the new and old groups do not interbreed. Some isolation mechanisms themselves involve changes in behaviour, so that behaviour-led isolation should be added to behaviour-led selection as a factor in evolution.

For evolution to proceed, reproductive isolation and niche change must occur together. In animals that *can* change their behaviour, new behaviours are likely to be the commonest way for that to come about. As the biologist C.H. Waddington observed:

> Animals ... live in a highly heterogeneous 'ambience', from which they themselves select the particular habitat in which their life will be passed. Thus the animal by its behaviour contributes in a most important way to determining the nature and intensity of selection pressures which will be exerted on it.[78]

It is through behaviour-led selection that animals may affect the future course of the evolution of their own species. Individual choices and preferences ensure that evolution does more than merely grope randomly into new areas. By way of recapitulation, here is how the philosopher Karl Popper summarizes this view:

> At first sight Darwinism ... does not seem to attribute any evolutionary effect to the adaptive behavioural innovations of the individual organism. This impression, however, is superficial. Every behavioural innovation by the individual organism changes the relation between that organism and its environment: it amounts to the adoption of or even to the creation by the organism of a new ecological niche. But a new ecological niche means a new set of selection pressures, selecting for the chosen niche. Thus the organism, by its actions and preferences, partly *selects the selection pressures* which will act upon it and its descendants. Thus it may actively influence the course which evolution will adopt. The adoption of a new way of acting ... is like breaking a new evolutionary path.[79]

The Origin of New Behaviours

If changes in behaviour have a role to play in evolutionary change, how and why do behavioural changes arise? Is behaviour completely inborn – fully programmed by the genes? If this were so, behaviour could only change if the genes changed, a given experience invariably stimulating an inborn sequence of actions. However, behaviour is never fully preprogrammed. There is always some flexibility, a flexibility which increases as we consider increasingly intelligent animals, and animals which have gained greater independence from their environmental conditions.

A very simple life is exemplified by the earthworm. It must swallow moist earth, avoid drying air and light, and quickly retreat if pecked. So it can rely largely on genetically programmed behaviours. The blackbird that seeks the worm lives in a far more complex niche. An infinite variety of images of the world are presented to it by its senses, and it has a vast repertoire of innate behaviour patterns, to be combined together to construct an action that fits the situation. But a bird's behaviour is not all innate. It also has an ability to learn from experience and from the traditions of its social group; it is able to choose from a range of possible behaviours, as the peahen does when she chooses which resplendent peacock to mate with; and it is even perhaps able to discover behaviours never tried before.

Whether or not animals have a potential for innovative behaviour is a fascinating and controversial question. In the broad sense of innovation, they certainly do, because new behaviours do somehow arise. Conceivably, these might be accounted for entirely by chance and a combination of the other genetic and non-genetic factors mentioned above,[80] but it does not seem unreasonable to allow a creative role for an animal's mind.

Very intelligent species can introduce novel behaviours by mental processes presumably akin to reasoning in humans, an example being problem-solving in captive chimpanzees as described earlier. It is important to notice that intelligent innovation need not require a self-reflective process of deliberate invention: being 'conscious' in the human sense is not necessary. The same is true of animal 'choice', a word which is no longer taboo among ethologists.[81]

Sometimes an animal stops. It pauses, looks around: more than one possible next action may be open to it, one of them perhaps novel. Where do the possibilities, so far only mental, come from? How is one chosen, to emerge into real action? Here, one can, I think, only speak metaphorically, in order to point to junctures in our minds that could be similar to the choices made by our animal relatives. The animal's mind is bounded because its own past defines a limited area of tried responses. But, however slowly, that mind could be an evolving mind. It might glimpse, if you like, an action beyond the boundary of habit, and somehow, somehow, dare to do it.

Less intelligent animals probably hit upon new advantageous behaviours partly by accident. Perhaps our primitive insectivore ran up a low branch without noticing that it was any different from a piece of rising ground. But even in such a case, the animal's mind must surely play a part. It must *recognize* the benefits of the behaviour, and be able to *repeat* the behaviour; we saw in the last chapter that recognition is a primary function of the mind. The pioneering insectivore learnt to associate the branches with safety or food, and so ran up them whenever it had the opportunity. In addition, the new behaviour needs to survive the death of its inventor. Either contemporaries must be able to adopt the new behaviour by imitation learning, or the innovating animal needs to succeed in *teaching* the new behaviour to its offspring. Both kinds of learning represent more demands upon mental capacity.

Whether its source is insight or accident, a novel behaviour has to overcome the time-honoured, habitual, and automatic response to the same situation. A space is needed, a postponement of habitual responses so that an animal just may, occasionally, choose a new response. As I said in chapter 3, waiting before acting is characteristic of the most intelligent animals. On another level, it is very relevant to higher evolution as well. Even human beings are dominated by impulsive, unthinking actions. The first step in higher evolution is to open up a space of awareness between stimulus and response, a space for creative choice.

The arising of new behaviours in animals depends upon two things. Firstly, the flexibility of the existing behavioural repertoire of the species, which I shall say more about later. Secondly, the preparedness of the animal to try out new behaviours and venture into new situations. The urge to explore new situations is popularly called curiosity. The proverb says that curiosity killed the cat, but the selectionist view is that some curious cats must survive, or natural selection would have completely eliminated curiosity in cats. Or would it have? It may be that curiosity can only be curbed if growth in mental capacity is restricted: my own suspicion is that the tendency to explore and innovate is a direct consequence of mental capacity. If this is the case, natural selection can only reduce curiosity by reducing mental capacity.

As I explained in the last chapter, it is now fairly well accepted that higher animals use their sensed experiences to build up an internal representation of all relevant aspects of their environment – a mental map. The mental map would then be the animal mind in its static aspect, a picture of what the mind holds, ready for news from the senses and ready to guide action. The inputs and outputs are the mind's dynamic aspect. On the input side, there is selective attention, the selection of experiences for inclusion in the 'map'; on the output side, the control of behaviour.

In this view, exploratory behaviour is accounted for by an animal's need to discover more about its environment, to improve its map. A greater mental capacity implies a more sophisticated map, and so a greater urge to explore and a greater ability to innovate behaviour.

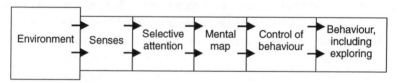

Fig.15 Exploring to update the mental map

There is plenty of evidence for curiosity – an urge to explore – in animals. Laboratory rats will explore the whole of an experimenter's maze even if they know already what part the food reward is in: an exploratory urge, not hunger, is driving them.[82] In one experiment, hapless rats were punished for putting their noses into certain boxes. The punishment conditioned them to avoid those particular boxes, but could not dissuade them from exploratory behaviour. Other boxes remained just as interesting to them.[83]

If exploratory and innovative behaviour are consequences of mental capacity, the behaviours themselves do not have to be selected for. It is the sophistication of an animal's mental maps and its general mental abilities that have a bearing on its fitness: mental capacity is the trait selected for. If it is beneficial for an animal to have an elaborate 'map', of course it will explore to fill in the gaps; if new possibilities for action frequently arise, it will have the potential to originate new behaviours.

In some circumstances, those animals which push their potential for exploration and innovation to the limits may frequently get themselves into trouble. If danger lurks around every corner, the cat would do well to restrain its curiosity. As a result, a certain degree of caution and fear of the unknown, inhibiting exploration and innovation, is apparent in all higher animals. It is partly innate and partly learnt from parents and from experiences of 'close shaves'.

MIND AND THE DIRECTION OF EVOLUTION

Behaviour-led selection gives exploratory and innovative behaviours a central role in evolution, at least in higher animals. The nature of these behaviours also shows why it is that an overall direction can be assigned to evolution: a continual increase, over the ages, of the highest level of mental capacity found among living things.

All other things being equal, the better an animal knows its environment, the more effectively it can live. So better and better cognitive mapping ability (i.e. mental capacity) will be selected for, so long as there is not too high a price to pay in other ways. The price is in the danger accompanying filling in 'maps' through exploration, and in the cost in time and energy in doing so when there are more basic demands to be met.

Considered in isolation, mental capacity is *not*, however, a characteristic that will automatically increase by natural selection, because all other things are *not* equal. Mental capacity that is not made use of is presumably an unnecessary burden. Mental capacity is to some extent related to brain size, and a brain bigger than is really needed is a physical liability. Unneeded mental capacity is also a disadvantage if effort has to go into preventing its full expansion in exploration and innovation, because of the drawbacks or dangers involved. A sheep, for example, needs most of the daylight hours just for munching grass and chewing the cud; it has no time to be clever and creative, nor even to have to keep restraining creative urges.

Mental capacity has certainly increased at the leading edge of evolution, though, and it is possible to see a cycle of behaviour-led selection that could explain why. Let us imagine a behavioural innovation that reduces the danger inherent in exploring, or which reduces the time and effort required for life-supporting activities like eating, finding a mate, or keeping warm. For example, if all its predators had been left behind on the ground, our pioneer insectivore could explore safely in the trees, and its new arboreal food sources might be more abundant than its former ones. There would be a selective advantage in the animal using its new freedom and leisure to explore everything in its niche as thoroughly as it could (including, incidentally, its social world). So much new knowledge would stretch to the limit its brain's abilities to maintain a full mental representation; it would be remembering all it could remember and associating images in the most sophisticated ways it was capable of.

In a safer and better-provided niche, exploratory behaviour is no longer limited by its danger and by competing demands on time, but only by mental capacity. So those animals with the greatest brainpower will be selected for, and the physical basis of mental capacity will increase over the generations by natural selection until danger and demands on time once more become the limiting factors. But the new cleverer animals will be capable of yet more innovations in their behaviour, some of which in turn may uncover less risky and more leisured ways of life in which cleverness can once again increase.

Mind and genes consequently form an interactive system, mental effects inducing new selection pressures which induce genetic changes, and genetic changes helping to improve mental capacity. Other forms of selection still operate in animals where mind has become important, but selection involving behaviour and therefore mind is the most likely factor explaining the continuous improvement in mental capacity observed at the 'growing tip' of evolution. The brain/behaviour interactive system seems to have been the overwhelming force which accelerated the evolution of modern *Homo*, as we shall see in chapter 5.[84]

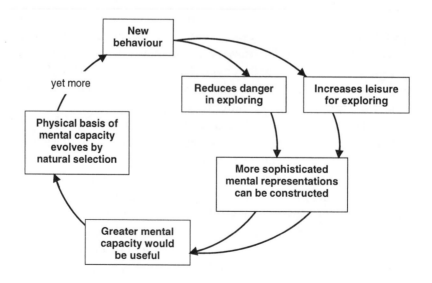

Fig.16: The hypothetical spiral of behaviour-led increase in mental capacity

DO MINDS CAUSE BETTER MINDS TO EVOLVE?

If this ascending spiral or positive feedback loop of mental development is a valid explanation for the known increase in mental capacity during animal evolution, it has some extraordinary implications. It is as if minds have a tendency to create new ecological niches in which better minds can evolve. Each mind encompasses a self-augmenting, even self-transcending, tendency probably not found in any other characteristic of living organisms. Other characteristics may develop along a certain direction, but they eventually meet with natural limits, or even reverse their direction of change. For example, animals get bigger along many evolutionary lineages, but very large animals breed slowly and sustain only small populations and so are susceptible to extinction if there is a big disaster.

It may be that the evolving mind has also encountered a limit; after all, nuclear annihilation is only possible because of the spectacular inventiveness of humans. But such a limit looks intuitively unlikely, since in general an individual animal with greater mental powers is more likely to find solutions to the problems it encounters than its duller relative.

Why, then, are all animals not rapidly catching up with humans in their intelligence? The answer probably lies in the lack of accessible new niches in which their minds could blossom. Such niches would have to have lower constraints on mental capacity; that is, exploring would be less dangerous or less costly than in the present niche. The very limited innovations in behaviour that even the brightest sheep could come up with are unlikely to free it from its prison of eating and watchfulness. And the situation for the less bright animals is exacerbated by the fact that the niches of greater freedom are probably all already occupied by more intelligent species. In the inequitable hierarchy of mental evolution, it is always the cleverest creature that has the most options for mental advance open to it. The others are trapped by the very narrowness of their outlooks. We humans have already won the race to self-reflective consciousness, and unless we destroy ourselves, where could another earthly species find the ecological space in which to make the same advances?

Behaviour-led Selection, Genes, and Evolution

Although new behaviours can arise without any genetic changes, the genes do have a role in innovative behaviour, in constraining the range of behaviours which are possible. For example, if our early insectivore had a gene which gave it a strong tendency always to run downhill, it would never run up a sloping branch! (This is not as far-fetched as it sounds: deep-sea sharks, say, have a genetic predisposition always to swim upwards, since otherwise they tend to sink.) Similarly, many behaviours are ruled out by the structure of an animal. A ground-dwelling insectivore can climb a tree, if rather clumsily, but it doesn't have the option to swoop through the tree tops like a bat, since it hasn't any wings.

Behaviour-led selection can operate, then, if there is sufficient flexibility in behaviour. The animal behaves in a new way, but in a way which is within its existing behavioural repertoire. Natural selection then modifies the animal in its new, behaviour-chosen niche. Now the new kind of animal will have a new behavioural repertoire, permitting behaviour-led selection to open yet more evolutionary doors for it. The new behaviours are not genetically determined, but the degree of flexibility – the range of behaviours possible, known as plasticity – is limited by genetic factors.[85]

The animals that we regard as higher tend to have the highest degree of behavioural plasticity, this being one of the ways in which they achieve independence from environmental changes. So a 'higher' animal can initiate much larger evolutionary changes through behavioural innovations than a 'lower' animal can. Consequently, behaviour-led selection is either absent or slow in simple animals. Either behaviour-led selection is only significant in advanced, flexible animals, and naturally selected chance variations govern the evolution of primitive animals, or, if behaviour-led selection is important in primitive animals, it only works in very tiny steps over very long periods.

However, the more flexible an animal is, the freer it is from the pressure of natural selection. Red deer, for example, can adapt quickly to unusually cold weather by seeking out the most sheltered places, and huddling together for warmth. Inherited physical adaptations for different climates, such as length of fur, are thus much less important in deer than in animals which cannot alter their behaviour.

The more one speculates over the origins of the breakthroughs in the evolution of animals, the more plausible it becomes to consider that behavioural changes played a major role in many of them. Improvements in mental ability have already been considered. Then there is the conquest of the land, the care of young, warm-bloodedness, the origin of flight, improvements in the sense organs and the associated parts of the brain, changes of food source, new social structures, the rapid exploitation of new habitats and the diversification of species there – these all may well have been initiated by behavioural changes. The great American biologist Ernst Mayr asserted that 'many if not most acquisitions of new structures in the course of evolution can be ascribed to selection forces exerted by newly acquired behaviours. Behaviour thus plays an important role as the pacemaker of evolutionary change. Most adaptive radiations were apparently caused by behavioural shifts.'[86]

Consider a fairly minor evolutionary change – the development of the otter from terrestrial ancestors. Alister Hardy asks which is more plausible: that ancestral otters mutated webbed feet, and *then* took to the water, or that they first started hunting in water, where webbed feet were subsequently selected for?[87] Surely the latter.

Behaviour-led selection has explanatory power, but is it generally accepted? There has been something of an orthodoxy in biology, explaining things solely in terms of chance and the actions of inherited chemical structures.[88] Some biologists committed to this orthodoxy are unwilling to implicate mental factors such as choice or innovation in the evolutionary process. But the orthodoxy is being challenged, or at least modified, as mind and behaviour capture the attention of increasing numbers of creative scientists. However, even for the biologist with his or her own exploratory and innovative tendencies unrestrained, it is difficult to come by evidence that behaviour may influence the course of evolution.

As always in evolutionary biology, there are only jigsaw pieces of evidence, no complete pictures. Behavioural innovation? – Yes, plenty of examples have been observed. Great tits and blue tits discovering how to open milk bottles for the cream is a famous one,[89] and Japanese macaques learning to wash dirt off the sweet potatoes and grain they were fed is another. The British myxomatosis-prone rabbits (see chapter 2) who abandoned their underground nests provide another example. But human observations have not been going on for long enough to give time for structural changes to follow in these cases, if any structural changes would have adaptive value. Future blue tits with bottle-opener-shaped beaks is perhaps too far-fetched a notion!

Is it possible for characteristics acquired during an animal's lifetime to yield new selection pressures which give rise to structural changes programmed in the genes? Again, yes; several examples have been observed in the laboratory, the process being known as 'genetic assimilation'.[90]

Unfortunately, looking at the fossil record, one cannot tell the source of the niche-changes that presumably preceded a new species. Dr R.F. Ewer gives an example of tooth-wear in fossil pigs, however.[91] The pigs look as if they changed their diet, and in later generations the structure of their teeth altered in adaptation to the new diet.

To sum up: like us, animals have minds – their 'insides'. Minds have surely evolved and become more sophisticated over the ages. And it is very likely that minds have played a major role in animal evolution, because of animals' potential to 'choose' to change their environments. Mind and structure interact to shape the life of the individual, and over many individual lifetimes behaviour, environment, and natural selection all interact to guide the process of evolution. Of particular interest is the possibility that innovations in behaviour can fuel increasing mental abilities, which in turn permit more radical innovative behaviour.

CULTURAL TRADITIONS IN ANIMALS

The previous sections have suggested that mind became a causal factor in evolution as soon as animals became capable of some flexibility in their behaviours. Being flexible in behaviour enabled an animal to choose, in a non-self-aware way, to change its ecological niche. Behaviour-led selection, mental in origin, was thus added to the blind groping of chance mutations in guiding genetic evolution. Behaviour-led selection shows the mind at work in genetic evolution. But as minds developed, a quite different kind of evolution became possible: cultural evolution.

At first sight, culture seems a uniquely human achievement. The term embraces traditions of stories, myths, and customs; industries and crafts; the development of art, science, and religion. Some of these elements of culture, however, are already present in some animals. As long as an animal sometimes consorts with individuals from other generations and can learn new behaviours, it is capable of starting traditions, of maintaining culture. In fact, learnt cultural traditions are quite common among birds and mammals, though they are not often found in lower animals.[92]

I have already mentioned tits learning to open milk-bottles. The behaviour is not innate, not in the genes, but neither is it discovered afresh by every new-fledged tit. What happens is that the young birds learn the behaviour as they follow their more experienced seniors. This is how young oyster-catchers learn from their parents the very tricky technique of opening a mussel shell to eat its flesh. There are two distinct cultural traditions: in one, the oyster-catcher disables the mussel underwater by stabbing through its still open shell; in the other, it hammers on the weakest part of a closed shell to break it open. Individual oyster-catchers are observed only to use one method, and it is this method which their offspring always learn.[93] Again, in bird songs and mating displays, regional and even family variations are found which are transmitted from generation to generation by a learning process.

TRANSMISSION BY LEARNING

Learning is sometimes a solitary business of trial and error, and fails to become part of any traditions. It is education – learning from others in the same species – which is the prerequisite of culture. An animal can get its education by imitation learning, by gathering information, and by training.

Imitation learning is the commonest way, where the learner is active, and the 'teacher' just continues with its normal activities. An animal observes another perform a particular behaviour and copies it, practising until it achieves proficiency. Some birds learn their songs, in the local dialect, in this way.

The transmission of specific and transient information is very widespread, but it could only be a truly cultural process if the information was not transient but of long-term value, and if it was preserved over a number of generations. A deer flashing the white underside of its tail and rump as it runs off in alarm is telling its comrades about a potential danger, but culture would be involved only if the meaning of the gesture had to be learnt: the specific danger being signalled will have passed within a few minutes.[94] An animal which attends to the actions of more experienced members of its social group is participating in a genuine culture if it thereby collects knowledge which will be of use in the long term. It might find out, for instance, which foods are edible or which other species are dangerous predators.

In imitation, the learner is active. In information-transmission, the learner passively attends. Training is the cultural mechanism in which both parties are actively involved. In the absence of true language, what happens is that the novice imitates and the teacher reinforces if the imitation is good, punishes if it is wrong. Most commonly, the trainer is a parent. For example, captive primates often train their young in the rules of acceptable behaviour. Training seems rarer among wild primates: it has been suggested that a captive animal pesters her offspring more to alleviate the tedium!

CULTURAL INNOVATION AND EVOLUTION

Animals are far more conservative in their habits than people. Nevertheless, their traditional behaviours can change, and new traditions can arise. I have already discussed the introduction of new behaviours. In higher animals, innovation is thought to be ascribable to individuals who hit upon, or even invent, new ways of doing things, ways which are then learnt and transmitted by relatives and neighbours of the inventor. Clearly, such innovations are unlikely to occur simultaneously to every animal in a population; it is single individuals, or at most a few individuals, who are likely to be responsible, as in the case of the bottle-opening tits.

As well as the tits and the potato-washing macaques, other examples of innovation have been observed. The ornithologist P.F. Jenkins watched singing inventions as they happened in a New Zealand songbird, the saddleback. Every so often, a bird would 'compose' a new song, based upon an old one, but with changes of pitch, repetition or elision of notes, or the addition of fragments from other songs. The new song would be copied by young birds and become part of the local song 'dialect'. Incidentally, male saddlebacks wander from district to district, always learning and using the song dialect of the locality they find themselves in.[95]

Are cultural changes haphazard? Perhaps they are in the case of the specific score of a bird's song, though one ethologist, W.H. Thorpe, insists that birds rely partly on a refined musical taste in choosing how to sing![96] But in general, animal behaviour is a matter of life or death. Behaviours are adopted because they are successful in promoting survival and reproduction; for example, learning to sip the cream on cold winter mornings, or learning to be very shy of humans carrying guns. A group of South African elephants whose forebears were hunted down one by one in 1919 but who have since been completely protected are still known as among the most dangerous elephants in Africa. The extremely shy and defensive behaviour which permitted a few to survive the hunting has been passed down unchanged over several generations. An elephant never forgets, so they say, and it makes sure its descendants don't forget, either.[97]

Behavioural innovations, such as this loss of tameness, generally arise and survive because they help the animals to be fitter in an evolutionary sense than other animals lacking the behaviour. In fact, we can say that the behaviours are selected, naturally selected. So cultural traditions can evolve by the natural selection of advantageous new behaviours. It should be added, though, that it may sometimes be possible for disadvantageous cultural forms to evolve and persist.[98]

However, there is a crucial difference between the way cultures evolve and the way that the physical characteristics of animals evolve. The difference is that cultural evolution does not depend on the genes. Animals can evolve radically new traditions of behaviour without any change at all in their genetic make-up. All the genes do in influencing cultural evolution is to constrain the repertoire of behaviours possible to an animal, and to affect the flexibility of its behaviour.

This means that cultural evolution can proceed at a much faster rate than genetically-based evolution: a new culture can be taken up by a whole group of animals within one generation. The speed of cultural evolution increases the plausibility of behaviour-led selection. Major new behaviours could spread rapidly through a population as a part of cultural evolution, taking the population into a new niche. There, the slow processes of natural selection could start to work on building a new structure appropriate to the new niche.

The increasing importance of culture is said to explain why evolution proceeds so much faster in 'cultural' types of animals. A.C. Wilson gives the following figures. Our own genus has evolved at four times the rate of hominoids, six times songbirds, fourteen times other birds and mammals, and forty times reptiles and amphibians.[99]

Very many specific behaviours in higher animals are not genetically determined at all, but are learnt, and these behaviours form a reservoir of information surviving from generation to generation which is quite distinct from the information stored in the genes. Genes are chemical structures copied into the cells of the body. But learnt behavioural traditions are mental structures preserved as habitual responses and memories.

It is generally thought that the genes alter only by chance, not through need, and usually gene mutations have deleterious consequences. But the mental traces which underlie cultural traditions[100] can alter as a result of an animal's experiences, even perhaps its 'choices' in a sense, as these traces are subject to innovations by individual animals.

Genetic changes are slow and unwieldy, but cultural evolution is limited in speed only by the quickness of an animal's mind and by how amenable its fellows are to modifying their traditions. Cultural and genetic evolution are distinct but not separate. The genes dictate the repertoire of cultures accessible to a population, and, as we have seen, new behaviours can direct the course of genetic evolution by introducing new selection pressures.

With cultural evolution potentially proceeding much faster than gene-based evolution by natural selection, cultural innovations can become the dominant force in the evolution of intelligent species, through behaviour-led selection. The slow process of natural selection is usually a conservative force, helping a species to settle down into an increasingly highly specialized way of life in a static niche. The only 'direction' that natural selection would seem to impose in evolution is one of increasing adaptation. It tends to promote changes which make an animal fit more and more snugly into its specialized niche. A highly specialized species tends to be very vulnerable to environmental catastrophes or new competitors, as we can see with modern animals like the giant panda. The panda eats only bamboo shoots, and in years when all the local bamboos flower and die, many pandas starve to death. However, natural selection cannot 'foresee' that overspecialization is risky, and no convincing mechanism for selection for adaptability, for being a generalist, has been proposed.

New behaviours, as well as environmental changes, keep disrupting the stabilizing influence of ordinary natural selection, and flexible generalists survive to move in if the specialists are overtaken by some disaster. Cultural animals can survive environmental upheavals because so much of their environment is of their own making – they live in partly 'cultural' surroundings. A baboon's social group is a culture-made environment (and thus is made by mind, the director of behaviour). With culture, an animal gains increasing independence from its physical environment. Natural selection working through the genes becomes of less and less importance because what might be an ill-adapted creature without its learnt traditions of behaviour may be well adapted in its clothing of culture. I mean metaphorical clothing, but real clothing is a good example: how would an Inuit survive in the Canadian winter without his fur coat?

Culture, rooted in fluid mental factors rather than in the intransigent crystals of the genes, has been the secret of the overwhelming biological success of the greatest generalist of all – mankind. We are highly adaptable largely because we can evolve cultural forms to cope with almost any environment. The faculty that underlies our cultural inventiveness is self-reflective consciousness; in Julian Huxley's words, 'evolution become conscious of itself'. We shall investigate its importance in the next chapter.

Chapter Five

SELF-REFLECTIVE CONSCIOUSNESS

*'It is very unhappy, but too late to be helped,' Emerson had noted in his
journal, 'the discovery we have made that we exist. That discovery is called the
Fall of Man. Ever afterwards we suspect our instruments. We have learned
that we do not see directly.' Wisdom interfused with compassion should be the
consequence of that discovery, for at the same moment one aspect of the
unexpected universe should have been revealed. It lies deep-hidden in the
human heart and not at the peripheries of space. Both the light we seek and the
shadows that we fear are projected from within. It is through ourselves that the
organic procession pauses, hesitates, or renews its journey.*
Loren Eiseley, *The Unexpected Universe*, 45

FOUR-DIMENSIONAL EVOLUTION

We all have the same roots. All human beings are products of a great
evolutionary process, and by appreciating this we can understand our
common humanity. Our physical forms have evolved, our minds have
evolved, and our cultures have evolved. These are three of the four
interwoven strands or dimensions of evolution that I outlined in the
Introduction, and these three dimensions have been our topics so far.

We saw that living organisms have evolved in their physical structures. We saw that as animals gained in independence and complexity, an activity within them called 'mind' gradually pushed apart the poles of sensation and action. Minds evolved. When organisms with minds gained the ability to learn patterns of behaviour and even mental processes from their elders, evolution achieved a cultural dimension too.

There is a fourth dimension in the universe of evolutionary change, and it is this dimension, individual or higher evolution, which forms the culminating theme of this book. It and the other three evolutionary dimensions are as incommensurate as time is with the three dimensions of space. Yet modern physics unites time and space (in general relativity), and perhaps higher evolution can, too, be reconciled with the other dimensions of evolution.

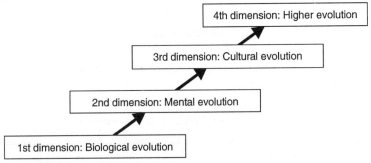

Fig.17 The four dimensions of evolution

The dimensions of evolution appear to form a hierarchical series. They can be ordered according to their recency of appearance, their complexity of structure, their apparent independence from the material base, and according to their potential value and importance to us as human beings. But each dimension or level rests very firmly on its predecessors, and each continues to influence the development of the others. Thus evolving life appeared in a lifeless physical world, its prerequisite being stable chemicals which could replicate themselves slightly unreliably. Evolving minds appeared in living organisms as they developed nervous systems mediating stimulus and response. Evolving cultures appeared among living animals with minds, capable of learning from other animals' minds.

Higher evolution had to be the last of the four dimensions to appear, because it is a possibility only to beings with minds and culture. Something quite novel, a mysterious new faculty, was necessary for the fourth dimension of evolution to begin. Animals with minds, interacting culturally with others, had to become aware of their distinctness from those others, and deliberately turn their attention to their own mental life. So the prerequisite for individual or higher evolution was the arising of self-reflective consciousness, the truly human level.

Rising consciousness

The human level of consciousness is a condition of mind that we all experience, but at times we also experience degrees of consciousness which are lower than this self-reflective level. They are lower in the sense that our awareness is more limited in its scope. For example, in deep sleep we are breathing, our heart is pumping, we are definitely alive. Alive, but not aware, not conscious. We remember nothing of deep sleep when we wake up: no experiences have been illumined around us during that period. As I write these words, however, I can see the pencil in my hand, feel my fingers on my cheek, and follow the thoughts as they jell into words on the page. Accompanying these processes is a general experience of the mental 'illumination' itself that reveals them to me – I am aware that I am aware.

In deep sleep, I am, practically speaking, completely unconscious. Writing at this moment, I am in a state of self-reflective consciousness; and I can assume that you, the reader, are too. I can assume it not because we are always fully self-reflective, but because drawing someone's attention to the possibility of self-reflective consciousness has the effect of inducing that very state, of making one aware that one is aware. The distinction between unconsciousness and self-awareness is quite plain, a matter of common experience. We all know what self-reflective consciousness is, but it's an extraordinarily slippery concept to try to define.[101] To define it clearly, one would have to find concepts which related to other experiences still more fundamental; there probably are no such concepts.

I have used the word 'consciousness' very broadly. It is present whenever an animal has *appropriate responsiveness* to the world it perceives, and so it correlates with being awake and alert. There is an evolutionary sequence of levels of consciousness, as well as a parallel scale of levels accessible to the human individual. Reviewing our experience, surely consciousness in general, and not just self-reflective consciousness, displays a full spectrum of degrees or intensities, right from the deepest sleep to the brilliant clarity of our most joyfully – or painfully – aware moments. There are the various types of dreaming sleep, a number of day-dreaming, bleary, and absent-minded states, and ones in which attention is intermittent and strained. What is excluded from consciousness? Answering this question pin-points how low or high the level is. When the focus to which perception impinges (the 'self') is included, then consciousness is self-reflective.

A dreaming level of consciousness is responding to a perceived world, the landscape of dreams, but a world lacking inputs from the physical senses. Dreams usually also lack self-awareness, until one recreates them from memory in the morning. Yet even in deep, dreamless sleep or coma, there is *some* responsiveness; the unconsciousness is not absolute.

An experienced car driver may cover the whole journey in a 'highway trance', so that the perceptions he has responded to so skilfully may not even seem accessible to later remembering. Anything unusual entices him out of the 'trance': a flashy sports car passing at speed; frustrating hold-ups; an emergency when he takes a corner too fast. Then he is present in his experience for a while, though not in a thoroughly satisfying way.

Consider eating. In a hurry or watching television, one may bolt the food down with only just enough presence of mind to ensure that the fork passes into the correct opening. Then there is an unpleasant crunch – a piece of grit in the vegetable – and the rest of the plateful goes down very gingerly, as one feels around with the tongue for any more stones. As with the driver, it is often something unexpected that triggers a stronger consciousness with a continuous sense that 'I am here doing this'. One faces a threat or an opportunity, affecting one's body, or more often one's ego, and one has to be on the ball to ensure nothing goes wrong. When things are back to normal, one sinks back into a less alert state, with relief.

There is another incentive to fuller self-reflective consciousness. Sometimes one finds oneself in a state that has been called by L.L. Whyte 'aesthetic awareness'. Aesthetic awareness is far from being a frustrating break in one's habitual dull reverie. It is a clear attention, that takes in a fuller than usual purview of present experience, savouring its finer aspects, appreciating its significance and beauty. The driver finds himself tingling with vitality as he races through the countryside, wondering at the play of light on the spring fields, happy to be alive. One gives that meal one's full attention, being present in every mouthful, eating with quiet deliberateness.

This aesthetic awareness is the beginning of higher evolution, 'man in his wholeness, wholly attending', as D.H. Lawrence has it. It comes unbidden, on occasion, to every human being. But one does not have to wait and hope: it can be cultivated systematically. The price to be paid is not to seek escape from periods of the more uncomfortable episodes of self-reflective consciousness. When they are present, instead of getting through them as quickly as possible, one can infuse them with the 'zest and ease' of full self-reflection, a process known in Buddhism as mindfulness practice. We shall consider it more carefully in chapter 9. Facing discomfort is one way of enhancing mindfulness. Another is finding experiences that stimulate one's aesthetic sense, for example the contemplation of art or nature.

Given the range of possible degrees of consciousness, it is not surprising that biologists, psychologists, and philosophers make so many apparently contradictory and even contentious assertions about consciousness. The reason is more often confusion of meanings than confusion of thought; in English, the available terminology in this field tends to be inadequate and loosely used. Returning to the metaphor of illumination, it is as if one word, 'consciousness', is used to refer to various intensities of mental 'light' illuminating various objects. Whenever the 'self' bearing the light is one of the objects 'illuminated', we are in a state of self-reflective consciousness.

Here, I shall continue the evolutionary account in order to build up gradually to the self-reflective level of consciousness. I hope that the significance of this level will become plainer as the elements which make it possible are seen to have been added one by one in our evolutionary past. Of course, we cannot know for sure what has happened in the minds of animals and people over past ages. But several fields of study combine to suggest how the full human level of self-reflective consciousness probably arose. These include the study of living animals, the record of the past of our own species, the mental development of human children, and individual introspection.[102] Surely it was not a sudden 'waking up' from something like deep sleep; surely it was a gradual development with recognizable and causally related steps.

THE CENTRE OF EXPERIENCE

I described above the stage in the evolution of mind at which some animals became capable of constructing mental representations or 'maps' of their experience. An animal takes in data about its world through its senses and compares sensed images with a representation of that world, previously built in its mind. The comparisons may yield certain associations, such as 'food' or 'danger', or they may show that the image is something new, missing from the mental map, which needs incorporating.

An animal with a mind sophisticated enough to retain mental representations has the beginnings of a centre of experience. Mental maps give enough structure and capacity to an animal's internal experience, its mind, for it to begin to distinguish an 'inside' from an 'outside', if only in a very vague way. The animal's attention can be switched from inside to outside and back again. It can replay its mental representations as it remembers past experiences or plans future actions, alternating between attending to its sensations and the mental models inside.

In this way, animals may sometimes have a rudimentary awareness that perceptions are entering an individual self which seems distinct from the source of those perceptions. And they may notice that actions originate in a self which seems distinct from where the actions have their effect. Experience then has a centre upon which sensations seem to impinge, and from which actions seem to emanate. Before this stage, awareness had been spread over a diffuse circle of perceptions. Now, for the first time, there is a central point, at which all impressions and experiences can be knitted into a unity.

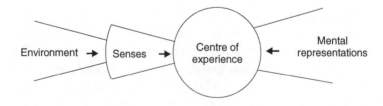

Fig.18 The centred experience

It is important to realize that the centre of experience, the 'self' in normal usage, is presumably not itself attended to at this stage, and that the boundary between external and internal is as yet very fluid and undefined. We are not yet talking about self-reflective consciousness. And it would seem that there is, so far, no realization that others too might find themselves as centres of experience.

An important result of experience being centred is that since there is an agent, a 'self' (though so far one which is not itself an object of awareness), the individual animal can experience its continuity in time. It does not live entirely in the present, but has a little awareness of past states and of motives directed to the future.

There is some evidence that the most intelligent animals experience themselves as the centre of their own attention in certain circumstances.[103] For example, captive chimpanzees, orang-utans, and gorillas quite quickly learn that the image in a mirror is their own, and they will wipe off smudges marked unbeknown to them on their faces if they notice them in a mirror. This would seem to imply a centred awareness of the type described above (though I would disagree with those researchers who claim that it indicates self-reflective consciousness of the human sort). Animals other than great apes never seem to learn that a mirror reflection is of themselves, and continue to grope behind the mirror, or threaten what they see as a rival. This is why you may have seen birds aggressively flying at house windows, sometimes stunning themselves: they are attacking a rival seen reflected in the glass, a rival precisely as belligerent as they are. Human babies, by the way, can recognize themselves in a mirror by the age of fifteen months.[104]

It is very tempting to regard animals as more human than they really are. This is particularly true for animals with which one has a close relationship: a devoted pet, a working animal, or any animal one knows well, even the subject of a long scientific research project. It conveys its own personality, often so active, hilarious, and spontaneous. If one is honest, though, does that dog really understand every word one says? Even chimpanzees and dolphins, marvellously quick-witted though they are, have nothing like the capacity for reasoning, communicating, loving, choosing, self-knowing, creating, or being nasty that people have. Animal language? The claimed successes in teaching language to apes have been called into question in recent years.[105] Bertrand Russell once remarked: 'No matter how eloquent a dog is, he cannot tell me that his father was poor but honest.' In any case, captive animals frequently display abilities never observed in the wild. We have seen, for example, how chimpanzee mothers in captivity train their young. This is doubtless partly due to the advantage of prolonged close contact with people.

In the discussion, we have now got as far as a rudimentary kind of self-awareness – awareness of a centre of experience – associated with the existence of complex mental maps. At this level, the 'self process' itself is not attended to, and other members of the same species are not recognized as 'selves', either. The next step very probably occurred as a result of more and more attention being paid to those other potential 'selves'. I would say that there is no really convincing evidence that it has happened in any species other than the human.

SELF-REFLECTIVE CONSCIOUSNESS

Human beings have always been intensely gregarious. One can infer too that they have always had the potential for great behavioural flexibility. The complex mental representations of our early forebears allowed them to try out strategies in advance mentally, and to review them in memory. It must have been in social situations that mental capacity was tested most stringently. So many characters to get to know: whom can you trust? Who is dominant, whom can you trick in some way? A constant manoeuvring for advantage in very complex social games can be observed in the most social of living non-human primates, the baboons, and a similar situation probably prevailed in the tribes of early humans.[106]

To win in 'games' of social advantage one needs constantly to evaluate one's performance, and so a capacity for increasing self-awareness would be of great value. There is a closely related reason for introspection of some kind being of great advantage to early man, an even stronger one than for checking out social strategies. This is what the experimental psychologist Nicholas Humphrey calls 'doing psychology'.[107]

Humphrey's conclusions are based on intensive studies of primates, particularly baboons in the wild. He believes that self-reflective consciousness evolved because introspection was such an effective way of predicting the behaviour of others. Early humans with the greatest insights into the 'psychology' of their fellows would be most successful in all relationships, and thus they and their relatives would reap the rewards in dominance, food, safety, and access to the best sexual partners. The discovery of the short cut of projecting one's own inner experience on to others was a great breakthrough, claims Humphrey, as it is a far more efficient way of predicting others' behaviour than 'behaviourism' – that is looking for patterns in their external actions. 'Reflexive consciousness, by giving each individual a picture of the psychological structures which underlie his own behaviour, provides him with a framework for interpreting the behaviour of others like himself.'[108]

It is a natural step from 'modelling' what one would do in someone else's shoes to actually imagining what it must be like to be them: the beginnings of empathy. And from there it is a small step to imagining how they see you. The anthropologist Margaret Mead believed that during the development of the child, reflective self-consciousness originates by such a sequence,[109] and perhaps something similar happened in evolution. What would seem most likely is that the ability to focus attention on one's own mind came about gradually as a result of several factors. The more alienated and anxious state of imagining how others see one, fittingly called being 'self-conscious', was one factor. Another was introspection for 'doing psychology' – for predicting others' behaviour. And a third was curiosity: people with mental capacities far higher than anything ever seen before on earth being naturally fascinated by their own minds.

At first the centred experience gradually consolidated into a recognition that one's own self is autonomous, and separate from other selves around one. Then the realization gradually dawned that one could attend to the workings of one's own mind, as well as being able to attend to sense-experience. (This is sometimes described as perceiving a model of the self in the mental map, but such a view is logically very problematic: what and where is this 'self' that is being modelled?) As language developed, probably in tandem with self-reflective consciousness, words were found to fix and objectify the awareness of being aware; words were found for the concept of 'self' that had arisen in the human mind.

Some authorities believe that a baby cannot at first distinguish its mental experience from the world around it. In the first four to eight months, the 'self' is confused with the physical world. Then the infant discovers, say, that if it bites its pillow it feels nothing, but if it bites its finger, it hurts, so it identifies itself with its body, its sensations and emotions. This 'body ego' is stable by around age two, and by two, the child seems to recognize itself as an 'agent': it discovers that its deliberate actions can affect its experience. Thus it might shake its rattle *in order* to make a noise. Gradually, the child learns to speak and to use symbols and ideas, including imagining things which are not present to the body's senses. Thus a mental identity emerges, learning to control the body and its instinctual responses, to manipulate aspects of the physical world, and to interact with others. The mental identity usually develops between four and seven years old. Finally, around adolescence, awareness develops the ability to separate itself from

Level of consciousness	Characteristics	Animals possessing it
7. Full self-reflection	Fully rational thinking, awareness of unity of life and possibility of directed transformation, independent individuality, highly creative awareness. Unselfishness. Mindfulness.	Some humans (first in the axial age)
6. Beginnings of self-reflection	Speech, verbal concepts, abstraction, deliberate altruism, deceit, conscious emotions, alienation from experience, systematic invention and planning. Deliberate transmission of culture – strongly group-based. Conformism.	Humans only
5. Centred experience	Simple consciousness. Dream experience. Associative 'thinking' with non-verbal concepts. Planning, problem-solving, complex communication. Flexible cultural traditions.	The most intelligent mammals
4. Representation	Images combined in ideas and mental representations; memory, anticipation, likes and dislikes. Communication and imitation learning, exploratory and innovative behaviour. Beginnings of cultural transmission.	Birds and mammals
3. Perception and association	Recognition of complex stimuli by comparison with innate 'images', goal-directed behaviour, association-learning, training.	Animals with central nervous systems
2. Recognition	Recognition of simple classes of sensations, fully stereotyped responses. Sensitization and habituation'learning'.	Animals with nerve-nets
1. No consciousness		Non-living matter, living things without nervous systems

Table 2: Levels in the evolution of self-reflective consciousness

whatever else is going on in the mind, an ego consolidates, and the child has, sometimes at least, self-awareness.[110]

As self-reflective consciousness developed gradually in the human species, so each individual today achieves it only after long and gradual development (and also in a pattern strongly conditioned by cultural factors). And self-reflective consciousness in the full sense can still be a mental level in which one feels awkward, precarious, and over-stretched, so that for most of one's life one gratefully sinks back into some variation of a dimmer, less conscious state. However, being self-aware is a necessary precondition for developing one's own consciousness any further, for higher evolution. This is why the Buddhist programme of self-development stresses the practice of mindfulness so strongly.

Mindfulness is the Buddhist term for sustained self-reflective consciousness. Fully developed self-awareness is more than the ability to follow one's own mental experience. It also incorporates qualities like sympathy with others, a sense of purpose in one's actions, and a creative imagination. We shall return to mindfulness in a later section. The table opposite updates the levels of consciousness surveyed in chapter 3, to include the levels of self-reflection.

Self-reflective consciousness was the greatest achievement of our ancestors and offers our greatest opportunities for further human achievement. It would be such a waste if we were not to put this legacy to use. The psychoanalyst Erich Fromm wrote:

> Man has awareness of himself, of his past and of his future, which is death, of his smallness and powerlessness; he is aware of others as others – as friends, enemies or as strangers. Man transcends all other life because he is, for the first time, life aware of itself. Man is in nature, subject to its dictates and accidents, yet he transcends nature because he lacks the unawareness which makes the animal a part of nature – as one with it.[111]

The real trouble is not that we are human, with all the anxiety self-knowledge brings, but that we are not human enough. We can become *fully human*, I would say, by strengthening our awareness, that is by consolidating our self-reflective consciousness. Chapter 9 gives the Buddhist account of how this may be achieved.

THE EFFECTS OF SELF-REFLECTIVE CONSCIOUSNESS

Some time in the last few-score thousand years, the occasional person occasionally awoke to self-reflective consciousness. For more than three thousand million years before that, the fecund 'ocean' of evolution had seethed with teeming forms of life, the characters in a wild, dreamerless dream. Gradually, dreaming minds had bubbled up in the sea-dream to play with parts of it like puppeteers. Now at last, a few dreamers burst out of the ocean in brief intervals of wakefulness, ungainly creatures, humans like us, thrown on to the beach of self-reflective consciousness.

We can look back over that ocean and see the marvellous organisms that break its surface and dive again; we can look back, in imagination guided by the discoveries of science, over our own evolutionary past. Looking back, that breakthrough of self-consciousness seems the most momentous transition that living forms have ever taken. Is it not the faculty of self-reflective consciousness that underlies every ability that distinguishes humanity from animals?

We are able to achieve things that animals cannot because we can act and think *intentionally*. We can act and think intentionally only because our minds can form intentions, of which we are *aware*, so intentional action without self-reflection is not possible.[112]

What has intentional action and thought given us? Mentally, it has given memory in the full sense: the deliberate recall of stored experiences, followed by conscious attention to them. It has given planning in the full sense: creating sequences of possible actions and evaluating them. It has given reasoning in the full sense: consciously following ordered chains of concepts to a conclusion, and checking that their succession is logical.

It has granted positive emotions a human status: love, in the recognition of the value and autonomy of others; concern, through conscious identification with another's experience; self-confidence through recognition of one's ability to cope with life; reverence as one becomes aware of the differences between people, and the fact that some people to some extent embody one's ideals.[113]

Self-reflective consciousness has also brought the negative emotions into the human sphere, by adding to biological drives an urge to protect and strengthen the self-reflected self or ego. So animal appetite becomes a craving for mental possessions that will fortify a wounded ego; animal aggression becomes a desire for the destruction of what seems to thwart this possessiveness; and animal fear of immediate danger becomes a more continuous fear, particularly of death.

These mental attributes made possible by self-reflective consciousness in turn transform the animal's socially maintained traditions into

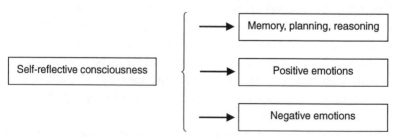

Fig.19 The effects of self-reflective consciousness

truly human culture. It was claimed in chapter 3 that language and conceptual ability evolved together in humans. Language is itself a form of culture, and it is also a vital precursor of nearly all other forms of human culture. Growing self-reflective consciousness must have influenced the development of language no less than it influenced the purely mental abilities already mentioned. The pronouns 'I', 'me', and 'mine' were invented to refer to the self-concept that now had its place in human minds. Communication could be far more subtle and extensive, since speakers could intentionally reflect to themselves the contents of their own minds, labelling what they found, and conveying it in words.

The new linguistic abilities could then be used to impart skills to others, notably in making tools, and to pass on traditional and ephemeral knowledge of food-sources, topography, and so on from person to person. As language grew in sophistication, it permitted greater self-consciousness by providing a conceptual apparatus for a mental commentary on experience. One can talk to oneself, putting one's feelings, actions, and plans into words, and so know more clearly what is going on in the mind. This increasing self-consciousness must have demanded more subtle distinctions in language, as well as encouraging other cultural advances, a feedback loop rather like that produced by behaviour-led selection, as described in chapter 4. With the new language abilities, stories could be told to strengthen group identity, and myths could evolve to describe and account for the structure of the world, society, and human life.

SELF-REFLECTIVE CONSCIOUSNESS AND THE DEVELOPMENT OF HUMAN CULTURE

There is evidence for growing consciousness in the history of human culture. Conversely, the development of human culture seems to have depended on the presence of some self-reflective consciousness. A baby, we are told, experiences itself as the whole centre and meaning of existence, since it cannot distinguish its mental world from its sensed surroundings. In order to start to learn cultural traditions from its parents, such as speaking, social rules, and the accepted 'meaning' of various experiences, the growing infant needs to recognize the existence and authority of things outside itself. Cultural transmission by learning requires at least the beginnings of independence.

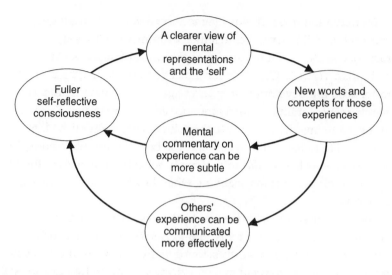

Fig.20 Language and self-reflective consciousness feedback loop

Even with animals, we could say that individuals have no real independent existence until they start to *learn* things. Without learning, every member of the species will behave in virtually the same way in the same circumstances. Once learning is possible, an animal has its own history, its own character, and it can even intervene (as it were) in its species' evolution. A pet-owner will confirm that two stick insects seem like each other's clones in terms of behaviour. Two goldfish may be distinguishable, but boredom sets in if you watch them for too long. Perhaps the more doting owner may decide to give each its own name. Two budgerigars can have quite distinct characters, and two dogs have personalities that seem to cry out for humanizing descriptions.

Once animals have some individuality, culture is possible. Once individuality is accentuated by human self-awareness, culture becomes a major part of life. Because, as it expanded, self-reflective consciousness allowed an increasingly effective transmission of customs, ideas, and especially values, it had a profound effect upon culture.

The variations in one's own state of mind indicate that the beginning of self-reflective consciousness was not a sudden switching on of a complete faculty. One should not imagine a scene of brutish ape-men all over the world rousing each other one morning from animal slumber to full human wakefulness. The process has been a long and gradual one, and it still occurs nowadays in every person, with varying degrees of intensity and persistence. The history of humanity has been the history of growing self-reflective consciousness.[114]

When it first appeared, self-reflective consciousness was no doubt a very occasional, private, and rather baffling experience. It was only gradually recognized in language and human culture. Attempts have been made to trace the infiltration of self-awareness into collective life by examining the myths and archetypal images of ancient peoples and of modern cultures regarded as primitive. The Jungian psychologist Erich Neumann, for example, uses his knowledge of myth to trace the changing contents of the unconscious mind. He infers the stages by which the self has disengaged itself from immersion in nature and the social group, a historical process recapitulated by each individual as he or she becomes psychologically mature.[115]

We do not have a complete picture of ancient mythologies, and it is doubtful to what extent modern tribal peoples are really 'frozen' primitives, and so a great deal of Neumann's work is speculation. The same applies, to a greater extent, to Ken Wilber, who attempts to extend Neumann's ideas by employing a framework for the evolution of consciousness derived largely from the Hindu tradition.[116] Nevertheless, both authors provide profound insights into the origins of modern consciousness, and remind us that we will understand consciousness and its history much more fully if we come to understand the contents of our own unconscious minds.

The rising influence of self-reflective consciousness did not only leave its record in the unconscious mind. Many of the innovations and advances achieved by human beings provide evidence of conscious intention; the innovations must often have set up a changed environment in which further developments in awareness became possible. Before the time of civilization and written records, we cannot be very certain about the chronology of changes in consciousness, but the following table gives an approximate idea.

The table of important events in the rise of self-consciousness is of necessity quite speculative, and the relevant dates are being constantly revised in the light of new evidence. Two particularly significant periods in prehistory are said to be the appearance of our own genus, *Homo*, about 2mya, and the 'neolithic revolution' which commenced soon after the end of the last ice age, about 12,000 years ago. For many thousands of years after that, self-awareness remained dim and evanescent, and only in historical times did full self-reflective consciousness become well established in some people. We shall see why this was so in the next two chapters.

Time	Event	Effect on self-reflective consciousness (src)	Influence from src
By 4mya	Walking upright	None directly, but freed hands for tool-making etc.	None
3–0·5mya	Co-operative behaviour (hunting, gathering, carrying and food-sharing)	Encouraged planning, language, cultural traditions and 'doing psychology'.	Permitted more sophisticated forms of co-operative behaviour.
c. 2·5mya	Tool-making	Required cultural traditions. Involved concentration, and deliberately modifying an object held in front of one. 'Ownership' may have strengthened the self-sense.	Conscious processes aided design and memory.
c. 2mya	Dramatic increase in brain size	Src may have required an increase in mental capacity, which correlates with brain size.	Since src was probably highly adaptive, any modification which permitted it would have been selected for.
Possibly some by 2mya (but possibly much later)	Language (conceptual)	See text (pages 62 & 105)	See text
1·9–1·4mya	Right-handedness	Unknown	May result from the left hemisphere of the brain specializing in functions connected with the more conscious activities, probably an effect of src. Other species (except parrots) seem never to have more right- than left-handed individuals, or vice versa.
By 0·6mya	Use of fire	Light at night and central hearth may have provided the time and circumstances for social rapport, which was probably important for src.	Overcoming the natural fear of fire.

Time	Event	Effect on self-reflective consciousness (src)	Influence from src
60,000ya	Deliberate burial of the dead	Bringing the importance and problem of death to the attention of all.	Implies a recognition of and valuing of the individual. Decorating the corpse and providing grave-goods may suggest a knowledge of the distinctness of mental and bodily processes, yielding a suspicion that bodily death does not necessarily imply a cessation of mental life.
30,000ya (possibly much earlier)	Visual art	Provides the artist with a sense of autonomy and creative power and objectifies mental images, showing how much different people's mental images have in common; all of this would strengthen src.	Requires conscious imaging ability, knowledge that an image can be represented concretely, and an intention to execute a particular work of art.
c.11,000ya	Agriculture and settlement in towns and villages	(a) Encouraged long-term view of human life and its relationship with natural cycles. (b) Extra surplus gave increased leisure to some, allowing time for reflection.	Careful long-term observation of the best way to grow crops demanded much continuity of attention, good memory and planning, and effective communication.
c.9,000ya	Domestication of animals	Possession of animals would have strengthened the self-sense, and possibly prompted the idea of 'possessing' human slaves or subjects.	Care of animals requires the long-term and autonomous stability of memory and planning provided by src.
by 5,200ya	Writing	The first purely mental production, since abstract symbols are now being preserved outside the mind.	A systematic invention requiring much thought, and demanding co-operation and understanding in order to spread.

Table 3. Self-reflective consciousness and human culture[117]

Chapter Six

CIVILIZATION AND THE AXIAL AGE

A civilization is simply a great metaphor which describes the aspirations of the
individual soul in collective form – as perhaps a novel or a poem might do.
The struggle is always for greater consciousness. But alas! civilizations die
in the measure that they become conscious of themselves....
Lawrence Durrell, *Clea* 143

HISTORY STARTS

Most of the landmarks in the rise of human consciousness listed in the
last chapter are assigned to what is called prehistory. Cultures can only
really have a history when they start writing down a record of the
events which are of importance to them, so history starts with writing.
And the ability to write, according to most historians, is one of the
hallmarks of a civilization.

It is very risky – productive often of both heat and prejudice – to exalt
one group of people as 'civilized' and dismiss another as 'uncivilized':
no rigorous definition of the term civilization can cool the partisan
feelings that the topic evokes. The civilizations were the main concern
of the great though controversial historian Arnold Toynbee

(1889–1975), and he provided what is more an evocation of the process of civilization than a definition of the term. No other recent historian of Toynbee's stature has dared to seek the common patterns (if there are any) in the rise and decline of civilizations.

Toynbee makes a sharp distinction between 'primitive societies' and twenty-one civilizations which have existed since the invention of writing.[118] Primitive societies as we see them, says Toynbee, are profoundly conservative, since their members are conditioned to imitate their elders and ancestors, not to seek change. However, as a civilization arises from a primitive society, people are prepared to look forward rather than back, and they imitate certain creative personalities who have the talent and independence to act as pioneers in new cultural developments. So the arising of a civilization is a period of unprecedentedly rapid cultural innovation.

Toynbee's simile for the distinction between primitive society and civilization is a vivid one:

> Primitive societies, as we know them by direct observation, may be likened to people lying torpid upon a ledge on a mountainside, with a precipice below and a precipice above; civilizations may be likened to companions of these sleepers who have just risen to their feet and have started to climb up the face of the cliff above....[119]

He warns, though, that this view is only a snapshot. The 'sleeping' primitive societies must have climbed to their present pre-civilized level by past creative efforts. Civilizations in their turn have a tendency to become static and moribund; and then they in due time become the camp of sleepers from which new civilizations awake.

Characterizing civilization, as Toynbee does, as a dynamic phase in the alternation of static and dynamic societies is unspecific enough for anyone to put forward his favourite culture as being truly civilized. However, Toynbee and other historians demand more specific attributes from a candidate for civilization. A primitive society is one which has not developed these attributes. The most characteristic and general of these is the coming together of a large group of people to achieve feats impossible at the family or small tribal scale, and their long-term unification under common, complex forms of culture and religion. Civilizations are recognized by their construction of such things as irrigation systems, great cities, and temples. They are also recognized by writing, an important tool in the organization of the new projects.

'Public works' are impossible if everyone has to work full time just to have enough to eat, so an agricultural surplus is a prerequisite for civilization. This is why most of the early civilizations arose in fertile and well-watered river valleys in warm regions.

Why, then, did civilizations not spontaneously arise in all such places soon after the adoption of agriculture? Toynbee says that more than the right environment was needed. He also presents evidence to reject the suggestion that certain races were naturally predisposed to be civilized and to bestow civilization upon others. Neither nurture (environment) nor nature (genetic race) fully explains civilization. Instead, Toynbee claims to discern a common pattern in the origin of all the better-understood civilizations, both early and late.

In each case, a static harmony was intruded upon by a strong stimulus, tending to give rise to variations in the old static order. This is a recurring theme in myth, the harmonious matrix perhaps being personified in a nature-bride and the stimulus in a potent deity, the creative result being, say, a great hero. Thus Zeus, in the form of a shower of gold, visited Danaë in her brazen tower, who as a result bore the hero Perseus. The initial harmony is too internally 'perfect' to generate change; a challenge, even a disruption, is required.[120]

Later we shall try to discern the type of human consciousness characteristic of civilized societies. I think it is reasonable to regard the new attitudes necessary to start to co-operate on a large scale, to develop new unitary cultures and religions, and to invent written symbols for words, as all indicating definite changes in human consciousness.

Knowledge of all the details of environment and racial character cannot, Toynbee says, allow us to predict whether or not a new civilization will appear. There is an unknown quality – 'the reaction of the actors to the ordeal.... Psychological momenta ... decide the issue.'[121] Toynbee is confident concerning the creative conditions for civilizations, but he is less clear concerning the actual stimuli which conceived the first ones; his concern to establish a law of historical progress tempts him to oversimplify the wide variety of probable causative factors involved in the birth of the different civilizations.[122] So let us look very briefly at the first literate town-dwelling societies, in Sumer, Egypt, India, Crete, China, and America, and see what challenges might have stimulated men and women to create the first civilizations there.

THE FIRST CIVILIZATIONS: IRAQ AND EGYPT

As far as is known, Sumer was the earliest civilization. Around 4000BCE a farming people moved into the jungle swamps around the lower reaches of the Tigris and Euphrates rivers in what is now Iraq and started opening them up for irrigated cultivation. What stimulated them to face such a challenge? Pressure on food resources due to drought used to be the favourite explanation, but it is now thought that there may have been no drought.[123] Agriculture was already being practised in oasis and stream-side settlements scattered over south-west Asia, but these were presumably too small to support civilizations, and provided no challenge requiring such an advance. But when people tried to settle the Iraqi river valleys, they found that agriculture was only possible with highly organized co-operative efforts. It was civilization or nothing.

Civilization was a real possibility here because of the geography of the land between the rivers; but the creation of civilization rather than nothing must be credited to the genius of the Sumerian people. 'The psychological factor responsible to no little extent for both the material and cultural achievements of the Sumerians', says the archaeologist Samuel Kramer, 'was an all-pervading and deeply ingrained drive for pre-eminence and prestige, for victory and success.'[124]

Sumer being the first civilization, it could conceivably have been the source of all others. This is not now generally believed, but there is evidence of some Sumerian influence on all the other early civilizations apart from those in America.

The Nile Valley in Egypt was more benign than the valleys of the Tigris or Euphrates, and agriculture advanced steadily there until a literate and centralized civilization is recognizable from about 3200BCE. The historian J.D. Evans ascribes its initiation to the unification of the country under the first Pharaoh, known in legend as Menes.[125] If this is the case, the lever which lifted Egyptian civilization from a primitive society may have been the authority of one man, stimulated in part by an awareness of the Sumerian advances.

THE FIRST CIVILIZATIONS: INDIA, CRETE, CHINA, AND AMERICA

The Indus Valley civilization was founded by 2500BCE in Pakistan and north-western India, when Egypt and Sumer were already well established and trade was flourishing. The archaeologist Mortimer Wheeler does not, however, believe that the Indus civilization was merely a daughter of either of its elders:

> The Indus civilization, with its individual technology and script and its alien personality, was no mere colony of the West. But ideas have wings, and in the third millennium the *idea* of civilization was in the air in western Asia. A model of civilization, however abstract, was present to the minds of the Indus founders. In their running battle against more spacious problems than had been encountered either in Mesopotamia or in Egypt, they were fortified by the consciousness that *it had been done before*. And in that consciousness, after one failure and another, – they won through. In some such manner may be reconstructed the initial phase of the Indus civilization, as the ultimate triumph of a village or small-town community, determined, well-led and inspired by a great and mature idea.[126]

In the valley of the Yellow River (Huang-Ho) in northern China, local people were once again confronted with the challenge of taming a marshy, thickly vegetated, and flood-prone river valley, and they created a civilization around 2100BCE. The Yellow River people were tested more rigorously than the inhabitants of other Chinese river valleys such as the Yangtze (where civilization did not penetrate until very much later), facing extremes of heat and cold in summer and winter. They seem to have solved most of their problems themselves, but a few cultural features were probably borrowed through trade with western Asia.

The next was the Minoan civilization in Crete, beginning about 2000BCE. It is possible that the Minoans were stimulated into civilization by contact with Sumeria or Egypt, but Toynbee suggests that migrating peoples broke through to civilization as they overcame the challenge of the sea in reaching Crete.[127]

Central and South America each saw the appearance of civilizations from primitive societies. By about 1250BCE there was a sophisticated culture, that of the Olmecs, in Mexico, building earth pyramids and carving jade, but without metals or large cities. Rather later, about 800BCE, another civilization emerged in Peru, from a culture known as the Chavin. The Chavins and their successors in South America right up to the Incas never invented writing, but the Olmecs of Mexico devised a script, which continued to be used later by the Mayans. Neither the Olmec nor the Chavin civilization grew in a fertile river

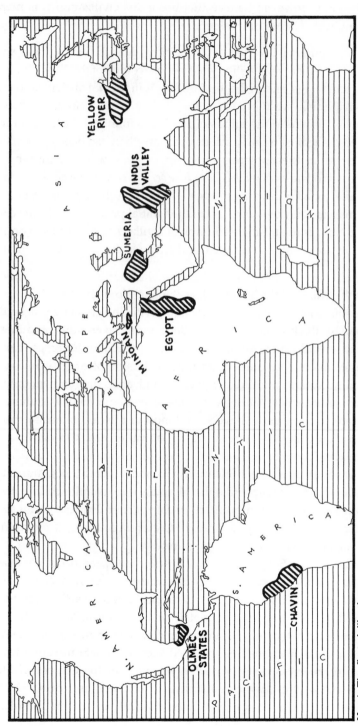

Map1: The first civilizations

valley: the cultivable land tended to be on high plateaux, choked with dense jungle. Toynbee speculates that the serious environmental difficulties in part provided the challenge needed to instigate civilization; in addition, the terrain was so varied that communities with very different life-styles might live in close proximity to each other, stimulating each other culturally.[128]

The Sumerians, Egyptians, Indus Valley people, Minoans, Yellow River people, Olmecs, and Chavins can be regarded as the seven pioneer civilizations. History starts with them. So far as is known, the 'civilized' attributes of all human civilizations can be traced back to one or more of these.

CONSCIOUSNESS IN THE TRADITIONAL AGE

First the settled life of farming and later the collective life of civilizations were great cultural breakthroughs, that is breakthroughs originating in human minds. They were the gradual and cumulative achievements of many people, often over many generations. Nevertheless, as with the evolutionary advances already considered, their originators could not just stand back and contemplate their achievement as, say, a sculptor can, for they had altered their whole world of experience and now had to find new ways of living and perceiving in their new environment. The beginning of history was the result of changes in consciousness, and it was the condition upon which further changes would take place.

It is very hard to imagine what experience must have been like in the early civilizations. All one has to go on is the evidence of social and economic life unearthed by archaeologists, together with objects of religious art and architecture; writing at first was used only to keep records of collective work, levies, trade, and so on. Later, written records give more insight into the mentality of the time. There are the annals of royal dynasties, royal proclamations, codes of law, texts on gods and their rituals, and heroic and tragic epics.[129]

Reviewing what is known of the ancient civilizations, one first notices the many disparities between them. Take the oldest three: Egypt, Sumer, and the Indus Valley. Egypt was rural, conservative, highly centralized, and ruled by a deified king (the Pharaoh), obsessed with the after-life. Sumer was much more urbanized, composed of warlike city-states with their own local gods, and was prone to more rapid cultural changes. The Indus civilization was also urban, but seems to have been admirably pacific (virtually no weapons are found in the older layers) and very well organized. Evidence can already be seen there of some of the later Indian cults of natural fertility deities; and pictures of figures sitting cross-legged have been taken to demonstrate that people practised meditation.

Nevertheless, a number of writers have seen enough in common between the ancient civilizations to speculate on what their predominant mode of consciousness was like. Ken Wilber, in his survey of the development of consciousness, *Up from Eden*,[130] says that consciousness in agricultural and early civilized societies was at a level characterized by a strong feeling of 'membership', that is, membership of a coherent group from which each person unquestioningly derived his or her values and world-view. This may be called the 'traditional age' in which rigid loyalty to cultural traditions best served the interests of human communities.

It is likely that full self-reflective consciousness was extremely rare in the traditional age. In an influential account of its appearance, Julian Jaynes finds no evidence of self-reflective consciousness before the second millennium BCE.[131] This may appear less surprising if one reflects upon how easily one can get by, even today, without bothering to maintain full self-reflection, and how much time most people spend in an 'unmindful' state, to use the Buddhist term.

Drawing mainly on the art and literature of the time in the Mediterranean and Middle Eastern civilizations, Jaynes suggests that the achievements of human beings in the traditional age are explicable without allowing for an ability to take deliberate decisions. People's mental representations of a complex (and highly social) world formed the basis for intuitive conclusions, which were then hallucinated as spoken instructions, ascribed to an ancestor, a social superior, or a deity. So in the *Iliad*, a poem which Jaynes thinks reflects the experience of people with this type of mind, the heroes hear and even see gods and goddesses instructing them in times of crisis. After excluding later interpolations, Jaynes claims that the author(s) of the *Iliad* demonstrate no inkling of the possibility of thinking a problem through, or even of the existence of mental acts. However, the *Iliad* shows signs of the voice-hearing mind breaking down, since its characters generally hear voices only when under great stress, as do schizophrenics today.

Unfortunately, Jaynes does not consider that self-reflective consciousness (which he just calls 'consciousness') might occur in several degrees, and so he sees it as arising rather suddenly, and much later than most other authors suggest. He is also hampered by apparently restricting 'consciousness' to the state in which one stands back from experience and provides a sort of mental running commentary on it. None the less, his theory of how people's minds worked in the traditional age rings true to me, if regarded as the norm and not the inevitable rule. After all, one does often use a verbal process to make complex decisions, talking to oneself in one's mind. Without self-reflection, any such mental talking would presumably seem to be a 'still small voice' with an origin outside the self.

THE BEGINNINGS OF RELIGION

Reading back what we now call 'religion' into a prehistoric past, we do not find one unified phenomenon. Instead, we are left with a number of subheadings forming part of a description of prehistoric cultures. Cultural traditions might have included a number of things now regarded as aspects of religion:

- myths of the origins of the world and the tribe
- an interest in how consciousness continued after death
- a sense of the 'numinous' – fear or wonder at mysterious or powerful aspects of experience
- the use of magic to influence people's behaviour, women's fertility, the success of the hunt, the natural world
- accounts of altered states of consciousness.

Only much later did religion become a separable part of culture, perhaps when it became institutionalized in the traditional age.

We feel that we can neatly divide our experiences into those with an internal, mental origin, such as dreams, emotions, and thoughts, and those with an external origin – events in the world, perceived through the senses. In a situation where self-reflective consciousness was only occasional and weak, such a clear-cut distinction would rarely have been made. The material world was probably seen as alive, and possessed of a personality, or many personalities. And mental experience also constituted a world, a world of mental representations, not fully distinct from the material world. The mental world was closer to the centre of experience that gave a feeling of location to each individual, but there was little of a defined boundary between mental and sensed experience. Both were characterized by light and power, sometimes capricious, mysterious power.

All experience must have seemed a complex web of relationships with various beings, various personalities. Some were one's real relatives, neighbours, rulers, or enemies. Some were the personifications of natural forces and places, spirits or gods of rivers, thunder, or a city, for example. Others were perhaps the admonishing 'voices' of dead ancestors and half-forgotten heroes, if we accept Jaynes's idea. It is all very speculative, but perhaps these were the roots of religion in traditional societies. The personalities of the gods were further filled out in the myths told about their roles in the origins of the world, of humanity, and of human institutions. Then superstition and fear helped the powerful or ambitious to consolidate their control by a sincere appeal to the support of the divine voices, confirming their rule and even their cruel intentions.

Religions in the traditional age were always associated with a particular community and a particular area, since their objects of veneration were a specific group's ancestors and heroes, and local nature deities. They spread by conquest. Thus Marduk, the city god of Babylon, eventually headed a pantheon of Mesopotamian gods as Babylon ruled all the Mesopotamian cities. A religion confined to a specific ethnic group has been termed an ethnic religion, in contrast with the universal religions originating after the traditional age, which appeal to spiritual capacities common to all humanity. I shall say more about this distinction in chapter 7.

THE AXIAL AGE

Compared with what had gone before, the couple of thousand years of the traditional age saw a ferment of human social activity. The early civilizations inspired other civilizations to emerge nearby. States warred, united, or carved out great empires. Ruling minorities were overthrown by oppressed groupings. Vigorous military nations from outside the civilized regions swept into them, sometimes replacing the ruling dynasties with their own leaders, sometimes rejuvenating decadent cultures, and sometimes just destroying the mighty collective achievements that they could not understand. Thus the centres of power and influence constantly shifted, civilizations fragmented and died, and new ones were born.

Much is known of this period: names and genealogies of rulers; accounts of conquests and migrations; the ruins of cities, temples, tombs; the remains of artefacts and weapons. But still it is shadowy. It is so difficult to imagine life in ancient times. People's minds, to the extent that one can glimpse their workings through the dust of millennia, still seem somewhat strange, even alien. When is it that we can start to recognize the emergence of our own kind of consciousness? It seems to be in the axial age.

The 'axial age' (German *Aschenzeit*) is the term the existentialist philosopher Karl Jaspers (1883–1969) employed to refer to the period of a few hundred years centring on about 500BCE. Jaspers saw this period as the axis of world history, because previous ages seem to be converging on its achievements, and human culture since has radiated into diverse forms of religions, philosophy, science, and so on, all of which can trace their origins back to the new departures of the axial age. 'In this age were born the fundamental categories in which we still think today, and the beginnings of the world religions, by which human beings still live, were created. The step into universality was taken in every sense.'[132]

This period is recognized as 'axial' by many authorities: some are listed in a note.[133] What they all notice is that a number of individual people in several parts of the world originated enormously influential systems of thought and religion, mainly in the sixth century BCE. I shall say something about changes in human consciousness in this period, and about who these people were and what they taught, but before that it is worth looking at the state of the relevant parts of the world in their time, the axial age. The axial areas were Israel, Iran, Greece, north-eastern India, and China.

THE AXIAL AREAS

In south-west Asia, Mesopotamia gloried in its last taste of hegemony under the Babylonian king Nebuchadnezzar. His huge empire was destroyed in 539BCE as Cyrus of Persia established an even vaster empire. The juggernaut of the Egyptian civilization still lumbered on, but in a rather dilapidated condition, and the American civilizations seem to have remained deep in their traditional age right up until the arrival of the Spaniards.

Meanwhile, several small nations had arisen on the western edges of Mesopotamian influence. One of them, by the time of the axial age calling themselves the Jews, had emigrated from Egypt about 1200BCE. The Jews had a very strong awareness of their own tribal annals. And they were militantly attached to a form of religion which started by

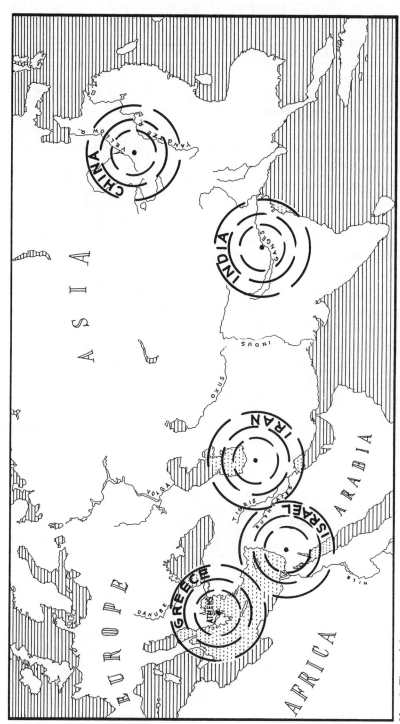

Map 2: The axial areas

exalting one of their tribal gods to a position of supremacy, then held him up as their only god, superior to the gods of other tribes, and finally asserted that those other gods did not exist at all, theirs having sole authority over the world and human life. There has, incidentally, been a suggestion, supported by Sigmund Freud and Joseph Campbell, that this form of monotheism originated with the Pharaoh Akhenaton (reigned 1379–1362BCE) in Egypt. He is said to have been the first to espouse monotheism, and Moses is said to have been an Egyptian noble who taught the doctrine to the Jews.[134]

The hills and plains of Greece shared with several islands and coasts around the Mediterranean a dynamic and shifting culture of small, independent city-states. Each supported a community with a strong feeling of political and sometimes individual independence. Each was very conscious of the variety of cultural and social traditions exhibited by its neighbours and more distant civilizations, since the region's geography encouraged travel, trade, and a generally outward-looking attitude. Greek religion was very rich in myth. It envisaged a fractious community of immortals subject to human emotions and weaknesses, and it sang of the deeds of half-divine heroes. It may be that the uncringing attitude adopted by the Greeks to the unseen powers accounts for the open spirit of rational inquiry characteristic of the axial age in the Greek culture.

In India, the Indus Valley civilization had vanished long before, as invaders calling themselves Aryans filtered in from the north-west. The successor culture to that of the Indus was more widespread in India, and centred on the valley of the river Ganges in the north-east. There, several states were vying for supremacy; some were small, some large, some were monarchies, and some republics of a sort. Also vying for supremacy were the two upper classes of the descendants of the Aryan invaders: the aristocracy or warriors, and the priestly Brahmins. The Brahmins were later to become the most successful, and the two classes solidified into two of the four main castes of Hindu India. It was a time of relative prosperity, of cultural and social unity, and of spiritual ferment. The Brahmins had taken over the Indus people's stress on ritual cleansing, and claimed a monopoly over the conducting of the extravagant and bloody sacrifices traditional to the Aryans. But while they entrenched their privileges in institutional religion, another category of people maintained an ancient tradition of 'non-conformist mendicant philosophers', the *shramanas*.[135]

In China, civilized culture had slowly diffused southward from the Yellow River basin, so that by 500BCE it was the common possession of scores of 'states' scattered across northern China, and had also reached the Yangtze Valley. Society was in general divided into a harsh and warlike landowning nobility and a mass of peasants who were literally anonymous, in that they had no ancestral clan names. The peasants worshipped nature divinities, while the nobility worshipped their clan ancestors, with the ruling house being responsible for maintaining the good will of these hidden ancestral powers. The Emperor functioned as a nominal feudal overlord. Dukes and princes were jostling for power and influence, trying to devise effective means of government and to maintain efficient armed forces. Wandering scholars moved from patron to patron, propounding their versions of the sources of virtue and power: the axial age in China included the time of the 'Hundred Schools'.

THE AXIAL SAGES

Karl Jaspers singles out five cultures which nurtured the sages who pioneered our current attitudes to life. These axial peoples were the Iranians, Jews, Greeks, Chinese, and Indians.[136] In Iran lived the sage Zarathustra or Zoroaster, somewhere around 600BCE. In sixth century Babylonia or Judea was the prophet known to scholars as Deutero-Isaiah, and several other great Jewish prophets flourished in the axial age. Ancient Greece is so familiar to us that dozens of names resound as authentic axial sages, for example Pythagoras the mystical mathematician (about 580–500BCE), Solon the lawgiver (about 638–559BCE), and Plato the philosopher (about 427–347BCE).

In China there were Confucius (traditionally 551–479BCE), Lao Tzu (about 604–531BCE: of doubtful historicity) and several others. In India, the unknown sages who wrote the Upanishads worked from about 700–300BCE, and there was Mahavira (about 548–476BCE) who founded or revived Jainism. Finally there was Siddhartha Gautama, who became known as the Buddha (about 560–480BCE or later), described by Arnold Toynbee as the most sublime and radical of the axial sages.[137] It could prove unfair and misleading to attempt to summarize the discoveries and teachings of each of the pioneers of consciousness in just a few sentences, and there is not space for more. There will be much more about the Buddha and his teachings on the higher evolution of consciousness below and in later chapters. First comes a general survey of the place of the axial sages in the advancement of human consciousness.

SELF-REFLECTIVE CONSCIOUSNESS IN THE AXIAL AGE

I described in chapter 5 how the 'centred experience', already present in the brightest animals, developed into human self-reflective consciousness. There was the need to evaluate one's performance in complex social interactions, and to predict the behaviour of others by 'doing psychology', both of which encouraged people to attend to the workings of their own minds. There was also the anxious tendency to imagine how others saw one, and natural curiosity about the mysterious inner dimension of experience.

All these factors combined to increase the recognition that one's own self is autonomous, distinguishable from other selves, and also to yield a realization that one can follow one's own mental processes as well as attending to sense experience. Meanwhile, skill in speaking was slowly improving, in tandem with the rising self-awareness. Words were found to describe, and so make more definite, concepts of self in the human mind. In particular, the 'knower' as a subject was called 'I' (to use the English word), and the self as illumined in self-reflective consciousness was called 'me'. The pioneer psychologist William James is still worth quoting, a hundred years on: 'The consciousness of self involves a stream of thought, each part of which as "I" can remember those which went before, know the things they knew, and care paramountly for certain ones among them as "Me", and *appropriate to these* the rest.'[138] These appropriated objects of consciousness are labelled 'mine'.

For a long time, people's self-reflective consciousness had been capable of attending to the conclusions of their own minds. But if one accepts Julian Jaynes's account of the 'voice-hearing' consciousness of the traditional age, it could not fully distinguish these conclusions from voices heard by the physical ear; not, at least, when there were decisions to be made. 'I' heard the voice, but did not know that it came from 'me'. A person could not yet conceive of himself 'as an independent person with the faculty of choice in accordance with his individual character'.[139]

Among the axial peoples, life was getting more complicated; life surprised people more often. Instincts could not cope with the constantly changing circumstances, nor could time-hallowed traditions. Even the divine voices of people's own minds began to falter – perhaps there was no single, straightforward solution that the hallucinated god could proclaim with its accustomed serene and resounding assurance. Matters needed to be thought through and discussed critically. People's thinking processes became more and more important, sometimes in matters of life and death, often in matters of personal satisfaction and advancement. As thinking became more important, people *noticed* it more. In their best moments, the most quick-witted people attained *full* self-reflective consciousness. This was not the beginning of self-reflection; awareness of the self as the originator of actions seems to have been a real capability much earlier, as a result of the factors enumerated at the beginning of this section. The self-reflection achieved by a minority in the axial age was far more intense, vivid, and continuous, though, and it cannot always have been a pleasant experience.

THE BUDDHA AND SELF-AWARENESS

What was it like to 'discover' full self-reflection? In the case of the north Indian aristocrat who was to become the Buddha, we are fortunate in having a fairly full account, scattered through the Buddhist texts. The stories of Gautama's early realizations purport to be his own reminiscence; in substance they probably do come from Gautama himself.

While still a boy, he was sitting one day in the shade of a tree in the countryside, watching ploughmen at work, when he found himself entering a spontaneous meditative state of mind. This state could be described as self-reflective consciousness *par excellence*. It is characterized by full, one-pointed awareness, with the ability to turn the thoughts to any chosen topic and to explore that topic undistractedly. The state is accompanied by a pleasurable awareness of the physical body (rapture), and a sense of profound happiness. Gautama's 'mystical' experience only lasted a matter of hours, if that, and was not to be repeated until he suddenly recalled it years later at a crucial time while he was striving for enlightenment.[140]

As he grew up, Gautama was pampered and protected by his wealthy family. However, he could not be protected from the facts of life and death. A legendary story describes him driving into the city park on successive days, and seeing for the first time an old man, a sick man, and a corpse. Whether or not the story is literally true, Gautama thought deeply about the apparent futility of even the most fortunate life when faced by the reality of suffering and death, and, crucially, applied his reflections to his own case:

Whilst I had such power and good fortune, yet I thought: when an untaught, ordinary man who is subject to ageing, sickness, and death, not safe from them, sees another who is aged, sick, or dead, he is shocked, humiliated, and disgusted, for he forgets that he himself is no exception.[141]

Inexorably, Gautama followed through his reflections on the human condition, on his own existential predicament. Like everyone else, he was subject to decay and the mysterious ending of life. He saw that this seemed so awful because of his strong identification with the 'ego' that had coalesced around his centre of experience. He saw the tendency to be 'enslaved, infatuated, addicted' by the things one values most and realized that he was seeking security in people and possessions that were just as subject to decay and ending as he himself was. It was such insight, combined with his keen sensitivity to the suffering of others, that led him, like other axial sages, to determine to devote his life to seeking wisdom, enlightenment, for the benefit of all.

The legend of seeing the old man, sick man, and corpse continues with a fourth drive to the park, during which Gautama saw one of the 'non-conformist mendicant philosophers', whose example prompted his next step. He left home and family to become a wanderer. He strove for several years to increase the scope of his awareness until he was satisfied that he had reached perfect enlightenment. He was discovering, virtually unaided, the process of higher evolution, and in later chapters we shall see the stages that he traversed.

A RUDE AWAKENING AND THE EGO

Gautama and the other axial sages stood out because of the heights to which they carried their discovery of the potential of awareness. But in all the axial areas there must have been thousands of people starting to reflect on their own experience. Imagine what an eerie and disorienting experience the new awareness was. Like coming to, out of a jolly blur of drunkenness, with a garish sense of self-consciousness, a wincing memory of what you've been doing and saying, and a painful sense of all that you are lacking. Like that, only it has never happened before.

A rude awakening it indeed proved to be. The literature and art of the centuries leading up to the axial age are characterized by anguish, and by a sense of loss, abandonment, and sin, as in much of the Old Testament of the Bible.[142] The history of the same period is characterized by chaotic social upheavals, and wars of unprecedented cruelty. Many then and since would not sustain the rude awakening, and they shook off the full consciousness of themselves like a nightmare face in a mirror. Of necessity, only a small fragment of the mind was able at first to enter the torch-beam of self-reflection, and this is why the event was painful.

Most of the composite being that had been accumulated by the aeons of evolution remained untouched, so the overwhelming *feeling* of the start of full self-reflection was likely to have been of the great gulf between the newly discovered self and the dark mass that lay beyond the edge of the new awareness. This is alienation; alienation from nature, the body, and the objective world in general; alienation from the unconscious parts of the mind which were the legacy of biological/mental evolution and of the traditional mythic age; and alienation from the great mass of other people, still defending ways of life conforming to their mass, pre-conscious traditions.

The result was – and still is, again and again – an 'ego'. For present purposes, the term 'ego' refers to one's strong identification with mental contents and habitual attitudes of which one is aware. Buddhism speaks of the 'I am I conceit', which is buttressed by habitual processes of 'I-making'. The ego's feeling of separateness from all that seems outside it led to the kind of desperate and futile projects that only human beings can conceive, all reducible to the twofold movement of attraction and repulsion; attraction being the drive to gather in and appropriate all that 'other' under the skirts of ego, repulsion being the drive to consign it all to darkness by denial or destruction, until no 'other' exists.

Neither greed for power and possession nor cruelty and wanton destructiveness were new in the axial age – they have other sources besides the anguished parturition of ego. What was new was the possibility of quite genuine, viable advances beyond the boundaries of a parochial ego. The axial sages were people who made such advances to various degrees, and managed to convey something of their discoveries to others. The next chapter will consider just what the axial sages achieved.

Chapter Seven

INDIVIDUAL ACHIEVEMENT
AND THE GREAT RELIGIONS

*Man is always, all the time and for ever, on the brink of the unknown. The
minute you realize this, you prick up your ears in alarm. And the minute any
man steps alone, with his whole naked self, emotional and mental, into the
everlasting hinterland of consciousness, you hate him and you wonder over
him. Why can't he stay cosily playing word games around the camp fire?*
D.H. Lawrence, *Phoenix*, 323

THE SEARCH FOR COMPLETENESS

It seems that certain axial age individuals were able to recognize the
profound implications of their growing self-awareness. Like their fellows, they were faced with an unbearable problem; but their names
survive because they confronted the problem in creative ways, initiating new forms of art, thought, and religion. In moments of self-reflective consciousness, people had sufficient awareness to perceive that
they were *not* fully aware of everything. They were only partially aware
of nature, parts of themselves, and other people, and therefore they felt

a separation from these things, a painful separation: this was their problem. They yearned to cross the divide and to heal the separation.

One way to do so would have been to repudiate full self-reflection and return to a pre-conscious union with 'other', a course chosen by many, from alcoholics to preachers of a return to the blissful ignorance of the Garden of Eden. In fact, some commentators dismiss all religions or mystical efforts as regressive. They see them as attempts to revive pre-conscious harmony by denying rationality (and therefore, by implication, suppressing self-reflection) and by resorting to strange hysterical techniques.[143] The higher religions do not typically conform to this pattern, but it is appropriate for some forms of religion. According to Ken Wilber, religions of the Earth-Mother goddess, while they were appropriate to the traditional age and before, became, around the axial age, sinister dark cults demanding the dissolution (sacrifice) of the separate self. Such cults always reappear in people's minds as 'that terrible inertia which prevented the emergence of a truly strong personality',[144] submerging initiative in a diffuse, undifferentiated state. Early axial age myths such as that of Perseus and Medusa describe heroes conquering or integrating the representative of the great Earth-Mother.[145]

Another way of trying to end the feeling of separateness or incompleteness was to engage in the games of ego that I have already mentioned. The ego is the strong identification of the knower, 'I', with the tiny fragments of mind which its torch beam illuminates. It tends to solidify into the illusion of an unchanging self, in a process recognized by Ken Wilber: 'as the individual began to identify himself with the recording and thinking and memory aspects of the organism, he began to form a conception of himself as a static, permanent, existing self.' The games of ego are still very much accessible to us: they attempt to strengthen the ego so that it feels complete in itself by appropriating or dismissing what seems outside it.[146]

The third method of dealing with separateness was the hallmark of the axial sages. They started to explore the regions of human experience opened up for the first time by self-reflective consciousness, to expand the light of awareness so that it took in more and more of the domains of mind and the world. Not dimming that torch beam into pre-consciousness, not jealously hoarding the small golden disc of first illumination, they shone it around a bit, even spreading the light out in a widening cone.

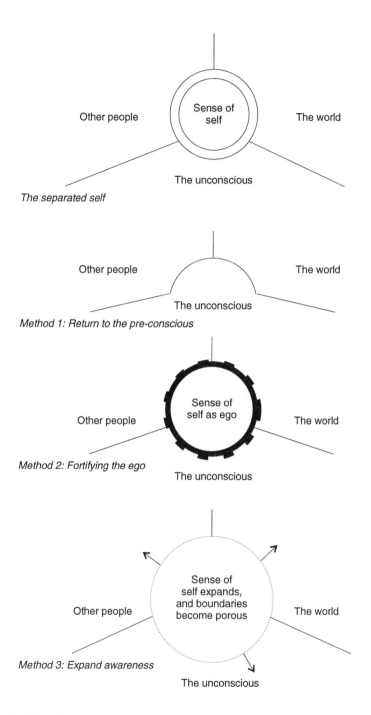

Fig.21 Dealing with separateness

The ego developed from the centre of experience; true to its roots, it tries to remain central, with all else in orbit around it. So it remains cut off from outer 'other' and inner 'other' (the unconscious). The psychoanalyst Carl Jung advocated a move from identifying with the ego to identifying with what he called the Self. Jung's Self resides on the border between conscious and unconscious; awake, yet open to the unknown. This border is the zone of further evolution. Evolution always works at the edge of awareness, testing and extending boundaries, and finally transcending them.

Through allowing their awareness to expand, the axial sages made the two great discoveries. They saw that one could initiate deliberate systematic processes for increasing the scope of awareness (i.e. for higher evolution). Looking within, they also realized how much their experience and their potential were the common store of every human being, so that, in the ways that really matter, humanity is one.

EVOLUTION FOCUSES ON THE INDIVIDUAL

Pioneering explorations of the edges of awareness must have taken enormous courage, because they threaten to dissolve the defensive boundary of ego. The first axial age people who took the third option had this courage, and it is only fair to call them heroes.

The axial age heroes did not only have to face terrors in their own minds, they also had to meet the reactions of others who could not understand their new way of seeing the world. Socrates, for example, was executed on account of his teachings. Unless they encountered other fully self-reflective people who could communicate on their level, they stood alone, and they must often have felt very isolated. Karl Jaspers says that they 'dared to stand upon their own feet as individuals.... Man opposed his own inwardness to the whole world.'[147] They lived as independent individuals, interacting with others as independent individuals, a characteristic which follows directly from consistently dwelling in self-reflective consciousness.

But why is it that full self-reflection has not percolated inexorably through the whole human race, like the use of metals or the knowledge of counting? The reason is that awareness is not infectious. Awareness can only be passed over, wholesale, to another if it is merely awareness of certain *facts* which can be adequately conveyed in words. On the whole, the significant contributions that the axial sages made to human evolution were not factual discoveries.

This is a very important point. Scientific and technological thinking is dominant in our own times, and it awards pre-eminence to facts which can be conveyed not even in words but in numerical ratios. Such an attitude impels us to ask concerning Pythagoras, for example, 'what new *facts* did he discover?' So we think of him as a man whose earth-shaking legacy was 'the square on the hypotenuse is equal to the sum of the squares on the other two sides.' Pythagoras gave us far more than that.[148]

So the advances in awareness made by the axial age individuals could not, in general, be passed on directly to others. Others could only use their guidance themselves to attempt the same feats independently, again as self-reflective individuals. Some of the sages succeeded better than others in getting their message across. Once they had died, the teachings of all of them were to varying extents watered down. They were often regarded as factual statements to be revered rather than as programmes for action and mental discipline, designed to produce the same real extensions of awareness that distinguished these sages as true individuals.

Their achievements were individual achievements, and they could only be genuinely emulated by individuals, prepared to act independently and not just to follow the mass. Consequently, the new form of 'evolution' they pioneered, higher evolution, is quite distinct from the genetic, mental, and cultural evolution I have been mainly describing so far. The work of higher evolution has to be carried out afresh by each individual attempting it. Once full self-reflective consciousness is achieved, evolution focuses down on to the individual. Many people may progress, but each does so in the noble independence (though no longer, one hopes, isolation) permitted for the first time by the ability to bend awareness back to one's own self.

THE CHARACTERISTICS OF THE AXIAL AGE INDIVIDUALS

The new type of people who, as one could say, created themselves in the axial age had consolidated and developed their awareness to such an extent that they could reflect autonomously on themselves and their world. For them, the customs, attitudes, and values of the traditional cultures were no longer completely fixed and inviolable. We can recognize and define these individuals primarily by the new degree of awareness to which they had attained: in their most lucid moments they had brought to completion the development of self-reflective consciousness which the first humans had started a hundred thousand years before. However, consciousness was capable of evolving far beyond complete self-reflection, as we shall see.

If well-established self-reflective consciousness is the primary characteristic of the axial age individual, then from it arise several secondary characteristics. In particular, there is a strength and independence of judgement and action (often with a consequent experience of isolation). There is a concern for and solidarity with other people, whatever their tribal allegiance. Finally there is a creative ability to initiate new movements in the individual's own consciousness or in society as a whole. As well as challenging the old social and intellectual norms, the new individual was prepared to create himself, mould himself, constantly working on his life, behaviour, thought, and of course on the scope of his awareness.[149]

All the axial age individuals that we have records of seem to exhibit this fresh intensity of awareness, and to varying degrees possess the secondary characteristics of independence, aloneness, solidarity, and creativity. Through reflecting on their own awareness, they freed themselves from their traditional group attitudes, gaining independence from their group, expressing fellow-feeling for others, whether in their group or not, and reaching some sense of creative responsibility for their future. Thus they were able to contribute to those revolutionary discoveries: the unity of humanity and the possibility of the conscious transformation of life and the world.

THE FIRST TRUE INDIVIDUALS

It could be, as Ken Wilber suggests, that the first to break through to full self-reflection were, or became, kings, or heroes in the military sense, but I do not find his argument very convincing.[150] The historical records we have tend to confirm that rulers are nearly always defenders of a narrow ego, not explorers of the frontiers of human creative awareness.

If they were not kings, one can make some fairly confident conjectures about what kind of people did break through. They probably had above average mental endowments. They had sufficient prosperity to leave the problems of subsistence for a while in favour of watching the world, conversing with many people, and swimming in their own thoughts. They had the luck to live in a time and place too stimulating, complex, and volatile to be handled in the old ways. And maybe they had a spark of something else, some intangible talent which marked them as the heralds of a new phase of evolution, higher evolution.

However, we can leave conjecture behind, and actually recall the great figures of the axial age. We remember them not for their private struggles and mental victories, but for the legacies they left, tangible fruits of a new kind of consciousness. They must have 'created' themselves by working on their own minds, but those whose names survive have left creations in human culture. They created themselves, but some also created great works of art, such as the dramas of sixth- and fifth-century BCE Greece, with their revelations of universality and personal responsibility, and the seventh-century BCE poems of Sappho, who illustrates well the light that art throws on advances in consciousness.

Sappho, one of the very few women we know of among the axial age individuals, seems to have been the first person to have described the anguish of love.[151] Such emotional upheavals, suggests the philologist Bruno Snell,[152] focused her attention upon her private, internal life. So she can speak of love as 'bitter-sweet' – mental conflict like this is inconceivable in her literary predecessors – and her imagination flies to friends in far-off places, as perhaps no one's had before her. She recognizes that she has a personal life, an intellectual, spiritual, and emotional life, yet that 'a community of thought and feeling is entirely feasible'.[153] The art of Sappho and the other axial age Greek masters, like the lesser-known art from the other axial areas, succeeded in conveying new values to its audiences, values capable of transforming their lives by stimulating greater awareness.

The evolution of new forms of cultural achievement received a great boost with the advent of people capable of deliberate creation, and not only in the field of art. Other axial age individuals created new systems of thought or philosophy which started to make rational sense of the 'new' world revealed in the light of self-reflective consciousness. (A.N. Whitehead is said to have remarked that 'the whole later development of Western philosophy can be regarded as a series of extended footnotes to Plato.')[154] Some of them introduced social and political innovations, such as the laws of Solon of Athens or the ethical guidelines of Confucius in China. Lastly, they founded great world religions, some of which endure and even thrive to this day.

KINDS OF RELIGION

Before the axial age, everyone is thought to have followed a religion. So how is it that Karl Jaspers is able to make the assertion that I have already quoted, that in the axial age 'the beginnings of the world religions, by which human beings still live, were created. The step into universality was taken in every sense'?[155] That word 'universality' provides the clue. Full self-reflective consciousness gave the axial sages the ability to see that tribal, national, regional, and racial differences between people were trivial compared with what they had in common. Full self-reflective consciousness provided a newly self-illumined experience of what it was to be a human being and to dwell in a fully human level of awareness, a level which is within the reach of any human being from any background. People's viewpoints traditionally highlighted local or ethnic interests; the new 'true individuals' each developed a more independent viewpoint, which naturally tended to feel and stress the universal interests of all mankind.

The cultures of the axial areas all possessed a strong religious component, and so the new universalist ideas cultivated by the axial sages inevitably influenced people's religious life. Religion remained a part of local, ethnic culture, but the existing ethnic religions could not incorporate the universal and personal attitudes discovered by the axial sages. Religion had to develop a wholly new, universal perspective. All religions have ethnic roots, and while some remain ethnic, some develop universal features. A religion with universal features may be recognizable as a new religion, quite distinct from its ethnic predecessor, and even cut off from it. The 'world religions' referred to by Karl Jaspers are of this sort. As it grows older, a universal religion shows a tendency to subside back into an ethnic matrix, losing its universal qualities. I shall give some examples of these various types of religion after having looked at what distinguishes ethnic from universal religions.[156]

ETHNIC AND UNIVERSAL RELIGIONS

The chief distinction, then, between the ethnic and universal components of religions is that ethnic religion serves the collective interests of a particular cultural grouping, while universal religion is to be followed voluntarily by the individual.

It follows that ethnic religions usually arise – evolve – organically, together with the other trappings of the culture they serve. An ethnic religion is part of the world view passed on to everyone born into that culture. 'For pre-Axial man religion was always ethnic in character,' writes the historian of religion Lloyd Geering. 'It could not be divorced from the tribe, city or people who practised it. It expressed the identity of the group rather than that of the individual.'[157] Ethnic religions tend to encourage a fairly static social order, in which conformism, submitting to authority, serving one's community, and bearing children in secure circumstances are the highest goals in life.

A universal religion, or a universal development from an ethnic religion, has a single founder, who is an exceptional individual. In principle, it is not tied to any culture or place, being potentially the religion of any individual anywhere at any time. Again, in principle, someone can only start to follow a universal religion after an experience of conversion to it, followed by a change of life. Non-degenerate universal religions tend to exalt individual freedom and independence, and to stress the value of personal responsibility. They often encourage attitudes and practices which go against the narrow interests of one's particular culture or community: for example sexual restraint rather than raising children, non-violence rather than defence and attack against rival groups, and contemplative effort rather than material productivity.

The stark contrasts I have given are not intended to dismiss ethnic religions as being 'wrong' or 'bad'. The two sorts of religion have quite different domains of relevance, and each can be healthy and appropriate in its own domain, with a supportive, tolerant attitude to the role of the other in human life. Ethnic religions, or the ethnic aspects of religion, belong to levels of consciousness below full self-reflection and so they have a social rather than personal relevance. They are traditions, products of cultural evolution. At their worst, however, ethnic religions provide a cruel and frightening backdrop to life, and they stifle individual initiative, the awakening of self-reflective consciousness, and the development of universal religions. One possible example is the reported witch-paranoia of the Zande or Azande, a modern African tribe.[158]

At their best, ethnic religions meet very important biological and social needs, particularly by instilling a sense of living relationship between a person and his or her natural and traditional environment. Ancient Greek paganism, for example, animated nature and natural forces with living personalities whom one could recognize and influence or worship: deities of rivers, winds, the moon, the harvest, and so on. This contrasts favourably with the modern tendency to treat the natural world as impersonal, even lifeless, to be ignored or exploited. Similarly, the Greeks connected the chief events of life with named deities and carried out the appropriate ceremonies: marriage, childbearing, war, death, and after death. Sporting, artistic, and civic occasions had religious significance, too. The Hellenic (ancient Greek) ethnic religion was largely a healthy one, and within its soil the shoots of universal religion could sprout and grow: young religions like Orphism and mystery cults such as that of Pythagoras, as well as imported religions such as Christianity, which was so unkind to its pagan mother when it gained ascendancy.

The universal religions need not compete for the same ground as the ethnic religions. The latter's ground is the collective religious life of a particular local culture. The former were founded to communicate visions of individual human emancipation; in fact they are characterized by the way they lead people into a dimension of higher evolution, quite distinct from the biological, mental, and cultural 'health care' administered by ethnic religions. However, if a universal religion tends to find that its converts arrive lacking a healthy ethnic background, as is increasingly the case nowadays, it may have to divert some of its energies into providing ethnic facilities. The new Buddhists in India, for example, are mainly ex-untouchables, who had experienced little but degradation from Hinduism, their former religion. As Buddhists, they are learning new rites of passage, and cultivating a new sense of self-worth.

When a universal religion takes on a predominantly ethnic role it can very easily lose its distinct universal features. Thus modern Mediterranean-style Catholicism is so exuberantly ethnic that a believer may pass his or her whole life without encountering the truly universal opportunities potentially present in Christianity.

An ethnic and a universal religion need not clash unless the ethnic religion holds the individual back from growing beyond it, or the universal religion seeks exclusive power over the psyche, even over the whole world, as can happen if a single jealous god is given command.

Decay and Revival in Universal Religions

All universal religions have shown a tendency to regress into ethnic forms as the lofty messages of their founders have faded with time. What presumably started as the plain and classical edifice of a universal religion has tended to become plastered with more and more ethnic adornments and encrustations, especially as growth and success have called for self-perpetuating institutions, and as living teachings have hardened into dogmas and empty formality. An example was the transformation of the early Taoist ideal of 'participation in the Eternal' into the search for foods and elixirs to prolong life.[159]

As a universal religion can be founded only by a truly independent individual, so its universal features can only be kept alive or revived by independent individuals. In fact, a universal religion, by the definitions I have given, can only be practised at all to the extent that the follower maintains self-reflective consciousness. This is why it tends to be only a small minority of the population who wish genuinely to practise the universal aspects of religion. Every so often, an unusually talented and vigorous follower is able to reinstate the universal character of a religion after a period of decay, and adapt its outward forms to new circumstances. Or more radically still, the reformer adapts it to new cultures. He or she can see behind all the colourful but non-essential ethnic accretions which festoon a great religion in a particular culture, and can discern its universal principles. It is these principles which need to be taken to the new culture if a healthy cutting is to grow in a dissimilar ethnic soil.

This is a vast and fascinating topic – how a universal religion fares when it is transplanted into a different country with a different culture. Perhaps it is enough for now just to notice that it fares differently according to whether it (1) tries to take with it all the exotic fittings of the ethnic religious background in which it grew up; (2) tries to root itself thoroughly in the ethnic religious culture of the new place; or (3) tries to remain aloof from the ethnic religions of both its homeland and its new soil.[160]

Ethnic and Universal Religions: a Summary

Ethnic religions, then, derive from levels of consciousness below full self-reflection, though they do not necessarily inhibit the extension of awareness. The purely universal aspects of religion are only of use to people who have a fairly consistent self-reflective level of consciousness: they offer teachings and practices which can to varying extents deepen and expand consciousness in the process called higher evolution. The distinctions between the two are summarized in the table below.

Ethnic religion	Universal religion
Part of lower evolution. Can promote biological, cultural, and mental health at and below the level of self-reflective consciousness.	Part of higher evolution. Promotes 'spiritual' growth, based in the level of full self-reflective consciousness.
Supports the ethnic group. Emphasizes fertility, obedience to authority, hostility to the 'out-group'	Supports the individual. Emphasizes independence, a recognition of consciously directed transformation of life and the world, and seeing the common humanity in all.
One is born into it.	One can join it only by voluntary conversion.
Evolves organically and is an inseparable part of the culture of a particular place, racial group, or nation.	Founded and revived by individuals, and can in principle be followed by any person, regardless of background.
Can provide the soil for a universal religion, or universal aspects of religion, if a true individual adds on universal innovations.	Can degenerate into an ethnic religion, in which case a true individual may revive its original universality.
Can give a healthy basis for individual growth, or stifle independence.	Can cherish healthy ethnic religion, or savagely reject it.

Table 4: A comparison of ethnic and universal religions

RELIGIONS IN PARTICULAR

I shall close this chapter by looking very quickly at how the better-known religions, roughly in order of their date of origin, seem to fit into the ethnic/universal classification. It is extremely difficult to evaluate a religion satisfactorily from outside its circle of followers, so the following paragraphs should be taken as tentative and personal impressions. I hope they give no offence.[161]

Hinduism. Being the religion of most of the Indian people, wherever they go, Hinduism is an ethnic religion. The Brahmin priests insist that one can only be a born Hindu: when the Mogul emperor Akbar asked to convert to Hinduism, the Brahmins showed him a donkey and asked him whether he could turn it into a horse. Hinduism affirms the values of the ethnic group, emphasizing caste solidarity and the performance of caste duties, as well as amassing wealth and the propagation of the species. Apparently, a Brahmin father who fails to find a husband for his daughter is considered guilty of as many murders as the number of children she might have had.

There are universal elements within the sphere of Hinduism. Spiritual teachers raised in the climate of Hinduism have often taught practices that take the devotee beyond the ordinary sense-based levels of consciousness. The fundamentally ethnic Hinduism of the great mass of Indians has repeatedly served as a matrix for philosophies and new religious movements with definite universal features: Maharishi Mahesh Yogi's 'transcendental meditation' is possibly a modern example. Buddhism and Jainism are completely un-Hindu, but both grew in a society which was Hindu.

Pagan religions. Every land once had its equivalent of Hinduism. I have already mentioned the pagan religions of some of the great civilizations. The uncivilized societies had and have their so-called 'primitive religions', which appear to be unequivocally ethnic, although some 'primitive' shamanistic practices may take a few individuals to higher states of consciousness. The related religions of the Celts, Teutons, and Norsemen in north-western Europe were also ethnic, as were the religions of South and Central America before the European conquest. Shintoism is Japan's ethnic religion, still thriving today.

Zoroastrianism. This religion was founded in Iran by one of the axial sages, Zarathustra. Its single founder and its strong ethical teachings, focusing on truthfulness, mark it out as a universal religion. Zoroastrianism spread very little beyond people of Iranian origin, but its influence has been enormous in that it gave to Judaism, Christianity, and Islam the idea of a cosmic conflict between Good and Evil, and a belief in divine judgement after death, followed by consignment to an eternal heaven or hell. It also influenced Buddhism and probably Taoism. Zoroastrianism had ethnic features too, right from the beginning, it seems, owing to Zarathustra's idealization of the life of the pastoralist.

Taoism. Taoism traces its origins to Lao Tzu, a Chinese sage of the axial age, who (if he existed) was definitely not an upholder of mass values. It advocates the quiescent life of a solitary contemplative, seeking a harmony with the intrinsic patterns of the cosmos. So far, universal rather than ethnic. One may wonder, however, whether the harmony of Taoism may not be a pre-conscious one, rather than a state which builds on full self-reflection. Lao Tzu wrote:

Being the stream of the Universe,
Ever true and unswerving,
Become as a little child once more.
... Return to the state of the uncarved block.[162]

Taoism gradually became more and more associated with superstitious beliefs and magical practices, so that today it is more ethnic than universal for the majority of its followers.

Buddhism. Buddhism is a universal religion, with an individual founder, affirming individual values rather than those of the ethnic group, and stressing independence of judgement and self-reliance. One becomes a Buddhist by deciding to practise its teachings. Buddhism has spread quite easily to cultures very different from its Indian roots, and it is interesting to see how it is adapting to the West at present. There is an essential unity between virtually all the forms that Buddhism has adopted through its history, a unity very obvious to someone who has practised Buddhism a little. Nevertheless, its basic ideals have sometimes been obscured by ethnic accretions. This is particularly evident in certain parts of the Eastern Buddhist world, where a monk may find that much of his time is taken up by demands for weddings and other ceremonies, blessings, and divinations. The universal and 'evolutionary' attributes of Buddhism are the subject of the next chapter.

Confucianism. Confucius was another Chinese axial sage, but the religious system he founded seems to contain a mixture of universal and ethnic elements. He stressed universal values such as mindfulness, individual judgement, and integrity, and recommended professional advancement on the basis of merit, not birth. But Confucianism has never spread to people outside Chinese cultural influence, and it lays great stress on loyalty to the ruler and filial piety, values tending to strengthen the social group rather than spiritual resolve. Over the centuries, Confucianism has gathered more and more ethnic features.

Judaism. Judaism is out of chronological sequence here so that it can be juxtaposed with Christianity and Islam. It starts with all the marks of an ethnic religion. It had no one founder, is associated with a particular tribal group and their particular homeland, and it strongly defends collective values, notably the importance of child-bearing and family loyalty. In its most orthodox forms there is no question of the conversion of non-Jews. However, a succession of great Jewish thinkers have incorporated universal elements into the religion, starting with the prophets in the axial age: Ezekiel, Amos, 'Deutero-Isaiah', and others. They were the originators of a universalist tradition which leads on to later universal 'prophets', particularly Jesus, Paul, and Muhammed.

Christianity. Only a rather patchy collection of the teachings of Jesus has survived. It seems fairer to give St. Paul most of the credit for founding Christianity, under the visionary inspiration of Jesus, whom Paul did not actually meet. Paul's theology and most of the teachings ascribed to Jesus, which formed the basis of the new religion, are emphatically universal in character. They are addressed to the individual, and say that a spiritual 'rebirth' is required if one is to join the religion. Certain values of the family and ethnic group are attacked very vigorously.[163] These universal features, however, were not entirely new to Jesus and Paul, being presaged in the writings of the great Jewish prophets of the axial age. We can say the same of Islam, too: thus both Christianity and Islam have their universal roots in the axial age.

Although a number of courageous reformers have tried to reaffirm Christianity's universal features down the ages, it would not be unfair to say that it has nearly always had a primarily ethnic significance, in practice, for the great majority of its followers.

Islam. This is even clearer in the case of Islam than in Christianity. Islam was founded by Muhammed in about 622CE; Muhammed saw himself as the last in a line of prophets which included Jesus and the prophets of the Old Testament. His teachings seem to have been directed primarily at the Arabs, but had at least a limited universality, preaching the equality and brotherhood of all believers, and the responsibility of the individual in willingly carrying out his duties of almsgiving and ritual observance. Muhammed's successors saw no need to restrict the new religion to Arabs, though unfortunately their means of spreading it were chiefly military; indeed Muhammed himself was a successful military leader. Islam has and had many strongly ethnic characteristics in addition to its belligerence, and perhaps only in the Sufi brotherhoods does one find a fully developed universal religion within Islam.

The new individuals of the axial age were great innovators. In particular, they showed in various ways how a higher evolution of consciousness can be started, building on the products of lower evolution. Some used the arts, some used philosophy, but here I am concentrating on the new systems of spiritual training, usually labelled 'religions'.

Any of the universal religions could be analysed to reveal how it helps the individual to continue to effect an evolutionary growth in his or her consciousness. Buddhism is the one that explicitly adopts the development of human consciousness as its primary aim. Chapter 8 discusses the origins of Buddhism's approach, and its perspective on the human situation.

Chapter Eight

BUDDHISM AS HIGHER EVOLUTION

*A progressive evolution with a definite ideal, its realization here and now,
making life cheerful, energetic, serene, worth living for the sake of doing good
for the welfare of others, this the Tathagata [Buddha] proclaimed.*
Anagarika Dharmapala, quoted in Sangharakshita, *Flame in Darkness*, 132

THE CULMINATION OF LOWER EVOLUTION

For over 3,000 million years, life had been evolving. In the axial age,
the old kind of evolution finished and a new kind of evolution became
possible. (I will justify this bold statement very shortly.) I have been
assessing the progress of evolution in terms of the progress of levels of
consciousness; the axial age saw a pinnacle reached in consciousness
that was also a limit, and only a new method of ascent could take the
mind higher still.

The evidence strongly suggests that it was then that the fully developed form of self-reflective consciousness first became accessible to
human beings, the highest achievement of biological and mental evolution. The nature of self-reflection implies that collective forms of
evolution cannot take consciousness any further. Lower evolution

encounters a natural ceiling, recognizable in one's own experience. Once one is fully aware of oneself, one is the pilot of one's own mind, and only a deliberate and specific programme of effort can improve the scope and clarity of one's awareness, that is, impel one's consciousness to a higher level. It is true that certain external influences, from drugs to the weather, can seem to improve one's well-being, clarity, or focus of mind, but, unless deliberate effort is involved, the effect is only temporary.[164]

In terms of consciousness, then, lower, collective forms of evolution can get no further than the self-reflective level, and in that sense, lower evolution finishes when self-reflective consciousness is achieved. The process can only continue by the voluntary effort of the self-reflective individual; from being collective, evolution has focused down on the individual.

However, in another sense, the process of lower evolution certainly did not come to a standstill as soon as a few of its products blinked and looked around with a new kind of awareness. Life goes on. Animals and plants are still subject to the natural selection of characteristics which help their survival, and over the generations their forms slowly shift and fade in and out in a never-ending magic spectacle. Will another of them one day become capable of self-reflective consciousness here on earth? I do not think it is likely, unless humanity becomes extinct. As I have said, we have already filled the 'ecological niche' of self-consciousness (a niche which tends to invade most other niches) and there is no room, I fancy, for another occupant. Humanity 'has a firm grip on this adaptive zone, and is fully able to defend it,' as G.G. Simpson puts it.[165] There is little opportunity for a less conscious being to become self-aware here on earth, unless we were to give it a helping hand.

So much for biological and mental evolution, the first two of the dimensions of evolution outlined in the introduction. What about cultural evolution – has that got no further in the last 2,500 years?

One could say that culture forms a bridge between lower and higher evolution. We have seen that cultural evolution began long before the advent of self-reflection. In that sense it belongs to lower evolution. But it continues into higher evolution. Cultural innovations are made by particular individuals, and when some individuals tap the enormous reserves of creativity opened up by full self-reflection, the effects on culture are enormous. Consider the achievements of great artists, poets, philosophers, religious teachers, scientists, and so on in the axial age

and since. Cultural changes, even cultural advances, actually accelerated in the axial age.

Lower evolution is a collective process which cannot take living
beings any further than self-reflective consciousness. Higher evolution
is an individual process, requiring voluntary effort: no one else can do
it for one; in a sense, one is on one's own. But the cultural environment
makes a big difference. Some cultural forms will stifle any urge to
higher evolution. Repressive governments, for example, restrict certain
aspects of life; there are ideologies which deny the possibility or value
of directed mental transformation, and some people have to live in a
social atmosphere which condemns independence of judgement or
which holds up as its highest ideals the gratification of biological urges
and the interests of the ethnic group. And it is clear that societies which
are so poverty-stricken that many people have to put all their energy
into avoiding hunger and disease are environments which hinder
higher evolution. Conversely, a prosperous and free society permits the
individual to experiment with methods of personal growth.

But the best climate of all for higher evolution is a culture which is
strongly pervaded by the influence of true individuals. Successful in
following the path of higher evolution themselves, they have contributed ideas, values, beliefs, and knowledge, in the form of works of art
and educational and religious institutions which actively encourage
others to attempt their own transformation.

THE FOUNDER OF BUDDHISM

To single out Buddhism as a cultural form promoting higher evolution
is not to belittle the many other systems and individual contributions
which aid personal transformation. Buddhist practices and teachings
have a proven effectiveness, and its system is particularly unequivocal
and comprehensive in its concentration on the development of all
individuals. But of course there is much of great value which is not
included under the label 'Buddhism'.

Around the time of the Buddha's spiritual quest in north-eastern
India, axial sages in other parts of the world were reflecting on human
life. They too discovered features of higher evolution, each, so far as
one can tell, reaching their conclusions largely independently. It is still
unclear why so much happened in those few axial centuries. Perhaps
the tenuous trading links between the areas were enough to put a
concern with the human predicament 'in the air'. Perhaps the time was

just right for it: some historians believe that city living was an important factor. Urbanization was associated with a growth in individualistic intellectual pursuits, which in turn promote greater self-reflection.

For a curious and courageous minority living in the axial age, full self-reflective consciousness offered dramatic vistas of unexplored territories of the mind. It offered new experiences in ideas, in the depths of human consciousness, and in communication with others. The world-wide bustle of exploratory activity is particularly evident in north-eastern India, around the basin of the river Ganges.

There was already a thriving tradition there, though probably a fairly new one, of men and women leaving their household ties behind them to wander in search of understanding and mystical experience. Sometimes they begged for food; they were generally accepted and supported by householders, and were recognized by their practice of staining their clothes yellow with mud. Sometimes they lived on wild plants in the forests. Some spent long periods alone, braving the fears of the forest and practising forms of meditation. Others lived in groups, either groups of friends trying the same experiments together, often experiments in extreme austerities such as fasting and self-torture, or groups living under a teacher with a reputation for spiritual attainment. Modern commentators see in these wanderers firstly a fierce independence, possibly inherited from the spirit of the Aryan peoples who had swept into India a few centuries before, and secondly a love of reasoning and rational discussion.[166]

'Buddhism' (a Western coinage) took root in this social climate. It refers to a diverse array of spiritual traditions, all tracing their origins to the Buddha's life and teachings. Like the other universal religions, it was founded by one man, known as the Buddha. His name was Siddhartha Gautama. We looked at his early reflections in chapter 6, where we saw how he described his spontaneous boyhood experience of full self-reflective consciousness. We saw how he considered the implications of human mortality and the effects of being attached to an 'ego', considerations arising from reflecting on his own life and comparing it with the experience of others.

He was motivated by these reflections to explore his own mind, its limitations, its tendencies, its strengths. After much experimentation with intellectual, ascetic, and meditational techniques, he found ways of promoting his own evolution beyond the self-reflective level. Eventually he concluded that his sufferings and yearnings had sprung from a powerful attachment to a very limited view of 'self', and his personal progress in higher evolution led him to transcend the spiritual blindness which had supported such an illusory ego. The very fact that radical development was possible proved to him that there was no unchanging self.[167] In transcending ignorance in this way, Gautama became known as the Enlightened One – the Buddha.

The Buddha is remembered today because his enlightenment led him to show other people how to follow paths of self-transcendence or higher evolution. Like the other axial sages, the Buddha taught. Like them, his methods and ideas were the starting points for thriving traditions of practice or thought. The axial age was an age of individuals. Identifiable people did things, said things, which had repercussions (not necessarily beneficial); they proved that history need no longer be only the story of surging mass movements. Human life could be changed for the better by exceptional individuals.

Later we shall consider why the Buddha adopted an evolutionary viewpoint, and see how developed Buddhism describes the process of higher evolution. First, though, let us see how Gautama shaped his own higher evolution.

GAUTAMA'S QUEST

Gautama's early reflections on the human predicament led him to decide to leave his family and home to take on the life of a wanderer. He later spoke of his 'going forth' from the household life as setting out on a 'noble quest'. Incidentally, he did not forget his family; soon after he had gained enlightenment, he visited his home town. Many of his relatives are said to have followed his teachings: his father, step-mother, wife, son, half-brother, and several cousins all eventually gained enlightenment.

The quest apparently occupied some six years. This time was a very difficult one for Gautama; one could say that he experienced failure after failure. He sat at the feet of at least two famous religious teachers and mastered their systems, but knew intuitively that what they taught had limitations, and he left them and continued alone. He faced the night-time terrors of complete solitude in the wildest jungles. He went to extremes in bizarre austerities, and fasted until near death:

And as I did so, my body reached a state of extreme emaciation; my limbs became like the joined segments of vine stems or bamboo stems, because of eating so little … my ribs jutted out as gaunt as the crazy rafters of an old roofless barn; the gleam of my eyes sunk far down in their sockets looked like the gleam of water sunk far down in a deep well....[168]

Eventually, disillusioned with these extremes, he recalled the 'zest and ease' of his meditative experience as a boy. 'Why am I afraid of such pleasure? It is pleasure that has nothing to do with sensual craving and [unskilful mental states]. Might that', he thought, 'be the way to Enlightenment?' He found 'a delightful stretch of land' with 'the river flowing clear ... and a village for support nearby', a delightful place in which to meditate and continue his quest. He sat on a heap of hay under the spreading branches of a peepul tree (later known as a bodhi tree or tree of awakening) and vowed not to arise until he had gained enlightenment.

His enlightenment coincided, we are told, with the ending of night. He fixed his eyes on the 'star of healing' – Venus – just rising in the east as the sky lightened before dawn. And, the accounts say, he knew then that he was enlightened, awake to an extent shared by no one alive that he could discern. 'He had reached perfection and he thought to himself: "This is the authentic way on which in the past so many great seers, who also knew all higher and lower things, have travelled on to ultimate and real truth.... Here I have found freedom."'[169]

The realizations which came to him under the bodhi tree were so far-reaching that he was satisfied that he had reached what he described as 'the unborn, unageing, deathless, sorrowless, undefiled supreme ending of bondage, nirvana',[170] the purpose of his 'noble quest'. However the realizations are described, they are always expressed in terms of a process first of expanding awareness, then of a recognition that he had surmounted a pinnacle of mental freedom, and, finally, of a process of the absorption of the experience to transform all the recesses of his personality.

The phase of expanding awareness is recounted in varying terms, often governed by the doctrinal forms that the enlightenment experience took on when the Buddha and others later tried to convey what it was like. Gautama started by generating mindfulness by concentrating on the sensations of his breathing, still perhaps the most popular of all meditation practices. In other words, clearing his mind of all distractions, he established himself in full, one-pointed, self-reflective consciousness.

It is a tenet of Buddhism that you cannot do without mindfulness – complete self-awareness – if you want any lasting access to still higher levels of consciousness. Thus Buddhism addresses itself to the person who is prepared to attend to his or her own mental and emotional states. It is not particularly concerned with the aspects of human life which do not demand reflective consciousness – sex, eating, social arrangements, and so on – except in so far as they are opportunities or pitfalls for the extension of consciousness. What Buddhism is concerned with is firstly the strengthening of self-awareness using mindfulness practices, as described in chapter 9, and secondly, the conscious process of higher evolution which extends awareness systematically into all the corners of human experience.

THE BUDDHA DECIDES ON COMPASSIONATE ACTIVITY

After spending several days just 'experiencing the bliss of release',[171] the Buddha, as we can now call him, reviewed the workings of mind and the world from his new vantage point, letting the whole experience sink in, as it were. The content of the enlightenment experience was later given the name 'Dharma'. 'Dharma' in Buddhism has several meanings, and in this context it refers to truth in two senses. Firstly, it means reality or truth as apprehended in states of mind completely free from emotional and cognitive 'veils' (*avarana*); secondly, it means the truth as communicated to others by an enlightened person, in the form of a path leading to enlightenment.[172]

Since the Buddha knew of no teacher who had achieved a more exalted level of consciousness than he had, he stated that he would utilize the Dharma as his teacher, 'living under the Dharma, honouring and respecting that'.[173] He later urged his disciples to do the same, exhorting them to 'abide islands to yourselves; taking refuge in none other: islanded by the Dharma, taking refuge in the Dharma, seeking refuge in none other'.[174] The description of the weeks following the Buddha's enlightenment certainly suggest that he continued to learn from his vision of reality, the Dharma. An enormous psychic momentum seems to have been established at the enlightenment, and this powered the Buddha through a series of further creative realizations. He worked with his new knowledge creatively, too, as it became clearer to him what a Buddha does.

It came to him that a Buddha engages in compassionate activity. A life of compassion is the natural external sign of a Buddha's internal realization. In his mind's eye, the story goes, the Buddha contemplated the world of living beings, and saw them like lotuses in a pool, in various stages of growth.[175] The buds of some were tightly closed and deep under water or sunk in the mud, but others stood clear of the water, their blossoms beginning to open.

The Buddha decided that he would spend his life trying to help such 'buds' to open fully, and would establish a system of spiritual practice and teachings which would continue to help people after he had died. The result was an extraordinarily successful religious movement. Our knowledge of early Buddhism comes almost entirely from contemporary Buddhist sources, but even if we make due allowance for partisanship, the Buddha emerges as a remarkably successful propagandist. His influence during his lifetime spread more widely and more deeply than that of any other religious teacher before or since.[176]

The Buddha continued wandering and teaching in northern India for another forty-five years or so, dying of dysentery at the age of eighty. He found that it was indeed possible to show others the way to gain the same enlightenment that he had gained, and he was very soon no longer alone. Many of his early disciples were themselves already on the 'noble quest' as wanderers, as he had been, and according to Buddhist records, they only needed a few hints to open their own flowers of enlightenment.

THE SANGHA AND THE IDEALS OF BUDDHISM

The Buddha once said that he felt like a traveller discovering an ancient, overgrown trackway in a forest. Following it, the traveller came to a ruined royal capital. He decided to persuade the local prince to repopulate the ancient city, and restore it to its former glory.[177] Similarly, the Buddha wished to open up the path of higher evolution, and to make sure that the way was kept clear. He wished to 'restore' the city of the human mind, too, but the image evokes more than the individual mind. His city was to be a mass movement, a collection of people working together to promote spiritual growth in others as well as themselves. The Buddha created this movement, it seems safe to say, because he wanted his discoveries to reach further than the people he encountered while he lived. He wanted to ensure that the path of higher evolution remained open after his death: a road only stays open if a stream of traffic continues to use it.

The movement that the Buddha founded, through which Buddhism has survived for so long, is known as the Sangha. A member of the Sangha is someone who 'goes for refuge' to the ideals of Buddhism. He or she takes the Buddha as exemplar, attempts to follow the higher evolutionary path (Dharma), and works to keep the Sangha a living spiritual community. In some Buddhist countries, the term Sangha is used only for monks and nuns, who take on rules of homelessness and celibacy, but originally it seems to have referred generally to all those sincerely practising in a Buddhist context.

Nowadays, the Sangha is divided into hundreds of independent spiritual communities, often following slightly different Buddhist traditions. How should the Sangha keep open the path of higher evolution? This is what the Buddha is recorded as saying to his first sixty disciples:

You and I are free from all shackles, whether human or divine. Go now and wander for the welfare and happiness of many, out of compassion for the world, for the benefit, welfare and happiness of gods and men. Go not alone, but in twos. Teach the meaning and the letter of the Dharma, lovely for youth, lovely for middle age, lovely for latest years; explain a holy life that is utterly perfect and pure. There are creatures with little dust on their eyes who will be lost through not hearing the Dharma, and some will understand. I myself shall go to Uruvela, to Senanigama, to teach the Dharma.[178]

THE THEORETICAL BASIS OF BUDDHISM:
CONDITIONED CO-PRODUCTION

Gautama's final breakthrough of awareness under the bodhi tree, the culminating insight of the enlightenment, was to survey the underlying evolutionary principles that drive the universe of phenomena. His vision was of a world in constant flux with nothing immutable in it, and of human experience as a stream of momentary mental states, with no stable central controlling 'Mind' set apart from those mental states. Yet both the flux of the world and the stream of the mind flow on in patterned, law-governed ways. The conditioned process is complex, Gautama realized, but its principles can be understood; it can be influenced. As a result, he appreciated how the deep yearning for higher evolution that so many people have can find expression in harmony with these principles.

Buddhism adopts a fundamentally evolutionary viewpoint on all topics. It is chiefly concerned with the cultivation of the human mind, higher evolution. But as well as seeing an evolving mind, its vision of what reality is like, on all levels and in all spheres, is of reality as process, as evolution. This was what the Buddha stressed when he tried to convey his enlightenment experience. All phenomena, he said, link together in a mutually conditioning network, and everything arises in dependence on the network of conditions present at its birth. This is 'conditioned co-production', the network of causality that gives life and the world its dynamic patterned structure.[179] In practical terms, the Buddha attempted to communicate as a path the conditioned stages that further cultivate the mind (see chapter 9). For the enquiring mind, he also translated his whole vision of conditionality into what one could call a theoretical or philosophical position underlying his practical teachings. The scholar Helmuth von Glasenapp goes so far as to claim that this 'philosophy of becoming'

is unique in the spiritual history of humanity, in so far as it explains everything that exists through the co-operation of only momentarily existing forces, arising and disappearing in functional dependence [on] each other. Due to this, Buddhism can renounce the concept of eternal substances (matter, soul, God) which in all other teachings form the basis.[180]

According to Buddhism, every event or phenomenon, including every event in the mind, arises in dependence on a network of other phenomena which are its conditions, and it in turn forms one of the conditions for innumerable other phenomena. The details of just *how* phenomena are connected together is incredibly complex and subtle. Buddhist psychological philosophers have debated the subject at great length.[181] In their own way, Western philosophers, scientists, and psychologists are also studying some of these connections, for example in evolutionary biology.

Fairly early on, Buddhist thinkers divided conditionality into five levels or orders: the physical or inorganic, the biological, the mental or psychological, the ethical (the order of deliberate, self-aware action – karma – with its moral consequences), and the transcendental.[182] Buddhism is a human-centred system, interested in what people can do directly to modify their lives, and so it has always concentrated on the fourth and fifth orders. Science deals with the first three orders.

It is tempting to home in on only one or two orders of conditionality, and try to account for everything within that level. Thus orthodox Hinduism tends to claim that all one's life experience is entirely a product of the karma generated in previous lives, a view which can encourage complacency and callousness. Reductionist science tries to reduce all phenomena to the physical, or inorganic, order. A more holistic approach sees that whatever happens may be due to conditions operating within any one or more of the five orders.

The universality of conditioned co-production favours an evolutionary approach to understanding all phenomena whatsoever, from inorganic processes to the workings of society and the human mind. The universe, according to this view, is not fickle or haphazard, it is law-governed, yet not necessarily fully predictable, not predetermined. Everything that happens is the outcome not of a single chain of cause and effect, but of a potentially infinite net of conditions operating in one or more of the orders of conditionality, just as a thunderstorm in Italy results from shifting weather patterns covering the whole globe.

CYCLICAL AND PROGRESSIVE CONDITIONALITY

Living creatures are usually even less predictable than the weather. An animal may allow its mind to be swept back and forth by the winds of conditionality, but just occasionally, by some mysterious process of recognition, its mind may give birth to a new idea, a new behaviour. As I suggested in chapter 4, novel behaviours can, under some circumstances, remove some of the restrictions on the scope of awareness, constituting an evolutionary advance in consciousness. Minds thus contain an inherent potential for self-transcendence, and give a direction to the evolutionary process.

The evolution of consciousness was a slow process, occurring only generation by generation, until the human species reached its mental maturity and individual people became capable of full self-reflection. Then choice became possible, and mental experience could be deliberately guided. Recognizing the implications of this fact, and reflecting on their own insight into conditioned co-production, the Buddha and his followers emphasized two crucial kinds of conditioned connection between mental events: reactive or cyclical conditionality, and progressive, 'spiral' conditionality. To quote an Indian scholar, B.M. Barua, this distinction was first made by...

the intellectually gifted early Buddhist sister Dhammadinna, whose views were fully approved and endorsed by the Buddha with the remark that he had nothing further to add to them. As interpreted by her, [the Buddha's conditioned co-production] admits of two different trends of things in the whole of reality. In one of them, the reaction takes place in a cyclical order between two opposites, such as pleasure and pain, virtue and vice, good and evil.... In the other, the reaction takes place in a progressive order between two counterparts or complements,... the succeeding factor augmenting the effect of the preceding one.[183]

If the cyclical form of conditionality is dominant in one's mind, then one tends to react to experience in a mechanical fashion, swinging between emotional extremes, acting in a blinkered and self-centred way, responding to pleasure by craving and attachment, and to pain by anger and fear. In short, one's life goes round and round in circles, as pictured in the symbol of the Tibetan Wheel of Life described in chapter 1.

The progressive form of conditionality connects the successive stages of higher evolution, since it permits a state of mind on one level to give rise to a state of mind on a higher level. Instead of bouncing or circulating between opposite factors, one uses skilful self-awareness to tap the tension between such factors, in order to transcend both of them. This process is the theme of chapter 9. It ends in nirvana; or perhaps 'ends' is not the right word:

Dhammadinna wisely said that Nirvana was generally regarded as the final step in the process, in order to avoid an infinite regress. But she has not failed to indicate that even if there be any further reaction, that also takes place in the line and whatever follows therefrom will also appertain to Nirvana and, therefore, will partake of its nature.[184]

The Buddhist doctrine of conditioned co-production says that the unsatisfactory and restricted aspects of life have identifiable causal origins, as do the satisfactory and open aspects. Consequently, it is possible for one to follow a path of deliberate self-transformation that gradually eliminates the causes of the unsatisfactory side of life, and promotes the causes of the satisfactory side.

If it were not for the assurance that such change for the better is possible, the vision of the universe as one great process of change could be an overwhelming, pessimistic creed, like the evolutionism of some influential Western philosophers of the last hundred years. Men like Herbert Spencer and Francis Galton saw humanity caught up in a tidal wave of evolutionary destiny, the strong and more perfect (i.e. men like them) thriving, and the weak being ruthlessly culled by nature. And if nature was too slow, then those who understood her plans best should intervene: Galton advocated eugenic breeding programmes to improve the race.[185]

This kind of evolutionism was prompted by the great success of Darwin's theory, but it has parallels in the ancient world. One of the Greek axial sages, Heraclitus, an approximate contemporary of the Buddha, taught, as the Buddha did, that all is flux. But he apparently fell into the trap of insisting upon an inexorable and immutable law of destiny, as a compensation for the world's instability. In addition, he rejected any universal foundation for ethics and recommended warfare as the best source of order in society.[186]

Opposing ideas of this sort, the Buddha taught that the advance of consciousness consists in the destruction of barriers, not only within the individual psyche, but between people as well. Some schools of Buddhism go so far as to claim that effort on the path of higher evolution ultimately fails to bear fruit unless it is for the sake of all, for reasons that will be considered in chapter 10. Consequently, Buddhism emphasizes compassion as much as wisdom, the unity of humanity – indeed of all life – as well as a vision of transformation. Conditioned co-production reveals the changeability of all experience, and so encourages attempts to direct change by conscious intervention. It also reveals the interconnectedness of all phenomena, so that actions for the benefit of others will redound to the benefit of oneself as well.

A balance between individual transformation and solidarity with others may seem a sufficient safeguard against one-sided views, but the Buddha did not stop there. He added warnings against literal-minded interpretations of any explanation, saying that any definite statements about what is really going on have only provisional validity, because reality is not circumscribed by words or concepts. If taken literally, they will eventually prove a barrier to further progress, a point that has had to be re-emphasized by most revivals of Buddhism, to the present day. The Buddha is reported as having warned that:

Even this view [conditioned co-production], which is so pure and so clear, if you cling to it, if you fondle it, if you treasure it, if you are attached to it, then you do not understand that the teaching is similar to a raft, which is for crossing over, and not for getting hold of.[187]

With this warning in mind, we can look at how higher levels of consciousness, the stages on the path of higher evolution, are accessible through putting the progressive form of conditionality imto practice.

Chapter Nine

THE SPIRAL PATH:
BUILDING ON SELF-REFLECTION

There is no landscape to see from the mountain-top except in so far as
you have built one up by the long effort of your ascent.
Antoine de St Exupéry, *Wisdom of the Sands*, 162

ASCENDING THE STUPA

Rising amidst the lush green farms and forests of Java is a huge Buddhist monument, the stupa of Borobudur. Arnold Toynbee describes it as

> ... one of the most lovely of all human works of art. Here in 772, the founder of the Shailendra dynasty encased a hill in a stupa, and the bas-reliefs that adorn the encircling tiers of terraces give a visual presentation of the whole world of Mahayana [Buddhist] mythology and metaphysics. The natural setting of this exquisite work of art is as lovely as the architecture and the sculpture. The sheer mountain that rises on one side is balanced by the green paddies that spread out on the other side.[188]

The first stupas were built as cairns to the memory of enlightened Buddhist teachers, but they developed into rich architectural symbols of the whole process of the development of consciousness. Borobudur is one of the most elaborate. Its six square tiers bear a series of reliefs carved in stone. The ones on the basal wall illustrate the disastrous effects of 'unskilful' (detrimental) deeds and the beneficial effect of 'skilful' deeds. Above them are narrative carvings of the progress of men and women towards enlightenment, including the Buddha's life (see chapter 8) and his legendary former lives. The Great Monkey birth story is there (see Appendix). The galleries on the higher square terraces illustrate the long pilgrimage of the youth Sudhana in his search for truth and enlightenment, Sudhana being the hero of the very popular *World Array Sutra*. There are three circular terraces above the square ones, where seventy-two Buddha images can be seen seated in meditation inside small lattice-work stupas. The whole is surmounted by a large bell-shaped cupola with a damaged spire, similar to the small stupas but originally containing a deliberately unfinished Buddha statue representing full enlightenment.

Since very early times, stupas have been objects of devotion for people in all Buddhist countries. The practice is to approach from the East, and walk around the structure in a clockwise direction, reflecting on an object of meditation, a sacred phrase (mantra), or on the symbolism of the stupa itself. If the stupa is tiered, like Borobudur, the pilgrim 'circumambulates in a sun-wise [clockwise] direction ... and ascends the successive terraces (representing various psychic levels)', gradually approaching the centre and pinnacle.[189]

According to the German Buddhist scholar Lama Govinda, the plan of Borobudur and some other stupas is designed to correspond exactly to a classification of the path to enlightenment into sixty stages. 'These sixty elements constitute a continuous way of ascending through the ... different states of existence in the form of a spiral, spiritual circumambulatory path.'[190]

The path of higher evolution is continuous, and so the number of stages one divides it into is partly a matter of convention. Buddhism alone describes a bewildering variety of paths: the Three Trainings, the Noble Eightfold Path, the seven Factors of Enlightenment, and so on; and other systems further add to the choice. How, then, can one decide upon a particular path to follow?

The Path in Principle

In a way, the intrepid evolver has no choice. Higher evolution goes by many names, but it is one process, one path: whatever leads from 'here' to enlightenment.[191] Segments, at least, of that path can be found in other belief systems. To the extent that those truly take one forward, they are in principle the same as the equivalent parts of the Buddhist path.

Although there is only one path of higher evolution, everybody's experience is unique: each person's life is made up of a flow of mental states which are unique to that individual. The possibilities of human life are endless, and both the succession of experiences and the details of the particular states must be different for each person. What is more, not all belief systems are equally effective in aiding one on the path, some indeed advocating goals which seem to fall far short of enlightenment and some not clearly teaching a path of transformation at all. However, one is faced each moment by a choice: either one seeks satisfaction on one's current level, hoping for happiness from habitual ego-strengthening techniques, or one creates out of present experience something unknown and new, of a more exalted nature. The latter ever-present potential for self-transcendence is something that everyone has in common, and in that sense there is only one path.

There is only one path in a more specific sense, too. The path of higher evolution is unique in that it always involves passing through a particular series of levels of consciousness, in a particular order. In essence, the path is an evolutionary succession of states of consciousness, leading on from the recognition – perception – centred experience – self-reflection succession which marks lower evolution. The main task of this chapter is to describe the sequence of levels which builds on self-reflective consciousness.

At first sight, levels of consciousness and active practices appear to be separate things. One tends to put what one *experiences* into a quite different category from what one *does*. The pattern in lower evolution is to have an experience and then to come out with the 'right' (i.e. habitual) reaction to that experience. The sea anemone is touched, and it defensively shrinks back. One could say that the action is designed to solve the 'problem' that the experience raises. Greater awareness allows one to reverse the link, to act first, in order to create a new type of experience.

However, the more intense one's experience becomes, the less one can separate action from experience. Instead of being passive, reacting to experiences, even instead of acting for the sake of desired experiences, one just acts creatively. One starts to construct the very path that one treads.

The path of higher evolution is an 'inner' journey, a sequence of levels of consciousness, of types of experience, if you like. It can also be described in terms of actions, the *practices* appropriate at each level, which lead one up to the next level. Yet the two merge. Each practice represents a certain experienced state of mind; each state is reflected in appropriate action. The most basic formulation of the Buddhist path is that of the *three trainings*, which are primarily practices: ethical behaviour, meditation, and wisdom. Other well-known Buddhist paths of practice are elaborations of the three trainings. Later we shall consider the seven Factors of Enlightenment, an equivalent path in which mental experience figures as strongly as type of practice.

Fig.22 The three trainings

In the three trainings, one is first advised to concentrate on one's ethics or life-style, ensuring that one's words and deeds have a beneficial effect on others and encourage wholesome mental states in oneself. While one is improving the ethical side of life one can certainly try to meditate, but one will probably find that meditation acts more as a support for ethical behaviour than as a means of access to higher states of consciousness. A straightforward life-style and a clear conscience is then said to lead on to contentment, happiness, and a clear mind.

With the mind sorted out on its present, conscious, level, it becomes easier to embark on a programme of mental training which directly promotes elevated states of consciousness. This is the second training, meditation. And once one's mind has been strengthened and focused by familiarity with absorption in meditation, one can direct it to the contemplation of reality itself. A contemplation of the real nature of the phenomena of the mind and the world leads to the first flashes of wisdom, the third training.

The third training takes place on a transcendental level: the division between inner and outer experience has been transcended. In deep meditation, one contemplates the subtle, interconnected processes of reality, and allows the resulting insights to influence all the activities of one's life, and to dissolve all the limited interpretations that overlay experience. Increasing access to an unveiled appreciation of reality – wisdom – is said to take one to liberation and the knowledge of liberation, that is, enlightenment.

THE PATH AS A SPIRAL

The devotee at Borobudur climbs to higher and ever higher levels, but has to travel all the way around each level before ascending to the next one if he or she is not to miss some of the glorious works of art adorning the walls. Similarly, each phase of spiritual progress needs to reach completion, needs to be fully absorbed, before one is ready to take full advantage of the next stage. A well-developed ethical life is a necessary basis for meditation, and the deep calm of meditation is a prerequisite if one's faculty of wisdom is to penetrate the subtleties of reality.

Lama Govinda gives a more profound reason for depicting the path in a spiral form. He points out that spiritual progress is not a vertical lift-ride to the 'roof' of enlightenment. It also has a circular dimension, so that overall it is a 'spiral-like progression'.[192] One passes again and again through a similar series of challenges and experiences, but each time on a more sublime level.

I described the three trainings of ethics, meditation, and wisdom as a broad division of the whole of higher evolution into three segments. Using the spiral image, however, Lama Govinda shows that one can regard the path as passing through the three trainings several times, 'in which the same elements reappear on each higher stage in greater intensity'.[193] He gives three to four turns to his spiral, but one can discern more and more turns if one focuses down to the streaming succession of mental states flickering past faster than the frames on a film.

Here, ethics, meditation, and wisdom merge into the states of consciousness that these practices correspond to. Each choice of a constructive action (deed, word, or thought – ethics) produces a more positive state of mind (meditation). In this state, experience can be appreciated a little more clearly and deeply (wisdom). A more adequate view of the world leads to a clearer insight into how best to behave, and if one chooses (ethics) to follow this insight, the spiral starts another turn, a little higher this time. One is making use of the progressive or spiral form of conditionality described in the last chapter. The sequence is easy enough to describe, but it is far from easy to achieve.

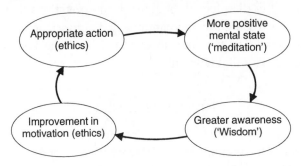

Fig.23 Spiral of ethics, meditation, and wisdom

The spiral way of progressing can be seen in a rudimentary form in lower evolution as well as higher. Like human beings, lower organisms normally follow a circular path of habitual responses to repeated situations. But occasionally a new factor is somehow introduced, such as the behavioural innovations discussed in chapter 4, and an evolutionary advance results. The biologist Robert Reid describes evolution as a spiral, or 'irregular gyre' in his excellent survey, *Evolutionary Theory: The Unfinished Synthesis*. He says that there is a sort of vertical jump as new qualities emerge, and then the species goes around in a cycle in which it takes advantage of and adapts to the new situation, specializing to its new ecological niches. In its scope, however, each cycle, Reid asserts, is progressively more adaptable than the last.[194]

The most remarkable example of the spiral of lower evolutionary advance was the loop between mental capacity, new behaviours, and mental maps described in chapter 4. It was probably a self-augmenting, self-transcending cascade of this sort that created the most spectacular product of lower evolution: self-reflective consciousness in human beings. And self-reflective consciousness, or mindfulness, is the starting point for a new spiral, most often described in Buddhism in terms of the seven Factors of Enlightenment.

THE SEVEN FACTORS OF ENLIGHTENMENT

The list of the seven Factors of Enlightenment must have been one of the central teachings of the Buddha and his early followers, since it is included so frequently in the texts of nearly all schools. The 'factors' are literally the seven limbs or branches (*angas*) of *bodhi*, (enlightenment, awakening, or wisdom), and they are:

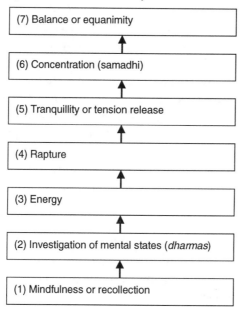

```
┌────────────────────────────────────────┐
│ (7) Balance or equanimity              │
└────────────────────────────────────────┘
                    ▲
┌────────────────────────────────────────┐
│ (6) Concentration (samadhi)            │
└────────────────────────────────────────┘
                    ▲
┌────────────────────────────────────────┐
│ (5) Tranquillity or tension release    │
└────────────────────────────────────────┘
                    ▲
┌────────────────────────────────────────┐
│ (4) Rapture                            │
└────────────────────────────────────────┘
                    ▲
┌────────────────────────────────────────┐
│ (3) Energy                             │
└────────────────────────────────────────┘
                    ▲
┌────────────────────────────────────────┐
│ (2) Investigation of mental states (dharmas) │
└────────────────────────────────────────┘
                    ▲
┌────────────────────────────────────────┐
│ (1) Mindfulness or recollection        │
└────────────────────────────────────────┘
```

Fig.24 The seven Factors of Enlightenment

All the factors are aspects of consciousness which can be cultivated at any time, and they reach perfection as seven faculties of the enlightened mind, as the name implies. However, they are repeatedly referred to as successive states of mind, or mental acts, constituting the path to enlightenment. They represent one way in which the spiral path of higher evolution has been expressed in words and concepts. The texts make it quite clear that each of the factors, in the listed order, can arise in dependence on the one before it by means of the progressive kind of conditionality explained in the last chapter.

One of the discourses preserved in the Pali language records the Buddha's explanation of the Factors of Enlightenment. When a disciple, says the Buddha, undertakes the mindfulness of breathing meditation and the general practice of mindfulness,...

... ardent, clearly comprehending and mindful, having overcome covetousness and grief concerning the world, then unremitting mindfulness is established in him.... on that occasion the mindfulness enlightenment factor is aroused in him, and he develops it, and by development it comes to perfection in him.

Abiding thus mindful, he investigates and examines that state with understanding and embarks on a scrutiny (of it).... on that occasion the investigation-of-states enlightenment factor is aroused in him, and he develops it, and by development it comes to perfection in him.

In him who investigates and examines that state with understanding and embarks upon a scrutiny of it, tireless energy is aroused.... on that occasion the energy enlightenment factor is aroused in him, and he develops it, and by development it comes to perfection in him.

In him who has aroused energy, unworldly rapture arises.... on that occasion the rapture enlightenment factor is aroused in him, and he develops it, and by development it comes to perfection in him.

The body and mind of one whose mind is held in rapture become tranquillized.... on that occasion the tranquillity enlightenment factor is aroused in him, and he develops it, and by development it comes to perfection in him.

The mind of one who is tranquillized in body and blissful becomes concentrated.... on that occasion the concentration enlightenment factor is aroused in him, and he develops it, and by development it comes to perfection in him.

He becomes one who looks with complete equanimity on the mind thus concentrated.... on that occasion the equanimity enlightenment factor is aroused in him, and he develops it, and by development it comes to perfection in him.

... thus developed, thus repeatedly practised, the seven Factors of Enlightenment perfect clear vision and deliverance [i.e. enlightenment].[195]

Before looking in detail at each of the Factors of Enlightenment in turn, here is an expansion of the Buddha's account of how they fit together. Full self-reflective consciousness, known in Buddhism as (1) *recollection* or mindfulness, is the starting point for the spiral path, and it is repeatedly stressed that mindfulness is vital for any spiritual practice.

In a state of clear self-awareness, one is in a position to carry out (2) *investigation* of what is going on in the mind, to get the flavour of different thoughts and emotions, recognizing which ones are unskilful (rooted in craving, aversion, and delusion) and which ones are skilful (rooted in content, goodwill, and wisdom).

Having sorted out one's stream of mental states, one then applies attention and (3) *energy* to the skilful ones, and withdraws it from the unskilful ones. This process of mental spring-cleaning liberates large amounts of psychic energy ((3) again) previously locked up in anxiety and mental conflict, and the free flow of energy is experienced as (4) *rapture* – an intense thrill or happiness of body and mind, which may be felt in meditation, human communication, artistic pursuits, or in daily activities intensely experienced.

Once the mind has been purified for the time being of negative, unskilful mental states, and the tensions and conflicts thus released have ceased gushing up in rapture, one emerges into a state of (5) *tranquillity* or tension release, a state usually only accessible during deep meditation. The clear tranquil mind is able to be fully one-pointed, with no distractions or disturbances, and it can expand and float gently up into successively higher or deeper states of meditative absorption or (6) *samadhi*. By samadhi here is meant a temporary state of very powerful, lucid awareness, in which there may be no conceptual thinking going on at all. The still transparency of samadhi encourages any mental processes not previously accessible to awareness (the sub-conscious and unconscious 'mind') to emerge into full consciousness. Any disharmonies within consciousness can consequently be gradu-ally resolved, and one's attitude to others can become perfectly un-prejudiced and even-minded. This is (7) *balance* or equanimity.

Balance begins as a state of mind present in deep meditation, but by influencing other aspects of experience, mindfully contemplated, it permits biases and obscurations of vision to be eradicated, leading to a growing non-dual awareness or insight. Once meditative balance has helped to transform one's fundamental view of existence, it becomes a complete equilibrium of being, a state of poise characterizing enlight-enment itself. 'Equanimity is an integral element of the experience of [enlightenment],' writes the Pali scholar Amadeo Solé-Leris, '... the fully realized human being is characterized by an unshakeable balance of mind and by the total openness and availability to others which are its corollaries.'[196]

(1) CULTIVATING MINDFULNESS OR RECOLLECTION

Full self-reflective consciousness is necessary as a starting point for the spiral path of higher evolution. In higher evolution, one is deliberately choosing to work to transform one's own mind, raising its level of consciousness step by step. So a reflective awareness of one's own mind cannot be dispensed with. In Buddhism the level of full self-reflective consciousness is called the state of 'recollection', more commonly but less literally translated as 'mindfulness'.

In chapter 5 we followed the origin and history of self-reflective consciousness, the seed of mindfulness, as man-like apes became ape-like human beings. We saw its foreshadowings as experience started to focus around a centre; and then the turning of awareness on to this centre itself, and a fixing of the observed centre by concepts and words: I, mine, and so on. We also saw that full self-reflection – mindfulness – was never a persistent feature of human experience. It has to be discovered anew by every child, and thereafter it comes and goes, illuminating the self fitfully, like lightning in a midnight downpour.

The arising of mindfulness is a mysterious process. For much of the time one is in a drifting or mechanical state, chasing dreamy thoughts or images, or performing familiar actions without being fully 'there'. Yet as soon as one notices this unawareness or unmindfulness, it has gone, like darkness, which cannot be seen by switching on the light. The process of drifting out of and snapping back into mindfulness is particularly noticeable during meditation, but it happens all the time.

The first task in spiritual practice is to improve the continuity of one's mindfulness. Mindfulness of one's surroundings, of one's actions and bodily sensations, of one's feeling-responses and emotional states, of one's thoughts, and of other people – all these are emphasized again and again by Buddhist meditation teachers.[197] 'Being here now' and not daydreaming of what was or ought to be is crucially important, yet this does not preclude a strong sense of one's continuity in time. Both memory and a clear awareness of purpose are aspects of mindfulness.

If one suspects that all is not right with oneself and the world, and that matters could be improved, that suspicion will have arisen when one was in a mindful state. In particular, one may become aware of just how unaware one usually is, and want to improve on that. Paradoxically, while self-reflective consciousness can be seen as 'not merely to know, but to know that one knows',[198] as Teilhard de Chardin defines it, it also brings with it a painful consciousness of how much remains unknown. So mindfulness includes a sober assessment of unsatisfactoriness, and a growing faith in the potential for transformation, even an intuitive response to the possibility of a non-dual form of awareness. (See chapter 10.)

The mysterious nature of the arising of mindfulness means that one cannot promote it unless one already has it (though one can help others regain their mindfulness if one notices that they are being unmindful). Whenever one is in a mindful state, that is the time for strengthening mindfulness, and for working on the higher Factors of Enlightenment. Mindfulness is particularly strengthened by avoiding distractions and by practising meditation exercises that bring about one-pointedness of mind. One is advised to shun, for the time being, those situations which scatter one's attention or disquiet one's mind, and to 'guard the doors of the senses': carefully noticing all the stimuli that enter one's senses and what effect they have, and acting accordingly.

Some Buddhist practices demand careful preparation and special circumstances, but mindfulness is possible in every situation. There is no time at which mindfulness is not appropriate, and a positive, skilful state of mind must invariably be a mindful one. This is why mindfulness (self-reflective consciousness) is the base and starting point of all higher evolution: it provides the necessary spark for every progressive act.

INTEGRATED AWARENESS AND THE EGO

The terms 'self-reflective consciousness' and even 'mindfulness' may seem to imply a condition of setting up a distanced 'watcher' in the mind, unfeelingly monitoring thoughts and movements like a time-and-motion study expert. Trying to become self-conscious in this way leads to awkwardness, tension, and sometimes heartlessness. Many authors describing the level of self-reflective consciousness are clearly describing this alienated state, and are not aware of the possibility of genuine mindfulness, which rather means being fully present in an experience.[199]

The kind of genuine mindfulness which Buddhist practices intend to bring about is a state in which one is completely *involved* in experience, without being swept away by negative emotions. Consider talking to an acquaintance as an example. Without mindfulness, one is thinking of other things, easily distracted from the other person, perhaps quick to get bored or become annoyed or dismissive. The conversation is unsatisfying and probably unproductive. With an alienated observer attitude, one is not distracted, but detached from the actual experience of communicating, watching oneself speak as if from a distance. There is no sense of flow in it, just a coldly evaluating commentary; no real feeling is involved (more likely, feelings are repressed). With true mindfulness, one is undistractedly *with* the other person, fully emotionally engaged and aware of one's feelings, responsive to the other. So practising mindfulness, one tries to become less entangled in habitual emotional reactions, without losing touch with one's actual feelings, whatever they are, cultivating a fully *integrated* awareness.[200]

When one is aware of one's own awareness, one has a partial control over one's mind. As well as being the only foundation for a positive development of the mind, this partial control can also result in emotional alienation if misapplied. The danger lies in the maintenance of a defensive ego.

Recall the origins of self-reflection, as described in chapter 5. Even when one is not self-aware, one experiences a 'centre of attention', a sense of 'I' which seems to attract all experience towards it. This centre may sometimes be present in higher animals, as I suggested in chapter 3. With self-reflection, one goes a step further. The centre of attention is now aware of itself as a centre.

Indeed, instead of seeing itself as it is – a 'point' in the metaphorical 'space' of the mind which happens to be central – the centre of experience tends to be felt as an unchanging and solid self or ego, or even an eternal soul. A traditional Buddhist account describes how self-awareness unfolds in the mind:

> ... depending on the [all-conserving mind], an evolution of the ego and consciousness takes place in all beings. What is meant by this? In the all-conserving mind, ignorance obtains; and from [this] non-enlightenment starts that which sees, that which represents, that which constantly particularizes. This is called the ego. Five different names are given to the ego.
>
> The first name is ... activity-consciousness, in the sense that through the agency of ignorance an unenlightened mind begins to be disturbed.
>
> The second name is ... evolving [*pravrtti* – 'progressing'] consciousness, in the sense that when the mind is disturbed, there evolves that which sees an external world.
>
> The third name is ... representation consciousness, in the sense

that the [mind] represents an external world.

The fourth name is ... particularization-consciousness, in the sense that it discriminates between different things defiled as well as pure.

The fifth name is ... succession-consciousness (i.e. memory), in the sense that continuously directed by the awakening conscious-ness (or attention) it retains and never loses or suffers the destruc-tion of any karma ... and also in the sense that it unconsciously recollects things gone by, and in imagination anticipates things to come.

... all ignorant minds through their succession-consciousnesses cling to the conception of I and not-I (i.e. a separate objective world) and misapprehend the nature of the ... objects of sense.[201]

Clinging to the conception of I, to a lump-of-concrete view of the self, does not accord with the fluidity of real life. The imagined self seems fragile, vulnerable, and incomplete. One is tempted all the time either to defend the ego against perceived threats, or to buttress it by accu-mulating 'possessions' from which it can derive a more solid identity. Such possessions range from a strong identification with the physical body, through material objects and social and sexual recognition, to the subtlest of views and attitudes. Defending the ego produces the emo-tions of aversion or hatred, and fear. Buttressing it with possessions produces the emotion of craving. Clearly, aversion and craving are our sophisticated, self-aware outgrowths of animal aversion and attraction.

With self-reflective consciousness, understanding dawns that one is indeed an autonomous self, capable of forming independent judge-ments and of choosing between courses of action. So far, this is an evolutionary advance, it is an expansion in awareness. However, as soon as the narrow causeway of independent individuality emerges from the tide, the twin whirlpools of what Jung calls alienation and inflation appear to the right and left. On the right, a shrinking from full-blooded, integrated experience. On the left, an anxious grabbing and rejecting of the liked and disliked elements of self-aware experi-ence. If one starts to slip into either whirlpool (and everyone sometimes does), a vain piling of sand into an island of ego begins. Without self-reflective consciousness, ego's obsessive constructions would not be possible. Nevertheless, without self-reflective consciousness, the evolutionary advance would be completely stalled, and we would languish in the world of dumb animals. Treading the causeway means

means consciously choosing an unflinching awareness of unpleasant realities as well as pleasant ones, and of uncomfortable emotions as well as clear observation. Turning back or turning aside means repudiating the pathway of increasing awareness, and choosing to strengthen delusion instead. The ego-view is deluded, but it is a very basic delusion, and one has not overcome it just because one can describe it. Delusion and its two main immediate effects, craving and aversion, are the fundamental vices in Buddhism – the 'three roots of unskilfulness'.

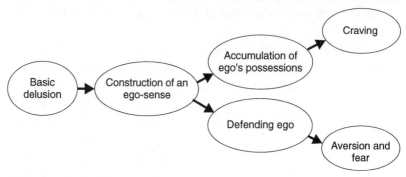

Fig.25 Delusion, craving, and aversion

Although the beginnings of self-reflective awareness are accompanied by these negative side-effects, in its fully developed form as mindfulness or integrated awareness, it has consequences which are entirely positive in the long run. By exercising mindfulness, one may dispel the darkness of ignorance. Integrated awareness effects further integration. The centre of experience, now fully aware of itself as a centre, can bring more and more elements of the mind constructively into its orbit. This integrating process is very noticeable if one takes up the systematic cultivation of mindfulness. The centred experience need not now be a fixed ego; nevertheless one recognizes a distinct but ever-changing 'self', growing in strength and continuity.[202]

One can only change and transform oneself if one's self-experience is made more vivid through practising mindfulness. Then one swings less between contradictory moods, one feels more solid, definite, and contented. Without mindfulness practice, one's personality can seem fragmented into what can amount to several competing 'selves', coming to the fore in different circumstances. Because mindfulness provides a strengthened sense of continuity, knitting the various selves together, it can be associated with the true individuality which has been a characteristic of the great pioneers of individualized consciousness in the axial age and since. A foundation of mindfulness must have been required for their independence of thought, explorations in awareness, creativity, and concern for others. The appearance of these qualities provides evidence of the first clear appearance of mindfulness in human history.

(2) INVESTIGATION OF MENTAL STATES

In the steady and focused light of mindfulness, it is possible to follow the waterfall of mental states in increasing detail. We progress from a general awareness, the first Factor of Enlightenment, to a sharpened discriminating faculty, the second factor.

Investigation can distinguish and evaluate one's mental states, and assess the flavour and quality of the different feelings, impulses, and thoughts present in consciousness. Some have 'the flavour of release', while some have the rank flavour of ego-fortification. The former are the seeds of further conscious evolutionary development, and if they are nurtured, they can flower and fruit as higher Factors of Enlightenment. So active investigation of experience is the next phase on from mindfulness: it makes possible a further conscious evolution of one's mind.

From a Buddhist point of view, mental events are either skilful (positive) or unskilful (negative); the level of consciousness corresponding to investigation of mental states can distinguish the two, as well as being mindful of mental processes in general.[203] 'Unskilful' is the technical term for states driven by those consequences of the early stages of self-reflective consciousness: craving, aversion, and delusion. 'Skilful' states are those driven by their opposites: content, good will, and wisdom. This distinction is used in Buddhism instead of our more familiar 'bad' and 'good'.

Actions and words are also labelled as unskilful or skilful, solely according to whether they arise from mental states which are unskilful or skilful. A deed is not condemned because it fails to conform to some external check-list of moral absolutes, but because it stems from greedy, malicious, or deluded *intentions*. Buddhist ethics exactly matches Buddhist psychology. Karmas are simply intentional actions; all of one's karmas are said potentially to have law-governed repercussions on one.

Craving and aversion spring from a fundamental mistake (delusion) about the nature of reality; so actions committed under their influence do not harmonize with the way things are. These unskilful actions

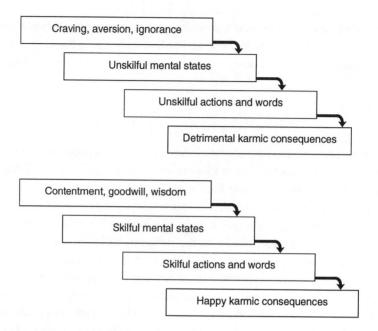

Fig.26 Unskilful and skilful states

eventually have a jarring, discordant effect on one's experience, according to the way karma operates. Karma ensures that unskilful mental states lead to suffering, especially if they are reinforced through bodily or vocal action. Similarly, skilful mental states harmonize with reality, and so they result in happiness.[204] A predominantly skilful person tends to progress up the spiral path from lower, more constricted levels of consciousness to higher, more expanded ones. Unskilfulness has the reverse effect, and one starts to regress into the circles of lower evolution. However, skilful behaviour alone is said to be insufficient for reaching the levels approaching enlightenment: a deliberate cultivation of insight is required as well, as we shall see in the next chapter.

It is possible to weaken unskilful mental states by ensuring that they are not translated into action. Buddhism is not advising that they should be hidden from view and repressed – that would contradict the theme of this 'investigation of mental states' Factor of Enlightenment – but that they should not be expressed physically or vocally. So Buddhist traditions have recommended various sets of precepts, or guidelines for ethical behaviour. The shortest and best known list of precepts is recited in virtually every formal Buddhist gathering: 'I undertake the training principle to abstain from: (a) harming living beings, (b) taking what is not given, (c) sexual misconduct, (d) untruthful speech, (e) drink or drugs which induce unmindfulness.'

(3) ENERGY

Successfully practising ethics assumes some degree of progress in the investigation of mental states. It assumes some ability to see which are skilful and which unskilful, with the help of traditional guidelines such as the precepts, and with aid from others familiar, from personal experience, with the spiral path.

The direct result of investigation is an upsurge of mental vitality – energy. It is an exhilarating achievement to be able to make the link between the feeling quality of a mental state and the direction in which that mental state is leading. There is a half-wilful ethical fog, which many people spend much of their lives immersed in, never quite willing to have a clear enough view of their thoughts and actions to let go of those which offer short-term selfish advantages, but harm self and other in the long run. This ethical confusion seems often to have a draining and debilitating effect. Practising mindfulness and investigation clears the fog, and clears the conscience. Energy is a powerful directedness, the excitement that comes from following the skilful. Wavering between skilful and unskilful locks up energy. As the trains of uninterrupted skilful states last longer and longer, energy is liberated: the impetus is all in one direction.

Energy, then, is the outcome of investigation. Like the other factors, it also corresponds to practices which yield the next factor up. The reason for investigating the mind is to be able to strengthen the positive and weaken the negative mental states. As well as doing this indirectly by behaving in an ethical manner, one can do it directly, by concentrating the energy of mindful attention on skilful thoughts and feelings, and withdrawing interest and energy from the unskilful ones. One can practise this at any time, whenever one is mindful enough to remember to do it, but especially in periods of meditation. An example of such a meditation practice is the Cultivation of Friendliness.

One begins by lighting and fanning a fire of loving-kindness for oneself, desiring one's own well-being and happiness. Then one allows the warm feelings to spread out from their centre of healthy self-love, first to a near and dear friend, then to someone one feels neutral towards, then to someone one dislikes or has some personal difficulty with. In the final stage, one calls to mind all four of the people in the previous stages, taking care that the loving-kindness is equally strong towards each, and then allowing the feeling to expand outwards, without limits.

Investigation involved an expansion of mindfulness until it could sort out the types of mental states. Investigation in turn expands into the next factor when one starts putting energy into skilful states and withdrawing it from unskilful ones. For example, the friendliness meditation, practised successfully, is not a tiring effort: it seems to liberate more mental energy than it uses. As we have seen, unskilful states of mind, since they go against the grain of reality, have a draining and exhausting effect. They lock up energy which could otherwise be released for full living and enjoyment.

Nevertheless, the evolutionary process is not spontaneous. At every stage of the spiral path, deliberate effort seems to be required to keep things moving. In the relatively early stages one needs effort just to keep mindful and aware. Go into neutral gear, and the car starts rolling backwards under the pull of primordial habits of craving, aversion, and delusion. Energy is needed at all stages, but there are two reasons why it stands as a separate Factor of Enlightenment following the investigation of mental states. The first is that there is a vital need to apply energy constantly in dealing with perceived positive and negative mental states in the following ways: (a) to *prevent* new unskilful states from arising; (b) to *eradicate* them if already present; (c) to *cultivate* new skilful states; and (d) to *maintain* existing ones.[205] The second reason is that as a result of living ethically, with conscience clear, there is a greater availability, even uprush, of mental energy.

(4) Rapture

The free flow of previously blocked psychic energy is an intensely pleasurable and exhilarating experience. Words like rapture or ecstasy come nearest to describing it. Rapture is closely tied up with energy release, and so it is not a continuous experience, more a rush of gladness and physical thrill whenever something breaks down mental barriers, conflicts, or tensions. It can come during a lively conversation, at the beginning of a close relationship, in seeing the solution to a personal or technical difficulty (as in Archimedes' 'Eureka!'), in the presence of artistic or natural beauty, and, most strongly of all, in meditation.

Intense effort in transforming the stubborn mind might be a demoralizing struggle if it were not for the reward of periods of great happiness. Happiness underlies the whole of the spiral path in any case, and someone who is genuinely promoting positive mental states always has an undercurrent of emotional positivity. This reservoir of happiness gives strength when effort becomes difficult or when the unsatisfactoriness of ordinary life comes to the fore. It is odd but true that an increasing awareness of the ills of oneself and the world can be accompanied by a growing deep resource of unconditional happiness, an exhilaration in the breeze of directed change. 'Joy and woe are woven fine,/ A clothing for the soul divine,' sings William Blake.[206]

(5) Tension-release or Tranquillity

When the sluices are opened to let a canal lock fill with water, the water at first gushes in, since there is a big difference in level between the two sides of the gates. Gradually, the flow slows down, until the water inside has risen to the same level as the water in the higher part of the canal. All is now calm and tranquil, and the lock gates can be opened with ease to let the boats through.

It is the same with rapture: the thrill comes from resolving mental conflicts and blockages. Once the pressure has had a chance to come down, all becomes calm and tranquil. What was a predominantly physical feeling of rapture ebbs away, leaving a very deep serenity, purely mental, described by the Buddha as 'a true but subtle perception of delight and happiness', the fifth Factor of Enlightenment.[207]

Tranquillity, serenity, is usually the most noticeable characteristic of someone who spends a lot of time deeply engaged in meditation. The feature that people find most attractive in a Buddha image is often his expression and pose of utter serenity. Before it becomes the normal dwelling place of one's mind, tranquillity is accessible only in deep meditation. This is because it is a level of consciousness quite independent of experience through the senses, a purely mental/emotional happiness and pliability of mind.[208] So long as one's life is dominated by sense experience alone, tranquillity in the full Buddhist sense can only be gained by temporarily withdrawing attention from the senses and focusing it inwardly, which is the method of meditation.

ABSORPTION: A NEW LEVEL OF CONSCIOUSNESS

Experience in meditation is often considered less objective than sense experience, in that it is less shared with others with a well-accepted common language of description, but Buddhists regard the meditative sphere of experience as no less 'real' than the sensual world. The meditative sphere is known as the level of 'pure form';[209] in it, brilliant archetypal mental images are perceived not with the senses but with the inspired visionary imagination. Buddhaghosha, the fifth-century author of a classic work on the practice of the Buddhist path, writes that when we see normally, even with the mind's eye, the object is flawed, imperfect in some way. But a mental object imaged on the level of pure form is

> a hundred times, a thousand times more purified, like a looking-glass disc drawn out from its case, like a mother of pearl dish well worked, like the moon's disc coming out from behind a cloud, like cranes against a thunder cloud.[210]

The level of pure form is characterized by the temporary absence of unskilful mental states and by the presence of certain skilful ones. It is traditionally divided into at least four sub-levels, called the 'absorptions' (Sanskrit *dhyanas*). Thinking dies away between the first and second absorption, and rapture is said to be calmed between the second and third, which are thus the levels of tranquillity. Equanimity or balance, the seventh Factor of Enlightenment, is developed in the third and is characteristic of the fourth absorption.[211]

Absorption represents a new and distinct level of consciousness. We saw in chapter 5 that full self-reflection involves a full awareness that internal experience is distinct from objective sense experience. Ordinary experience is always of something perceived as separate from the experiencing 'I'; it is always dual, even when it comes from the mind, in the form of memories, ideas, feelings, and mental images. But the senses generate the loudest clamour for attention. So the level of self-reflective consciousness – human life – is dominated by sense experience. Explorations of the expanding limits of sense experience characterize nearly all human creative activities, and the negative side of human life is marked by craving or aversion prompted by neurotically handled sensations.

The inner world where the senses are quietened is far more difficult to survey than the sensed world, since its objects of attention are far more subtle. Only in meditative absorption does one undistractedly abide in this subtle but no less real world. There one has achieved a level of consciousness which encompasses the self-reflection level – one is still self-aware – but exceeds it: one can attend to experiences normally masked by the clamour of the senses. In absorption, experience is still subtly dualistic, however, and internal and external worlds are not fully reconciled until a still higher level of consciousness: the stage of non-dual insight. A table in chapter 10 shows the full range of levels of consciousness considered in this book.

In absorption one has not necessarily transcended negativity entirely. Grossly unskilful states have been temporarily left behind, but until the attainment of enlightenment there are said to be conditions present in the mind which will bring them back. When they do start to return, one falls out of this meditative level of consciousness. It is like taking a hot-air balloon to rise above the choking smog of your home city. When the fuel has run out, down you sink again, but it was lovely while it lasted, and you come back to street level with an improved perspective.

The stage of insight relies on a quite different approach to the 'smog': actually converting it into pure air, at first just around you, but ultimately in the whole city (see the next chapter). An attachment to the transient bliss of the level of pure form (which may correspond to the 'oneness' ecstasies experienced by mystics of many traditions) is thus a serious pitfall from the Buddhist viewpoint, especially if the feeling of bliss and oneness are mistaken for insight, or even enlightenment itself. The eleventh century Tibetan teacher Milarepa warns:

Alas! Those proficient yogis who long have practised meditation
Mistake the psychic experience of illumination
For transcendental wisdom,
And are happy with this form of self-deception.[212]

A verbal description alone is unlikely to distinguish the two, but in the long term, as the Buddha remarked, 'wisdom shines forth in behaviour'.[213]

(6) CONCENTRATION OR SAMADHI

'Samadhi' is one of those Buddhist terms like 'Dharma' with many subtle shades of meaning. Sometimes it means the concentration of the mind on a single object, or it can mean meditation in general, but the English Buddhist teacher Sangharakshita explains that in this context,

Samadhi … is the spontaneous merging of all the energies of the psyche in an experience so intensely pleasurable that thought and volition are suspended, space vanishes, and time stands still. It is in fact a state of total integration and absorption rather than of 'concentration' in the more limited and artificial sense of the term, and as such can be compared best, though still inadequately, to the experience of the musician rapt in the enjoyment of a piece of music or of the lover rapt in the joys of love.[214]

The fourth enlightenment factor, rapture, arises because of the newness of the purely positive level of consciousness, the level induced by effort applied in the previous factors. Tranquillity is, strictly speaking, the *calming down* of the thrills of rapture as the level of pure form becomes more familiar. Samadhi here is the state of dwelling, quite at home, in the absorption level of consciousness. Being familiar with the absorptions, if one avoids the danger of becoming attached to their heavenly delights as ends in themselves, one is advised to work in them to achieve balance and eventually wisdom.

(7) BALANCE OR EQUANIMITY

The Buddha spoke of his system of spiritual training as being a *middle way*, between and above pairs of opposed experiences such as the desired and the rejected, self-indulgence and self-denial, heaven and hell, longing for unchanging eternal bliss and longing for nothingness, subject and object, self-interest and other-centredness, and so on.[215] The middle way is another name for the spiral path of higher evolution, for the path of progressive conditionality in which the tension between apparently irreconcilable opposites is used constructively to transcend both and reach a new, higher level.

When a person has completely transcended all such opposites he or she is described as enlightened, and is in a condition of perfect psychic balance, which is equanimity in its highest sense.[216] It is said that virtually the last obstacle facing someone on the verge of enlightenment is the fetter of 'wavering' or 'restlessness', the last vestige of imbalance, which continues even after craving and aversion have been quite overcome. However, as the seventh Factor of Enlightenment, balance normally means a very strong and imperturbable equilibrium of mind, developed in the absorptions.

There are special meditation practices for cultivating balance, including the last stage of the development of friendliness meditation, in which unlimited goodwill is developed for all equally, with no conditions attached. Balance is the mark of the highest two of the four meditative absorptions, and with its attainment the absorption level of consciousness has been perfected.[217] Yet it is still only a temporary equanimity of mind, lost when one comes out of meditation. To induce a permanent transformation of consciousness, equally at home in the world of sense experience as in the inner world of pure form, calls for a breakthrough into insight – balance in its transcendental sense, the theme of the next chapter.[218]

Chapter Ten

TRANSCENDING SELF AND NON-DUAL INSIGHT

All force strives forward to work far and wide
To live and grow and ever to expand;
Yet we are checked and thwarted on each side
By this world's flux and swept along like sand;
In this internal storm and outward tide
We hear a promise, hard to understand:
From the compulsion that all creatures binds,
Who overcomes himself, his freedom finds.
Goethe, 'The Mysteries', trans. Kaufmann, *Nietzsche*, 209

SENSE FACULTIES AND SPIRITUAL FACULTIES

Like animal life, human life is dominated by the sensed experience of a material world. But both reflective communion with oneself and sympathetic communication with others demonstrate that life has intervals in which the senses fade into the background. They become no more than receivers, initiating imaginative sequences in the mind which transcend material facts, or they play no part at all, as imagination,

imagination, feelings, evaluations, aspirations, and reasonings construct non-sensory worlds.

Thus the blind Milton 'looked' within, and declared:

So much the rather thou Celestial light
Shine inward, and the mind through all her powers
Irradiate, there plant eyes, all mist from thence
Purge and disperse, that I may see and tell
Of things invisible to mortal sight.[219]

An early Buddhist tradition also calls for an inner sight, for new 'sense' faculties to perceive the non-material aspects of reality.[220] The first and most basic of these faculties is full self-reflective consciousness itself. It is the uniquely human sense of autonomy, a sense which can attend to all mental activity whether originating from normal sense experience or from within the mind. We have seen that an established self-reflective consciousness is called *mindfulness* in Buddhism, and forms the indispensable starting point for a progressive series of mental states, the Factors of Enlightenment.

Like mindfulness, energy, the third Factor of Enlightenment, can be regarded as a spiritual faculty as well as a level of consciousness, and so can samadhi, the sixth factor. Samadhi, the faculty of concentrated meditation, only 'shines inward' when the outer senses are stilled. It 'senses' meditative experience, the levels of absorption or pure form. And like a normal sense organ such as the eye, samadhi can be first opened, and then trained and improved in acuity.[221]

The seemingly endless heavens perceived by a visionary faculty detached from fleshly troubles might appear a satisfactory goal for a religious life. But Buddhism says they are not. One needs another faculty, one that can transcend the ups and downs of levels of consciousness, replacing a dependence upon external conditions and internal ideas with a direct vision of things as they really are. Wisdom is this faculty.[222] Samadhi opened up a new level of consciousness, the absorptions. The faculty of wisdom can be regarded as revealing a higher level still – the transcendental or uncompounded level.

The absorptions are the foundations for wisdom. We saw in the last chapter how a training in wisdom is based in the trainings of ethics and meditation. However, Buddhist tradition does not depict wisdom as a more refined version of absorption. It is not a state of consciousness stacked on top of other levels of consciousness. Really, it is a quite different dimension of experience, accessed by cultivating all the non-

Level of consciousness	Characteristics	Animals possessing it
10. Enlightenment	All aspects of the personality transformed in the light of transcendental wisdom, all actions springing from compassion.	Some humans
9. Non-dual insight	Some experience of insight, incorporating transcendental wisdom and compassion. Third training: wisdom.	Some humans
8. Absorption, level of pure form	Highly concentrated, integrated, unified and blissful consciousness. Not sense-based. Absorption in object of awareness, so subject–object split attenuated. Negative emotions in temporary abeyance. Increasing calmness and balance. Enlightenment-factors (4)–(7). Second training: meditation.	Some humans
7. Full self-reflection or mindfulness	Fully rational thinking, awareness of unity of life and possibility of directed transformation, independent individuality, highly creative awareness. Unselfishness. Mindfulness. First training: ethics.	Some humans (first in the axial age)
6. Beginnings of self-reflection	Speech, verbal concepts, abstraction, deliberate altruism, deceit, conscious emotions, alienation from experience, systematic invention and planning. Deliberate transmission of culture – strongly group-based. Conformism.	Humans only
5. Centred experience	Simple consciousness. Dream experience. Associative 'thinking' with non-verbal concepts. Planning, problem-solving, complex communication. Flexible cultural traditions.	The most intelligent mammals
4. Representation	Images combined in ideas and mental representations; memory, anticipation, likes and dislikes. Communication and imitation learning, exploratory and innovative behaviour. Beginnings of cultural transmission.	Birds and mammals
3. Perception and association	Recognition of complex stimuli by comparison with innate 'images', goal-directed behaviour, association-learning, training.	Animals with central nervous systems
2. Recognition	Recognition of simple classes of sensations, fully stereotyped responses. Sensitization and habituation'learning'.	Animals with nerve-nets
1. No consciousness		Non-living matter, living things without nervous systems.

Table 5: Levels in the evolution of consciousness[223]

transcendental levels of consciousness, all of which remain 'visible' with the new faculty of wisdom. Nevertheless, a depiction of the evolution of consciousness has to place the transcendental, non-dual level of wisdom somewhere. So let us complete our table of levels of consciousness by placing wisdom and enlightenment (wisdom's consummation) at the top.

LONGING FOR THE REAL

The faculty of wisdom, created through 'man in his wholeness wholly attending', requires an integration of all the other human faculties on a higher level. It penetrates the obscuring veils which generations of dark emotions and faulty 'vision' have woven. So the physical senses subserve the purposes of wisdom, as do mindfulness and samadhi.

Another 'sense', too, is called for to complete the set of precursors of wisdom. It is the sense that there is more to life than the material world of the physical senses, more even than the inner worlds revealed by mindfulness and absorption. This intuitive faculty that consistently yields the intimation that 'this is not it, there is yet more to discover', is known in Buddhism as *shraddha*. The scholar Herbert Guenther renders *shraddha* as 'confidence trust',[224] a translation which avoids the anti-reason connotations of 'faith', but misses the heartfelt emotional yearning quality of this faculty. Traditionally, 'it is a deep conviction, lucidity, and longing for those things which are real, have value, and are possible.'[225] Anyone may experience this bright longing; in Buddhism, it is particularly directed to the Three Jewels (the fundamental ideals), especially the Buddha jewel, and so combines a growing attraction for the ideal of human enlightenment with an intuitive conviction that the transcendental faculty of wisdom can indeed be developed.

Real *shraddha* evokes a practical response: one is inspired by the possibility of higher evolution, so at some stage one is likely to commit oneself to a chosen path. In Buddhism, this act of commitment ('going for refuge') is the nearest thing to conversion in other religions, and it is what marks someone as a Buddhist.

Unlike the sometimes credulous faith of conventional religion, *shraddha* is strengthened by rational consideration as well as by inspiration from contemplating the beauty of the ideal. If one reflects on the human potential for enlightenment, considers the inadequacies of ordinary existence, observes the sufferings of others, and contemplates the qualities of enlightened men and women, then, some schools teach, *shraddha* will grow into an altruistic 'will to enlightenment' which is the dominant directing influence of one's life.[226] We shall return to this will to enlightenment later in the chapter.

WISDOM

One reaches the non-dual level of consciousness by reconciling and transcending the emotional and intellectual sides of one's nature. Thus the faculty of wisdom is marked by a desire for enlightenment (for the sake of all) dominating one's heart, and by a clear insight into things as they really are dominating one's perceptions.

The kind of reflections which lead to non-dual insight are more than just rational considerations. However, one probably needs to encounter some kind of conceptual account of what reality is like, to stimulate the mind in an appropriate direction, until one's own faculty of wisdom can apprehend reality directly. Reality cannot be conveyed in words, so how does an enlightened person describe the indescribable? Warnings against a literal-minded attachment to words echo throughout the Buddhist texts, such as this one ascribed to the Sanskrit poet Ashvaghosha (first or second century CE):

> All things in the world from the beginning are neither matter nor mind, nor intelligence nor consciousness, nor non-being nor being; they are after all inexplicable.... [The Buddha] only provisionally makes use of words and definitions to lead all beings, while his real object is to make them abandon symbolism and directly enter into the real reality.[227]

All the assumptions of the ordinary level of consciousness are deeply embedded in the words and concepts we use. After all, language and self-reflective consciousness evolved together in interdependence, as we saw in chapters 3 and 5. In particular, virtually every sentence we utter reassures us, through the subject and object intrinsic to its structure, that we should continue to see the world in terms of 'I' and 'not-I'. Words are generally the hirelings of the ego. So how can one use language to describe the insights of a quite different level of consciousness? It is a level in which the distinctions that sentences rely on, particularly the distinctions between thing and process and between subject and object, are no longer valid.

Broadly, Buddhist texts have adopted two approaches to describing the transcendental level. One is to use myth and imagination, by painting in words (and indeed in visual art) fantastic pictures of magical events in brilliant colours on canvases of cosmic dimensions. This approach is intended to stimulate the sense of wonder and delight, pointing beyond people's ordinary way of thinking by transporting their imaginations to mythical realms. There, every aspect of enlightenment is embodied in a regal personality made of light, and every step on the path is an adventure in a grand archetypal quest.[228]

The second approach makes use of concepts, but offers a fluid and provisional account of experience. The Buddhist texts frequently point to the impermanence of phenomena, ever coming into being and passing away as parts of conditioned processes. Being impermanent, no element of ordinary life can offer ultimate satisfaction, and no ultimate, abiding essence can be found in any phenomenon, either in the material world or in the human personality.

On the path to wisdom taught in Buddhism, such ideas are first to be fully understood, and then reflected upon in the light of one's own experience; the faculty of self-reflective consciousness is applied to the limits of understanding. It is then that meditation, the faculty of samadhi, comes in, as the medieval Tibetan teacher Milarepa explains:

> This non-thought, this radiant and transparent experience,
> Is but the feeling of dhyana [absorption].
> With this good foundation
> One should pray further to the Three [Jewels],
> And penetrate to Reality by deep thinking and contemplation.
> He thus can tie the non-ego Wisdom
> With the beneficial life-rope of deep dhyana.
> With the power of kindness and compassion,
> And with the altruistic vow of the Bodhi-Heart,
> He can see direct and clear
> The truth of the Enlightened Path,
> On which nothing can be seen, yet all is clearly visioned.[229]

Thus one starts by travelling up the spiral of the Factors of Enlightenment as far as one can, achieving as much mental absorption and balance as possible. This process of psychic integration and energizing is followed by highly concentrated reflection on one's experience of oneself and the world. One becomes increasingly familiar with all the levels accessible to consciousness, and works appropriately in each level. One ranges up and down the seven Factors of Enlightenment, repeatedly coming back to the 'investigation of mental states' level, working intensively on awareness of experience, until direct insight dawns.

The Experience of Insight

If one is familiar with absorption, then one has access to a whole sequence of states of consciousness, ranged above the self-reflective level like the storeys of a building. A highly directed and unclouded mind, reflecting on the conceptual pointers to reality provided by the teachings of Buddhism, has a chance of breaking out of the sequence of levels of consciousness that it inhabits into an additional dimension of experience: insight. Thus, in dependence upon the combination of absorption and reflection, non-dual insight eventually arises. The eye of wisdom opens. It may happen in imperceptible degrees, or in a great upheaval of consciousness, as in the case of one of the most revered of the Japanese Zen Masters, Hakuin (1683–1768). He was contemplating one of the non-rational, existential problems known as koans:

> I assiduously applied myself to it. I did not sleep days and nights, forgot both eating and lying down, when quite abruptly a great mental fixation (*tai-i* – the great doubt) took place. I felt as if freezing in an ice-field extending thousands of miles, and within myself there was a sense of utmost transparency. There was no going forward, no slipping backward; I was like an idiot, like an imbecile, and there was nothing but [the koan]. Though I attended the lectures by the master, they sounded like a discussion going on somewhere in a distant hall, many yards away. Sometimes my sensation was that of one flying in the air. Several days passed in this state, when one evening a temple-bell struck, which upset the whole thing. It was like smashing an ice-basin, or pulling down a house made of jade. When I suddenly awoke again I found that I myself was Ganto (Yen-t'ou) the old master, and that all through the shifting changes of time not a bit (of my personality) was lost. Whatever doubts and indecisions I had before were completely dissolved like a piece of thawing ice. I called out loudly: 'How wondrous! how wondrous! There is no birth and death from which one has to escape, nor is there any supreme knowledge (*bodhi*) after which one has to strive....'[230]

THE POINT OF NO RETURN

Hakuin's breakthrough came when the bell sounded: his perception became clear, his experience fluid and free, and his sense of a goal external to himself dissolved. The biographies of other Buddhist spiritual heroes and heroines typically contain a pivotal episode of this sort, in which a profound realization of non-duality, in one of its many manifestations, flashes forth in consciousness. There is usually still a long way to go until full enlightenment, but from this point on the rest of the path is clear. The insight experience is so vivid that it provides a touchstone for later mental states. In its afterglow, one can recognize whether a state of mind is a continuation of non-duality, or whether it is a remnant of the old distorted attitudes, to be worked on and transformed.

On the level of insight, the mind is for the first time more attuned to non-dual awareness than it is to those unskilful habitual urges that humanity acquired along with self-reflective consciousness. People with insight, writes Conze, 'are those whose conduct is largely determined by the urge for the Unconditioned.'[231] As a result, the Buddhist tradition says that for one with insight there is no falling back. He or she is beyond the point of no return. Further progress on the spiral path still requires effort, but effort now comes quite naturally – what else could one possibly wish to do but evolve further? And in the texts, the Buddha is frequently represented as encouraging his disciples by assuring them that if they only apply themselves earnestly to the practices he has recommended, then non-dual insight is a very realistic goal, attainable before too long.[232]

Beyond insight is enlightenment itself, the utter freedom which follows from the quenching of the 'fires' of craving, aversion, and delusion. After her enlightenment (*nibbana* in Pali, which literally means extinction), Patachara, a disciple of the Buddha, described her struggle for self-cultivation and its denouement in this poem:

With ploughshares ploughing up the fields, with seed
Sown in the breast of the earth, men win their crops,
Enjoy their gains and nourish wife and child.
Why cannot I, whose life is pure, who seek
To do the [Buddha's] will, no sluggard am,
Not puffed up, win to nibbana's bliss?
One day, bathing my feet, I sit and watch
The water as it trickles down the slope.

Thereby I set my heart in steadfastness,
As one does train a horse of noble breed.
Then going to my cell, I take my lamp,
And seated on my couch I watch the flame.
Grasping the pin, I pull the wick right down
Into the oil....
Lo! The nibbana of the little lamp!
Emancipation dawns! My heart is free![233]

The detailed stages of the continuing path beyond the point of no return are rather too remote to concern us here. It is sufficient to say that it represents a permeation of every nook and cranny of one's being by the light of non-dual insight, until one's nature is wholly transcendental, at which point one is enlightened. It is still a spiral path of successively higher states of consciousness, advancing through the self-augmenting kind of conditionality described in chapter 8, but now the progress is of an irreversible kind. As a spiral path, it can be seen as a repetition of the stages already traversed, now imbued with a new kind of non-dual consciousness.[234]

And how long will it all take? In some texts, it is said that millions of lifetimes are required for the process of conscious human development. In others, particularly of the Zen and Vajrayana forms of Mahayana Buddhism, it is said that there is only one time to gain enlightenment – here and now!

SELF-TRANSCENDENCE

We saw in chapter 1 that perpetual self-transcendence is the key to the whole evolutionary process. Insight is described as non-dual, so, more than any previous development in evolution, it transcends the limitations of the existing self. If only intermittently, the person who has reached the point of no return does not treat his or her experience in terms of a hard duality between subject and object, self and other. Dualistic self-reflection is being abandoned.

First the centred experience and later self-reflective consciousness were great evolutionary advances. The floating fragments of mind had coalesced to form human individuals. The new individualized minds then discovered kinds of interpersonal harmony that far transcended the herd unity of their ancestors. Moreover, they found that they could gently pilot the flotillas of their mental impulses, and evolve further, to more fully integrated states of consciousness, and at last to non-dual insight.

Insight of this sort is very hard to reach, because of the bewilderment which threatens as the viewpoint undermined by insight is abandoned. This 'safe' viewpoint is the almost universal habitual obsession with self, self as a centre of experience, seen only in a highly restricted way, and difficult to leave behind.

A developing concern for others is an important route to overcoming self-centredness, as we shall see, but it is also important to tackle the deep-rooted mental attitudes which maintain the narrow view of self. In Buddhism, they are known as the Three Fetters: (1) self-view, (2) doubt, and (3) dependence on moral rules and religious observances (as ends in themselves).[235]

(1) First is self-view. One tends to regard oneself as a particular kind of person, playing a particular role in life. 'That's the way I am, I've got a bad temper, there's nothing I can do about it.' This, claims Buddhism, is just a habitual self-view preventing progress towards the freedom of the transcendental level, and, like all habits, it can be broken. Being prepared to continually create a new self, refusing to be limited by the past, is the way to burst the fetter of self-view. It is said to require a strong commitment to self-transformation, ensuring that one's friends and life-style do not constantly reinforce one's old habits and views of oneself.

(2) Doubt is the second fetter. It does not refer to reserving judgement on something through a rationally-based independence of thought, but to wavering because of a lack of single-mindedness, confidence, and decisiveness. This kind of doubt is a half-deliberate vagueness that holds one back from effective action. It generally comes from a fear of the difficulty of making real progress on the spiral path – fear of having to let go of the old habitual self. Doubt is overcome by thinking things out clearly, so that one can see real choices and make decisions in the light of definite priorities. Until insight, one cannot clearly see the next step on the path of higher evolution, and one is bound to be a little uncertain. When the path is clear, illuminated by one's own experience, one gains a firm confidence.

(3) Third is the fetter of dependence on ethical rules and religious observances (as ends in themselves). Ethical behaviour is of great importance to any Buddhist, being the foundation of the spiral path (see last chapter); religious practices too are strongly recommended, a great variety of them. But once one knows all the standard, accepted

conventions, it is very easy just to keep up appearances, go through the motions, while permitting nothing to have any deep impact on one. Ethics and practices are not ends in themselves for Buddhism, but means helping one towards enlightenment. If they become just superficial gestures made to keep up appearances, they have become fetters, routines that tie one to the spot, rather than aids to transformation.

Habitual self-view, doubt, and dependence on rules and observances are all quite tangible forces pulling one back as one tries to move along the spiral path of higher evolution. They reinforce habits appropriate to lower, more familiar levels of consciousness, and one becomes passive, relinquishing responsibility for one's life and one's influence on the world. One can easily slip back, and lose any gains. The old habits are so deeply ingrained – because of their long evolutionary and psychological history – that they feel like a real gravitational force exerted by more constricted and fixed states of mind.

However, the Factors of Enlightenment represent positive countervailing 'habits' promoting self-transcendence. Eventually mindfulness and the other factors become so strong, and one's contact with a non-dual ideal so much a part of one, that the transcendent habits do not slip away, even in difficult circumstances. One's attitudes and perceptions are now mediated by the faculty of wisdom, and it is as if one were being swept along in the stream of one's creative effort. Effort continues, but becomes continuous and spontaneous, because 'evolving' is what one wants to do, unceasingly and above all else.

THE BODHISATTVA

A person with the faculty of wisdom is regarded by Buddhists as the ideal human being, someone to revere, learn from, and emulate. As I explained in chapter 8, the three chief ideals of Buddhism, the Three Jewels, include the Sangha, the spiritual community of those committed to following the path of higher evolution. As an object of reverence, the Sangha is specifically these exemplary people who have reached the transcendental level. In early texts, they are referred to as the Noble Sangha, and in some later texts as the Company of Bodhisattvas.

'Bodhisattva' means 'bodhi-being', that is, one striving for enlightenment, or one whose nature is enlightenment.[236] At first, the word was used to refer to the Buddha-to-be while he was still treading the path to enlightenment. It was soon extended, possibly by the Buddha himself, to the heroes of the birth stories, which purport to recount the

Buddha's previous lives as a bodhisattva (see Appendix). They always describe him performing acts of kindness, self-sacrifice, or heroism, perfecting his qualities in preparation for his final birth. Buddhists of all persuasions have always gained great pleasure and inspiration from the birth stories, especially those Buddhists without a relish or talent or the leisure for pursuing the intricacies of Buddhist philosophy and psychology. The stories clearly embody moral teachings, and one is intended to learn lessons of selflessness from them.

Some of the early Buddhists, quite possibly preserving a tradition from the Buddha himself, drew a reasonable conclusion. They insisted that the bodhisattva is the ideal Buddhist, the pattern for all committed Buddhists to follow. The most noble goal was surely not some private state of quietude, but the attainment of enlightenment as a Buddha, arising from a balance of both compassion and wisdom, the preparatory path of a bodhisattva having been undertaken for as long as necessary. This bodhisattva ideal became the most important basis for the birth of the Mahayana or Great Way movement in Buddhism. It was proper to call someone a bodhisattva once he or she had generated an overwhelming aspiration for enlightenment for the sake of all; that is, once the will to enlightenment had arisen.[237]

The nature of the bodhisattva ideal in Mahayana Buddhism helped to ensure that the compassion side of the goal was not neglected in favour of a self-centred and escapist sort of wisdom, which, from its one-sidedness, could not be non-dual wisdom at all.[238] As a safeguard against such spiritual individualism, the Mahayana writers always describe the bodhisattva as working tirelessly for enlightenment for the benefit of all sentient beings, and the will to enlightenment is defined accordingly. Here is a dialogue said to have taken place between the Buddha and one of his disciples, a king:

'In whom is there the [will to] Enlightenment, Master?'
'In him, O king, who has the intact resolve to gain it.'
'And who has such a resolve?'
'He in whom is the spring of great mercy [or compassion].'
'In whom is this?'
'He who never neglects all sentient beings.'[239]

The will to enlightenment is praised in many Mahayana texts as an infinitely precious faculty, a vision of the ideal of enlightenment for the sake of all. Always accessible to inspire and guide one, 'it is the star to every wandering bark.' It is said to be wholly of the transcendental level.[240]

THE BODHISATTVA PRINCIPLE

The bodhisattva is the ideal Buddhist, representing an uncompromising determination to transform his or her own life and to transform the world in the direction of universal freedom and happiness. To the extent that the bodhisattva's consciousness courses on the non-dual level, no distinction is made between self and other, and every action is fitted for the highest benefit of everybody. The 'wound' that keeps self and other apart has been seen by the bodhisattva's wisdom for what it is: an unnecessary result of ignorance. The wound has been healed in the warm balm of developing compassion, by the bodhisattva taking every opportunity to identify with others. Now whole and spiritually healthy, the bodhisattva is not tempted to relax into the spurious balance of a personal peace. Since others' welfare is no less a matter of vital concern than his or her own, the distinction does not arise. So the bodhisattvas are always active, trying to heal the wound in the world, motivated by compassion and illuminated by wisdom.

Such people, living and working in today's world, do not advertise themselves, but use whatever talents they have for the benefit of others, and are always prepared to learn and change. The message of the bodhisattva ideal is not 'find these heroes and adore them', but 'become one yourself'.

It is one's own deliberate effort to transform oneself on the path of higher evolution that ensures that the will to enlightenment will continue to arise in the world: nothing else can do it. According to Buddhism, every action, even every thought, counts. It is either creative and ultimately conducive to the welfare of all, or else it is wasted, and thus retrogressive. During every creative, generous, and fearless act and thought, including the smallest, one is momentarily a bodhisattva – the will to enlightenment has half awakened within one. I find this a message of great optimism: we each have the power to transform the world radically, if only we can start here and now to act from our noblest impulses.

Every phase of evolution has its active 'bodhisattvas'. On our own level, that of self-reflective consciousness, we can act creatively, and begin a wave of self-transcendence that rolls on towards the meditative and transcendental levels. Even lower evolution displays its heroic deeds of self-transcendence. Every animal that pioneered a new environmental niche ensured for itself and its descendants a place in a main stream of the evolution of consciousness. It transcended the legacy of static 'self' which had been passed on in its genes and behavioural traditions, and so in a rudimentary sense it manifested that same bodhisattva principle. In some of the (non-canonical) stories of his former lives as a bodhisattva, the Buddha-to-be is actually portrayed as an animal, who gives a lead to his fellows.

Every phase of evolution has its growing tip, and, symbolically at least, every group or class of beings can likewise be seen as having a particularly enterprising member, who takes the lead and opens up a way to new and more fulfilling areas of experience. Lower evolution and spiritual development are sections of the same upward movement in life and consciousness, and if the bodhisattva is the pioneer of spiritual development (higher evolution), the bodhisattva spirit can be regarded as the pioneering principle in all evolution.

In the axial age, the bodhisattva principle was embodied in the sages who demonstrated advances in consciousness and proclaimed the unity of life or the common potential for self-transcendence of every human being. Today, the bodhisattva principle manifests in the heart of each person, every time one takes a step which overpasses the limits of one's current state. 'What saves a man is to take a step,' writes the French author, Antoine de St Exupéry, 'then another step. It is always the same step, but you have to take it.'[241]

The Buddhist vision of existence sees the inadequacies of life, sees that they can be transformed, and sees the bodhisattva principle operating to transform them at all levels and in all that lives. The image of the bodhisattva clarifies the whole process of the evolution of consciousness by bringing it into an all-embracing, even cosmic, context. It portrays an urge to enlightenment in all spheres of life, urging individual human beings to help create a dynamic world characterized by compassion, beauty, and openness.[242]

CONCLUSION

The teaching is only of whither and how to go, the vision itself
is the work of him who has willed to see.
Plotinus, *Ennead* VI, 9. 4, Robert Bridges' translation

DECIDING TO EVOLVE

Through the pages of this book, we have been following the thread of consciousness, from its beginnings, through its human level of self-awareness, and into its expansion in higher evolution. As human beings, *here we are now*, on the threshold of the higher evolution. That phrase, 'here we are now', is incomprehensible to every animal except one, the human being. The processes of lower evolution that produced us moved steadily through a growing awareness of each animal's 'here', as animals evolved and encountered increasingly useful ways of finding out about their worlds. Awareness of 'we' is much more recent. It has been a great struggle for people to tame the startling lightning of self-awareness into a tended hearth, giving continuous light. Each person has to repeat the clumsy course of self-discovery, even with the benefit of the examples of pioneers of consciousness such as the sages of the axial age. Now we are being challenged: can we pull the 'here' and the 'we' together into a comprehensive grasp of our changing situation?

Rising to the challenge means deciding to evolve. Here we are now, but what comes next? There are ways of life suited to one's present level of consciousness, a level of intermittent self-awareness. Maybe there is sufficient fulfilment for one in these ways of life: raising a healthy family, progressing in a career which provides financial security, casting a considered vote at the election, and absorbing the current forms of entertainment. At times, there is comfort in these things, and satisfaction.

Alternatively, it may be that a whisper from one's possible future tells of unrealized worlds beyond the horizon, potentials open to the courageous. I think there is a sort of imperative in knowing about the possibility of higher evolution. The mountaineer must climb Everest 'because it's there'. The individual who suspects that the heights of wisdom and compassion are surmountable feels a similar pull. Self-respect keeps reminding one that there is yet more to do with this precious life.

So one takes stock. One considers one's circumstances, one's shortcomings, one's aptitudes and preferences. And one takes a step. Maybe one starts to disengage from constraints imposed by obsolete ambitions. Or one takes up compassionate voluntary work. Or one learns meditation, or resumes one's education. Whatever it is, one is beginning an effort to transform oneself to the core, no preconceived limits being placed on the transformation. Later, unless the urge to evolve is allowed to wither, one takes further steps. All the steps are creative movements, and no one can preordain precisely what they will be. Yet one can be confident that they will yield improvements in awareness and extensions of fellow-feeling.

In this secularized, industrialized society one may feel remote from one's roots in nature and isolated from other people. Values which have matured in more tradition-bound periods seem anachronistic; a self-seeking individualism appears best suited to the times. Are these ideal circumstances for higher evolution?

Of course, one has little choice. This is the world, this is one's personality, and this is where the path ahead has to start. Certainly, one faces greater isolation than in past ages. Cheerful companionship is rare; it is difficult to find straightforward enjoyments in simple things and one's reasonable mistrust of the supposedly wise may cut one off from the advice of guides on the path. However, nowadays there is not so much ignorant dogmatism to overcome as there once was, and the clear unsatisfactoriness (and worse) of much that modern unevolving life offers is a great spur to exploring higher evolution. And there are living spiritual communities (sanghas) which provide the elements of co-operation and friendship that is so important, at least on the Buddhist quest.

I believe that treading one's pathway of higher evolution is greatly aided if one can see the whole course of the evolving mind. I hope that this book has been of some help in introducing the levels that consciousness can traverse as it evolves. To conclude, I would like to climb through the levels once again. Hosts of wonderful beings populate our world, some lower in the scale of consciousness, some higher. What are they like?

Before I run through the phases of evolution, I feel it is worth re-emphasizing the hierarchy of evolution. It is very useful to recognize that it exists. Some living beings are more advanced than oneself, some less so, and it can be valuable to bear this truism in mind.

To be part of the evolutionary world is like being at a swimming pool, to make a fanciful comparison. Some cannot swim, some are just learning, some can dive off the side and swim fairly well, and some graduate to the springboard or even brave the high diving boards. There is a real gradation of expertise, but it is not fixed, and it need not lead to despondency on the part of novices, nor to disdain from the experts. Whatever level one has reached, one can progress further, doubtless overtaking some who are quite satisfied with a few lengths of breaststroke. One can learn from the best, and help the newcomers. So the pool can be a supportive community of learners, all prepared to increase their skills. Similarly, evolving humanity is a community. The differing levels of skill and experience simply demonstrate that progress is possible.

EVOLVING BEINGS

Consciousness appears in minute sparks in the hidden inner dimension of the simplest living things. If there is anything going on between a creature's experience of the world and its responses, that is mind, that is consciousness. And mind has evolved. The levels that consciousness evolves through were set out in a table in chapter 10: recognition, perception and association, representation, centred experience, the beginnings of self-reflection, mindfulness, absorption, non-dual insight, and enlightenment.

At first, the animal mind was capable of no more than a dim distinction between nice and nasty. Try to enter a primitive consciousness. You are a sea anemone living in a rock-pool. Your senses are stimulated in a certain pattern. Does the pattern signify (in the ancestral memory of the genes) food? Nice – grab it. It signifies attack or poison? Nasty – shrink back and reject it.

Evolution proceeds. Soon, the nerves knot together so that patterns of sensation can be played with in an opening mental space. You are, perhaps, a bee, and shifting shapes cross your honeycomb eyes. Wait – that shape is like the inborn image that means 'flower' – snap! And an impressive sequence of actions is set in train: fly nearer, land, sip the nectar. You have found that only yellow flowers ever have nectar? Then your mental image of flowers is modified; yellow and food are associated together. Something has been learned about your little patch of world. Awareness has expanded.

Look higher in the scale. Mind-space contains galleries of images, shifting, linking and unlinking in networks of associations. All that matters to you about the world is there in your mind like a map – a mental representation. Perhaps you are a squirrel: this tree is where your nest is; that one is in your rival's territory – be cautious. That clump has some sweet-barked saplings. Here, and here, you buried acorns last autumn. Now you gingerly explore the tree that fell in the gale last night. Over there is the farmer's garden, the place your mother taught you to fear. In fact, you can recognize a human a quarter of a mile off, even though they all look quite different – an idea of that menace 'man' has condensed in your mind from a hundred sightings. There is even a very dim sense of the world as surrounding you, as if a woodland clearing of awareness magically opened up around you as you leaped through the trees. But you don't take any notice of that!

Evolution ascends. Perception is brighter and more detailed, the world displays its riches. For some animals, there is a complex social world too, with rule-bound games, sometimes comic, sometimes tragic. Dreams and ponderings dance across the expanding mental arena, clothed in longings, terrors, enmities. Who are you now? Go back to a time before humanity: you are a bit man-like, part of a group walking cautiously through the waving equatorial grass to a clump of trees. Thought of the fruit there elicits an excited murmur, which the rest take up. Someone sees a hyena and gives the hyena-yelp of alarm.

You understand well and quicken your pace, drawing a youngster to you, holding his hand, making soothing noises. Language is on its way.

BEING FULLY HUMAN

Animals always lacked a crucial trick that would have freed them from the tyranny of hidebound tradition. Then a clever kind of animal, with sensitive hands freed by upright walking, found the secret. Pre-humans became humans by turning consciousness back on itself, so that mental processes themselves could be brought into awareness. With awareness, mental processes can be transformed.

The range of one's own levels of awareness extends over everything from the dream-world of pre-humans to full self-reflection. Can you remember when self-awareness first lit up when you were a child? Richard Hughes has a wonderful description in his novel of childhood, *A High Wind in Jamaica*. Ten-year-old Emily is playing happily, when for no apparent reason, 'she suddenly realized who she was':

[She] was thinking vaguely about some bees and a fairy queen, when it suddenly flashed into her mind that she was she. She stopped dead, and began looking over all of her person which came in range of her eyes.... She began to laugh, rather mockingly. 'Well!' she thought in effect: 'Fancy *you*, of all people, going and getting caught like this! – You can't get out of it now, not for a very long time: you'll have to go through with being a child, and growing up, and getting old, before you'll be quit of this mad prank!' ... The contact of her face and the warm bare hollow of her shoulder gave her a comfortable thrill, as if it was the caress of some kind friend. But whether the feeling came to her through her cheek or through her shoulder, which was the caresser and which the caressed, that no analysis could tell her.... What agency had so ordered it that out of all the people in the world who she might have been, she was this particular one, this Emily: born in such-and-such a year out of all the years in Time, and encased in this particular rather pleasing little casket of flesh?... It must not be supposed that she argued it all out in this ordered, but rather long-winded fashion. Each consideration came to her in a momentary flash, quite innocent of words: and in between her mind lazed along, either thinking of nothing or returning to her bees and the fairy queen. If one added up the total of her periods of conscious thought, it would probably reach something between four and five seconds ... spread out over the best part of an hour.[243]

Hughes captures very well the wonder of self-reflective consciousness. Emily's realization is followed by apprehensiveness: will some disaster result? Is she perhaps God? Will someone find out that she is *she*?

Self-reflection is accompanied by anxieties, frustration, and the growth of a protective ego. On the other hand, it has yielded noble discoveries: that humanity, even life, is intimately interconnected, and that individuals can accept responsibility for the future course of the world and themselves. Thus everything that makes us human is a consequence of this type of consciousness; religion and science, art and wisdom, as well as love, self-sacrifice, cruelty, alienation, and fear.

One can become *fully* human by strengthening self-awareness. The rare fully human person, a true individual, begins to see things and his or her self objectively, with a free and loving emotional attitude and with an uninhibited vitality in every action. He or she is independent-minded, and encourages others to free themselves from mass conditionings. Above all, perhaps, there is a sense of what I have called higher evolution in the fully human person, an excitement with unfolding all that is now only potential, an urge for self-transcendence.

EXPERIENCING THE ABSORPTIONS AND INSIGHT

The Buddhist route to self-transcendence that I have outlined in this book uses specific practices to cultivate higher levels of consciousness. Strengthening and focusing awareness in various ways prepares one for meditation, and for the absorptions. These levels also require an ethical shift, so that skilful mental states (rooted in contentment, well-wishing, and clarity) displace unskilful ones (rooted in craving, aversion, and ignorance). In chapter 9, I mentioned four levels of absorption; even without meditation experience, it is possible to get an inkling of what they are like.

In the first, one is 'rapt', thoroughly integrated into the chosen object of one's awareness, so that the attention is steady and bright, and rapturous feelings move in the body. Think of listening to uplifting music, or gazing with new love into a lover's eyes, or admiring the sweep of an ocean sky, or even rhythmically turning over the garden soil with a spade.

The second absorption is stiller, with no mental commentary, so that the mind's depths become transparent to the surface of consciousness. It is reminiscent of the lucid dream, which marries the waking self with the unconscious mind. A steady welling up of inspiration makes this absorption a well-spring of creativity, and the artist's muse dwells there. The third is profoundly tranquil; vast spaces open out in which the mystic contemplates mind, filled with a limpid happiness far deeper than bliss, since it cannot be contrasted with any pain. The fourth absorption is so firm and balanced that it is said to reorganize the mind and fill it with a kind of power. Saints and gurus with teeming followings sometimes seem to derive their charisma from this layer of meditative consciousness. Explorations of the fourth absorption can, we are told, yield an impression of infinite Mind, of oneness with a loving godhead, or even of apparent loss of the self in an unbounded cosmos.

According to Buddhism, such experiences can be snares for the unwary, side tracks for an inflationary ego. Yes, strengthen consciousness in the absorptions, but keep coming back down to earth. Reflect on all dimensions of human experience, investigating the whole length of the thread of evolving mind. With persistence, a breakthrough is possible, into a quite new way of appreciating experience: non-dual insight. Climb to the top of the flagpole, said a Zen master, and then take another step.[244]

Now insight is inexpressible, and it is not something I have achieved in any great measure, a double handicap in trying to convey what insight is like. Chapter 10 provided some traditional teachings, as well as Hakuin's account of his realization, triggered by the ringing of the temple bell. Insight is explained as an entry to the final path. For so long, one has wandered on the Wheel of Life, turning, turning. 'Dark path upon dark path treading, when shall we escape from birth and death?' wrote Hakuin in his 'Song of Meditation'.[245]

Yet now one has opened up a bright, preliminary path, developing mindfulness, an ethical life, meditation, and a longing for the real. At last one's eyes open and one visions the transcendental path, the final one.

> A person has entered the path that pleases the Buddhas
> When for all objects, in the cycle or beyond,
> He sees that cause and effect can never fail,
> And when for him they lose all solid appearance.[246]

For the revered Tibetan master Tsongkhapa (1357–1419), whose words I have just quoted, these two new perspectives sum up insight: seeing completely the processes of conditioned co-production (here translated as 'cause and effect') that interconnect all phenomena, and letting go of all labels for whatever is perceived, 'beyond taking any position', as Tsongkhapa says in the next stanza.

The bodhisattva

Insight is described as non-dual. It parts the curtains that divide self from all that one regards as other. So how could a path guided by insight remain a personal quest? Any feeling that 'this is me, developing myself, transforming my separate personality' must soon fade in the light of non-duality. Someone with insight, then, will wish to participate in a grand evolutionary stream, in which all beings are potentially aligned with enlightenment. Many, however, are overwhelmed by suffering and a fog of self-limiting attitudes; they need help. Sooner or later one will absorb the reality of others' needs, and wish to evolve for everyone's benefit, not just for one's own.

Altruism is a sort of inescapable metaphysical outcome of non-duality. But long before the opening of non-duality, the human heart can respond; altruism becomes a motivating force, and in Buddhist terms one is inspired by the bodhisattva ideal. The bodhisattva is an evolver *par excellence*. Single-mindedly, unwaveringly, he or she is set on enlightenment for the benefit of all. Compassion and insight are united in the bodhisattva: his or her actions are not merely kind, but far-seeing, clear, balanced, in short, wise. When one encounters wise kindness (or kind wisdom), that is the bodhisattva spirit operating, even if the kind person is not a true bodhisattva in the complete sense. A true bodhisattva is simply someone who is chiefly motivated by the altruistic urge for higher evolution; that urge is now permanently stronger than the ego-defending urges that rotate the Wheel of Life.

I would have liked to give you a brief biography of one of the remarkable men and women whom posterity has accepted as bodhisattvas because their lives were so consistently filled with the bodhisattva spirit. However, their lives are complex and full, and brief extracts cannot do them justice. Reading the biographies of Xu Yun in China, Shinran in Japan, Yeshe Tsogyal in Tibet, Dharmapala in India, and so on, I am struck by how rich and individual those bodhisattva lives are.[247] The more creative a person is, and the more the ego sense is lost, the less predictable they are, so their approaches to their own and others' problems are often astonishingly fresh and unexpected.

What of today? Are full bodhisattvas rare in these short-sighted times, or is it that they help people under cover, secret agents for enlightenment? (I am thinking of explicitly Buddhist bodhisattvas, but of course the same spirit can manifest in people from all backgrounds.) I do not know the answer.

THE GOLDEN THREAD

Perhaps it is most helpful to see the bodhisattva life as a way of being, a choice that anybody can make by selecting the kinder and wiser option in every situation. In this way, one inches forward along the thread of evolving consciousness. It is a golden thread like the one Ariadne gave to Theseus so that he could find his way out of the Cretan labyrinth. William Blake, in 'Jerusalem', says:

> I give you the end of a golden string,
> Only wind it into a ball:
> It will lead you in at Heaven's gate,
> Built in Jerusalem's wall.

One who knows something of the way out, like William Blake, may place the thread in one's hands. But that is not really necessary. It is already there; it is one's own evolving mind.

We are accustomed to using the evolutionary vision to look backwards. The backward gaze revealed our inviolable connections with each other and with the whole natural world, connections of kinship and ancestrally shared struggles to evolve. We are less accustomed to projecting the evolutionary view forwards.

The future is unknown and, it appears, unknowable. It is hidden because it is subject to personal choices, and so it is a future to be created rather than foreseen. Yet self-reflection discovers a unity of human experience which surely implies some correspondence of human potential. We cannot discover precisely who we may become or how this world may be reconstructed, but we can envisage the types of consciousness that we have not yet dwelt in, by getting to know the testimony of others who have dwelt there.

They have had an evolutionary vision, a vision of guided change. Change is real and inescapable, but it is like an intractable horse: it takes courage to resolve to govern it. Like it or not, one is entangled in its reins, and if one does not ride the horse of change it drags one along the stony road. To respond realistically to the changes that one is faced with, one requires a world view, a systematic attitude and emotional relationship to the world, which assumes change as its basic tenet. One requires an evolutionary world view.

Evolving further – the noble quest – is an enormous task, but I think that other quests just take one round in circles and are ultimately completely unsatisfactory. The path of evolution is there; from the dawn of life to the awakened sage. As self-aware human beings, we are at a crossroads, and, if we wish, we can participate in the path. The eighth century Indian philosopher-poet Shantideva wrote:

> If they develop the strength of their exertion,
> Even those who are flies, mosquitoes, bees and insects
> Will win unsurpassable awakening
> Which is so hard to find.
>
> So if I do not forsake the bodhisattva's way of life,
> Why should someone like myself who has been born
>   in the human race
> Not attain awakening, since I am able to recognize
> What is beneficial and what is of harm?[248]

One thing I am certain of: nothing, no, nothing, that one does is lost. All one's actions speak, and their utterances echo back, in discord or in euphony. Like the sea anemone, one tends to evaluate experience and then react. The task of an evolving individual is to discover how benevolent actions can yield a lucid mind, and how the lucid mind can find wisdom. Then one need not react to the bombardments of life, but act first, like the bodhisattva, and create a world in which the very rivers, the very birds, sing of limitless evolving.

Appendix

AN EVOLVING IDEA:
EVOLUTIONARY THINKING THROUGH THE AGES

EVOLUTIONARY IDEAS IN THE ANCIENT WORLD

Some of the ancient creation myths seem to describe a progressive sequence, each new entity or kind of substance giving rise to a further and different one until the contemporary state of affairs was reached (e.g. *Rig Veda*, x, 129, or the Greek myths of Chaos begetting earth and heaven, who begot the Titans, who in turn made Mankind).[249] Perhaps myths of a growing Cosmos came naturally to people who, as primarily farmers, would have observed the ordered growth of crops, animals, and themselves. Such myths, incidentally, contrast with the typical myth of monotheistic religions like Judaism, in which a single creator-being, displayed as permanent and unchanging, is personally responsible for the production of the Universe, living things and humanity.

Ancient records suggest that, as soon as men started using reason to speculate about the origins of the world and humanity, evolutionary ideas were incorporated. Such speculative theories differ from myths in that they were worked out by individual people, many of whose names we know, but then, as now, they tend to contain strong imaginative overtones, with abstract principles intervening more or less as if they were supernatural personalities. Here is a brief survey.

In China, one writer claims, the sage Confucius (551–479BCE) held that 'Things were originated from a single, simple source through gradual folding and branching.' And Joseph Needham states that Taoism definitely espoused evolutionary ideas concerning the development of biological form.[250]

In Greece, Anaximander in the sixth, and Heraclitus in the fifth century BCE both emphasized continuous change and a gradual emergence of life. Anaximander went so far as to trace human ancestry back to aquatic creatures. Even philosophers like Empedocles (fifth century BCE), who rejected change as a final reality, saw an evolution of life through a mixing of the basic, unchanging elements. Indeed, evolutionary doctrines predominated among the Greek philosophers before Socrates, and theories of social and cultural evolution were also current in fifth-century BCE Greece. For example, Democritus stressed the importance of the evolution of language. Democritus and the other classical atomists (including, later, Lucretius) envisaged evolutionary change as resulting from the chance combinations of atomic entities. Anaxagoras, however, believed in an evolution intelligently designed.

Plato (428–347BCE) and Aristotle (384–322BCE) were both opposed to applying evolutionary ideas to life or the Cosmos.[251] However, Aristotle saw individuals as evolving in their own lifetimes, and held that the end stage of a process 'attracts' the earlier stages to it, owing to its greater perfection. This doctrine of *final cause* (the most important of Aristotle's four causal factors), or teleology, introduced the notion of potentiality into philosophy, a crucial component of some later trains of evolutionary thinking. Aristotle emphasized 'higher' and 'lower' forms of life (plants – sponges, jellyfish etc – worms – other animals – man), but in terms of everlasting degrees of perfection, not as any historical succession. Aristotle's ideas, melded with medieval Christian theology, gave rise to the medieval 'Great Chain of Being', in which all forms of existence were ranged in a static hierarchy.[252] It was thought that the 'less perfect' can never generate the 'more perfect', a view radically challenged by the biological theories of evolution. Over in India, unknown sages were composing the Upanishads, very roughly between 700 and 300BCE. They, or one of them, anticipated Aristotle with an account of the 'rope of development', reeled in by the Absolute (Brahman) at its top end.[253]

One can already discern two kinds of evolutionary description. In one, all that is to be is already present as a potential, hidden within the apparently chaotic substance of the primal cosmos, or as a blueprint in the mind of a creator. The biblical genesis and the theories of Aristotle and the Upanishadic sages fall into this class. For them, evolution (which literally means a 'rolling out') is like the unrolling of a Persian carpet, where the pattern was long ago woven in, but is gradually exposed to view. The designs at the innermost part of the carpet don't develop *from* the designs on the part which is seen first; they just happen to be concealed for longer.

The second kind of evolutionary account allows some sort of creativity to the very things which arise in the process of evolution. Laws of development combine with some source of either originality or randomness to bring forth descendants which differ in unpredicted ways from their ancestors. The things evolving may be plants, animals, societies, human characteristics or anything else you care to mention. Potential is there, but not the inevitable destiny implied by Aristotle's 'final cause'. Instead of a carpet unrolling, perhaps this second evolutionary account is more like the unrolling of a dream, in which each event comes somehow out of the event that preceded it, but not by following a written script. Those pre-Socratic philosophers usually preferred an evolutionary theory along these self-creative lines, as did Confucius and some of the *Rig Veda* accounts.

If human minds can watch things maturing and get the idea of evolution, they can also remember, or mis-remember, how life has deteriorated since a past Golden Age, and call it *de*volution. The 'descending' view of the universe is represented in myth by the story of the Fall in the Old Testament, and in thought by the works of Plato and the Neoplatonists. Plato taught that people have lost sight of an ideal world of pure forms, or divine perfection, and sit in the cave of matter watching the mere flickering shadows of reality on the wall.

So some thinkers believed in evolution, some in devolution – and some in both! Combining evolution and devolution yields a cyclic view of the universe. While Anaximander was teaching evolution in Greece (sixth century BCE), the dominant approach in India seems to have been a cyclic one. It was thought that consciousness becomes grosser (devolution) until conscious beings are so gross as to need material bodies, while matter evolves into more refined and differentiated forms, until consciousness and matter are thoroughly interdependent, as in today's world. Then the process reverses, the material world gradually disintegrating, and conscious beings gradually disengaging from it.[254]

These evolutionary accounts of origins are stories rather than theories based on objective research. (Even Darwin's theory is envisaged most vividly if it is received in part as a story; its mythic appeal enhances its 'truth' for us. An origins story is not the same as a falsehood.) In this spirit, the evolution/devolution accounts of early India were taken up and used in a semi-humorous way by the Buddha.

INDIAN BUDDHIST EVOLUTION MYTHS

In the 'Dialogues', the Buddha is represented in several places as telling stories of 'beginnings' (Pali *aganna*), as he calls them. His listeners must have been highly amused by his tongue-in-cheek explanations of the origins of various current customs, sayings, and phrases. The intention seems in part to have been to satirize the solemn creation stories of contemporary Indian religious traditions, especially those involving a creator god or justifying the pretensions of the Brahmin priesthood.[255] The longest text has a more explicit message; the Buddha is linking unethical behaviour with degeneration, and ethical behaviour with further evolution, both in the cultural sphere and in the spiritual life of the individual disciple.

The overall framework is similar to the cyclic Hindu myths mentioned above: an unimaginably protracted cycle of alternate involution and evolution of the cosmos and consciousness.[256] At the limit of involution, says the myth, beings were reborn in an immaterial heaven world called Streaming Radiance. After ages, they were reborn on the youthful earth, but were still non-material; they were androgynous, dwelling in the sky, needing no food but rapture, and they shone brightly, immersed in their own radiance. The world was then 'just one mass of water', and dark so that sun, moon, and stars were not visible.

After a very long period, mighty winds whipped up and evaporated the water, and a rich, creamy essence solidified on its surface. One of the beings was of a curious or exploratory nature (alternatively translated as 'greedy'); he dipped his finger in the essence and tasted it. He found it delicious and very sweet, like pure wild honey, and others followed his example. Craving grew in them, until they were breaking off lumps of the stuff to eat. Consequently their radiance dimmed, and the sun and moon could be seen, and so the days, months, and seasons came into being. At the same time, the world's land-masses arose from the oceans: mountains growing like swelling bubbles on porridge as it cooks.

As the beings feasted, their bodies gradually coarsened, those that ate most becoming noticeably uglier than the norm. This induced conceit in the rest, who despised the ugly ones. As a result, the creamy essence disappeared, much to the dismay of all, and in its place a sort of fungus grew, also delicious (bitter according to one account), which became the beings' food. The coarsening of body and disparity of beauty increased further, giving rise to more conceit and spite, so that the fungus, too, vanished, being replaced by a fast-growing creeper, and then rice. The rice could be eaten straight off the plant, and always grew again in time for the next meal.

For the first time excretion was necessary, and coarsening and distinctions increased further, until the sexes could be distinguished in some, 'and the women became extremely preoccupied with the men, and the men with the women'.[257] Thus they desired each other, and later had sex, first in public, but later in private because of the disapproval of the beings who were still androgynous, who threw cow dung at anyone seen *in flagrante delicto*. Hence the invention of huts!

An unusually lazy being could not be bothered to gather wild rice before every meal, and so started the practice of hoarding it for longer and longer periods. This once again affected the food supply; perhaps it was being over-exploited. The rice developed husks, and did not regrow when cropped. The beings held a mass meeting, lamenting the results of their 'unskilful ways', and decided they would now have to invent farming, and cultivate the rice. This led to property, as each had his own plot with a marked boundary, and to theft, when one greedy being stole rice from a neighbour's field.

Now all the features of society as we know it crowded in apace. Caught, the thief promised not to steal again, but relapsed twice, and was seized, rebuked, and beaten up. Thus stealing, lying, censuring, and punishment all appeared. Another meeting was called, and the consensus was to elect the most handsome, capable, and kind-hearted of their number as a judge, to censure or banish wrong-doers. This first ruler was named 'the People's Choice' (the Buddha in a previous life, according to one version). The 'Beginnings' text goes on to explain the origins of the various trades and occupations.

At first sight, this myth is describing a degeneration rather than an evolution. There is something in this, but I prefer to see it as a co-evolution of the perceived and social worlds as human nature comes to terms with external reality. The radiant beings at the beginning are completely subjective, self-absorbed, and passive; they may hint at the pre-self-aware state. A perceived world grows around them as they interact with it.

They carry through pre-human greed into a self-aware, social existence, and so the perceived world evolves to match that greed. (Objective reality is still, in a relative sense, objective, but how we perceive it stems largely from our emotional attitude to it.) Thus, for example, farming and property do not evolve in the myth until the wild rice is over-exploited. The greed and ignorance were already present in the shining beings, but it took active intervention in the world before evolution could solidify these tendencies into the social structures of self-interest and self-protection that we know today. At first, self-awareness gave expression to greed and delusion, but it is also the foundation for higher evolution. The shining beings were not enlightened, and were too passive to work for enlightenment. The human state, for all its faults, is said to be best for that.[258]

A different fable in the 'Dialogues' gives an account of the evolution of culture. A golden age is described first, which ends when the ruler allows poverty to arise in his realm. This leads in stages to stealing, capital punishment, widespread violence, lying, and other evils. After many generations, people have lost their beauty because of the increase in antisocial behaviour, and their life-span has decreased to ten years. And here the nadir comes. Morality is unknown. Even those with the closest ties feel a ferocious enmity and murder one another. A bloody 'sword period' comes to pass, a time of unrestricted slaughter of each by each. A few survive by hiding in the forests, living on roots and fruits.

It is with the survivors, horrified by the world they remember, that 'evolution' restarts. They start to meet each other, and they rejoice that some are still alive. They realize that the catastrophe of the sword period was due to their former 'addiction to evil ways', and they agree to eschew all taking of life.

Consequently, the next generation is more beautiful and longer lived. Ethical behaviour is reinforced as such benefits are noticed, and people progressively adopt more and more 'wholesome practices': refraining from stealing, sexual misconduct, lying, slander, harsh speech, idle chatter, covetousness, ill will, and wrong views, abstaining from incest and excessive greed, and respecting parents, the religious, and the head of the clan. Gradually, over many generations, beauty and life-span improve, and the world becomes an ideal society with no disease – overeating, undereating, and old age being the only causes of death.[259]

This second myth illuminates the first, I think. It shows how a realization of the consequences of actions can reverse the degeneration of a society. In the first myth, awareness of an external world and of other beings active in it dawned in beings who before were wholly subjective. They built a perceived world around them that reflected their greed, ignorance, and later hatred, as those unskilful states came out in their behaviour. In the second myth, a utopia is created, also by self-aware and social beings, by giving expression to skilful states instead. What is stressed in both myths is the responsibility that one has for one's world as one experiences it. No outside agency, neither a god nor an abstract physical law, foists the environment upon one; in fact, in other sources, the Buddha explicitly repudiates creation by a god or Brahma.[260]

A BIRTH STORY

In Sri Lanka, Thailand, China, and other Buddhist countries, the most popular introduction to the evolutionary message of Buddhism is through the birth stories. These tales take for granted the standard Indian belief in rebirth, which I shall attempt to clarify before we look at a birth story.

Although it is a very widespread belief, rebirth is difficult for a scientifically-minded person to accept, because scientists tend to believe that mentality is dependent upon a material base (the brain), and is localized in space and time in the same way that matter is. But according to Buddhist tradition, consciousness possesses a certain momentum, and the death of the brain is said not to be capable of halting this momentum. One living consciousness 'knocks on', as it were, to the consciousness of a newly-born person, in the same way as one's present consciousness is the precursor of a different but continuous consciousness 'reborn' in the next instant from now. No 'thing' continues from life to life, but there is a continuity, so that memories of past lives are possible. The circumstantial evidence for rebirth is fairly strong, but it inevitably consists of anecdotal reports and not reproducible experiments: I do not see how it could be proved conclusively. More compelling for me is the complete unanimity of Buddhist teachers down the ages. They have challenged every fixed and cherished view, including Buddhist views, yet remained convinced of rebirth.

There would seem to be three main viewpoints on the connections, if any, between death and birth. Besides the belief in rebirth, there is a belief in an eternal soul created by God and eventually coming to rest in an eternal abode of torture or bliss, and there is the materialist view that consciousness is merely an attribute of the brain, and so completely ceases when the brain dies. Of the three, rebirth would seem the most 'evolutionary' view. It certainly seems that some people start life with psychological advantages over others, as if they have already done some preparatory work on the path of higher evolution. However, I have a peevish inner voice that complains: 'Never mind what the great teachers say, why can I recall nothing of previous lives?' Personally, I incline strongly to the rebirth view, but want some further proofs!

In any case, it is the belief in rebirth that gives rise to hundreds of different tales, biographical sketches depicting the former lives of the Buddha. In each one, the hero demonstrates how a life of virtue or self-sacrifice moves one closer to Buddhahood. Some tell of cultural innovations in former periods; many represent the Buddha-to-be (bodhisattva) as an animal, seeming to reflect, at first sight, events in biological or cultural evolution. However, the texts give virtually no clue as to the chronological sequence of the different lives they describe, and there is no suggestion that the 'animal' births were necessarily earlier than the human ones. Indeed, the animal stories are clearly fables, rather like Aesop's fables or the stories of Brer Rabbit, though generally with a much loftier and clearer ethical message.

No, the birth stories are not intended to reflect a biological evolution: the animals in them are engaging and entertaining ciphers for human types, as with Aesop and Co. Nevertheless, according to one of their translators, they represent 'the greatest epic in literature of the Ascent of Man'.[261] This is because they evoke advances in consciousness, encouraging the listener to be like the hero, and push his or her own consciousness to evolve.

Here is a fairly typical example of one of the animal birth stories.

Long ago, before men had tasted mangoes, the bodhisattva was reborn as a monkey, near the banks of the Ganges. Growing up strong and vigorous, he became leader of his troop. The monkeys found a huge mango tree on the river bank: 'Its sweet fruits of divine flavour were as large as water jars, and from one branch the fruit fell on dry ground, from another they fell into the Ganges.' The troop feasted eagerly on the fruit, but the bodhisattva pondered, and decided that he must not let the ripe fruit fall into the river, or there would come a time when disaster would befall his followers.

So after the next blossoming, he made the monkeys eat or discard all the fruitlets on the branch that overhung the river. However, one single fruit ripened because an ants' nest hid it from view, and it fell into the water.

Meanwhile, many miles downstream in the great royal capital Benares, King Brahmadatta was idling away his life. His many wives did their best to keep him amused, his courtiers flattered him and devised elaborate feasts, and the king himself grew more fat and more bored. In the afternoon he would go with his court to his bathing place on the Ganges. Nets were strung across the river, upstream and downstream, to keep out the crocodiles, and the king would wallow in the shallows to his heart's content, and then emerge for a picnic.

One night, after the king had returned to his palace, the fisherman who put away the crocodile nets found a strange object caught in the mesh. Was it the egg of some huge water bird? Red and green it was, weighty, soft to the touch; swollen, blushing, and fragrant. Did the fisherman know what it was? no! – So he gave it to the chief queen. Did the queen know what it was? no! – So she gave it to the king. Did the king know what it was? no! – So he asked the queen, who asked the fisherman, who did not know. The fisherman fetched the woodman: he would know. He said to the king 'Eat it, sire.' Suspiciously, the king made the woodman taste some first, and an enchanting perfume filled the palace as the fruit was cut.

Yes, it was the very mango that had fallen from the monkey's tree, and the king was soon guzzling its flesh, leaving some small pieces to tantalize his wives and courtiers. He was delighted, and the fragrant essence pervaded his body. They were ecstatic, and the fragrant essence pervaded their bodies. But when the mango was finished, the sensuous king craved more; the whole gourmand court were obsessed with mangoes. So Brahmadatta ordered an expedition for the next morning. They would all go up river to look for the tree. The bodhisattva monkey's worst fears were about to be realized.

The king's boats stopped under the mango tree, its branches bending with ripe fruit, and Brahmadatta and his wives and courtiers feasted to repletion, all falling asleep under the great tree. The moon rose. At midnight, our monkey troop arrived for their mangoes, not noticing their new and deadly rivals snoring contentedly on the ground. The noise of the monkeys woke the king, who saw them and smiled. 'The mango is an ideal fruit, but it lacks a savoury. Tomorrow we will eat mangoes and roast monkey!' Brahmadatta awakened his men and had the tree surrounded by archers, ready to shoot at first light.

Trembling, the monkeys came to their leader – 'What shall we do?' 'Do not fear,' he whispered, and climbed to the very end of the bough which overhung the river. With a prodigious leap, he made the far river bank, landing in a bush. There, he carefully calculated the length of his leap, broke off a long bamboo pole to reach the branch, tied one end to the top of the bush, and tied the other end to his waist. The great monkey gathered every sinew for a mighty leap, and 'with the speed of a wind-torn cloud' he sprang for the branch. But oh! the pole was just too short. With a despairing convulsion, the bodhisattva clutched the branch as he fell. 'O monkeys, my back must be the bridge. Run swiftly to the pole and safety.'

So the troop escaped the dreadful fate of adorning Brahmadatta's breakfast table. But look – the last monkey to cross is the bodhisattva's great rival, and he stamps on his chief's back as he passes, causing his heart to crack in a wave of pain. The cruel rival fled, laughing. The bodhisattva was alone, lashed to a bamboo pole, hanging on to the tree.

Brahmadatta had seen all in the growing light. 'This is but a beast, yet he risks all to save his kin!' and at daybreak he sent his boats into midstream and had a platform built on them. Gently, the dying monkey was taken down and tended. The king sat next to him on the ground and spoke, his heart full. 'You could have saved yourself, great being. What are you to those chatterers, what are they to you?' 'Those monkeys are my charge, king. In terror of your brutal arrows, they looked to me, and so I saved them. Neither death nor bondage will disturb my breast, since those I ruled are now safe. I tell this to you, O king, that you may learn that a wise ruler seeks the welfare of all in his domain.'

And so the bodhisattva died, and Brahmadatta gave him a monarch's funeral, enshrined his bones, and abandoned his own luxurious ways to rule righteously, following the instructions of a monkey.[262]

Tibetan Buddhist evolution myths

The temples of Paro and Punakha in Bhutan have series of beautiful frescoes on either side of their main gates, showing a myth of the origin of the world-system. B.C. Olschak and Thupten Wangyal describe their significance in *Mystic Art of Ancient Tibet*, calling each of the five designs a 'cosmic mandala'.[263]

In mandala number one, a first movement is symbolized by a three-footed spiral, like a threefold yin-yang symbol. Around it, a rotating 'wind' condenses into the four primordial elements: mobility (wind), temperature (fire), fluidity (water), and solidity/resistance (earth). The symbols for the elements are shown in a circle, in shapes that will become the continents, and the rest of the mandala is filled by an all-pervading blue, symbolizing the space that contains them all and is their source. Intersecting coloured circles represent, according to Olschak and Wangyal, the orbits of the celestial bodies. The whole is surrounded by a ring of fire.

In mandala number two, an axial mountain arises from the centre of the cosmos, with the abodes of celestial beings visible on it. Surrounding its base is an ocean, with twelve continents and subcontinents, and clouds and birds can be seen in the sky around the mountain.

Plants have started growing in a fertile landscape of hills and waterfalls in the third mandala. The fourth and fifth depict animals, people, and all the attributes of a mature world on the continents and in the ocean.

These Bhutanese frescoes are intriguing, and also exasperating; the commentary is very sketchy, and I suspect that the illustrations have been placed in the wrong order. A story from Tibet (clearly based mainly on Indian sources) helps to fill out the origin story upon which the frescoes are based.[264]

From voidness there arose two opposing winds, which, after countless aeons, grew thicker and heavier. The winds coalesced into the foundation of the universe, the great double vajra (diamond sceptre) 'Dorje Gyaltram'. From the double vajra, clouds arose, and rain fell from the clouds. After many years, the rain filled the primeval ocean. Then all became peaceful.

Slowly the winds moved again, churning the ocean, until a foam appeared on its surface. As butter forms in the churn, the earth gradually solidified from the ocean. It rose up as a great axial mountain, and more rain fell, forming the salt oceans. Around the mountain were the twelve continents and subcontinents, and trees and plants appeared there. Presumably animals and people evolved later, though the story just takes their presence for granted. The rest of the account is much as in the first Indian myth.

Our last myth tells of the origin of the Tibetan people.

An intelligent monkey once dwelt in the mountains of Tibet. Under the influence of his patron, the archetypal Bodhisattva of Compassion, he meditated on wisdom and compassion, which grew in him. A mountain demoness lived near his cave; she fell in love with the monkey. She begged him to live with her, but he refused. She pleaded and said she would die, and finally threatened to marry a demon instead, and conceive innumerable demon children who would devour all the living beings in Tibet. The Bodhisattva of Compassion advised his protégé to marry the demoness, and performed the ceremony. They had six children, one representing each of the realms of the Wheel of Life, and each consequently of a quite different disposition. All lived on the wild fruits of the forest.

The hybrid beings rapidly multiplied. Soon, there were 400 descendants, and the food supply gave out. Some cried with hunger, some took to fighting and quarrelling. The monkey, now an ancient patriarch, separated them into smaller groups, which became the tribes of Tibet. The bodhisattva came again to advise the monkey, who realized that food could be grown from seed. Season after season understanding grew, and the tribes were soon farming independently.

After generations of changes in diet and habits, the beings' appearance changed (one source says this happened before they invented agriculture). They lost their fur and began to cover themselves with leaves and bark, their tails fell off, and they walked erect. Language gradually developed. Distinctive customs emerged, interactions grew more complex, and concern for the welfare of the whole group increased. They were fully human.

Some of the tribes resembled the demoness in character, some the monkey, and some inherited traits from both. The story ends by relating that people eventually began to recognize that beauty and grace were connected with virtue, and so beneficial practices were encouraged in Tibetan society.[265]

Buddhism tries to instil an interest in spiritual development in its followers. They see their lives, therefore, in terms of an evolution of consciousness, an evolution which may have started in former births, and could continue in future lives. This evolutionary picture of life has probably influenced Buddhist myth, so that the myths envisage a development, too. In addition, the compassion teachings of Buddhism, as well as ideas of rebirth, stress the unity of life, animal as well as human. Man is never seen as a special creation apart from the rest of life. Human beings have a privileged position in the sense that only a human can make the deliberate decision to work for enlightenment.

This is why modern ideas of evolution in the West cause no alarm even to the most traditional of Buddhists. They may make the old myths look quaint, but the background is already evolutionary.[266]

EVOLUTION REAPPEARS

Now we return to evolutionary ideas in the West. Plato, Aristotle, and Christian theologians combined to put such doctrines virtually to sleep until around the eighteenth century. Then we find that several of the editors of the great French Encyclopédie, who were known as the Philosophes or Encyclopedists, held explicit or implicit evolutionary views, as did the French mathematician de Maupertuis (1698–1759). The ground had been prepared for them by the great scientists of the previous two centuries such as Kepler, Galileo, and Newton, who had undermined doctrines of immutability. The Philosophes believed in inexorable human progress, and explained evolution as an increase in complexity. One of them, Condorcet (1743–94), originated what was probably the first fully-fledged account of the evolution of mankind, though some of his ideas came from Voltaire.

Also in France, the great naturalist the Comte de Buffon (1707–88) applied evolutionary ideas to the living world, suggesting that species arose, altered and died out through climatic and other natural changes.[267] He even proposed that mankind's nearest relative was the ape. By the end of the eighteenth century, the biological evidence for evolution was so strong that theories of biological evolution sprang up in several parts of Europe. Charles Darwin, in a footnote to the introduction to his *Origin of Species*, wrote: 'It is a rather singular instance of the manner in which similar views arise at about the same time, that Goethe in Germany, Dr Darwin in England and Geoffroy Saint-Hilaire in France ... came to the same conclusions about the origin of species in the years 1794–5.'[268] This was also about the time that the German philosopher Herder (1744–1803) was proposing that each human society grew and developed in response to environmental conditions, like a living organism. And Hegel, also in Germany, was describing history as a 'progressive manifestation of the Spirit', an evolutionary process.

In general, the European intellectual community was now focusing more and more on the possibility of biological evolution, and the subject was hotly disputed. Let me just mention one unsung and two influential thinkers: Blyth, Lamarck, and Chambers. In Scotland, Robert Chambers published anonymously *Vestiges of the Natural*

History of Creation (1844), a journalist's polemic for evolution, carelessly researched but very widely read. (Its influence spread to Germany, where the philosopher Schopenhauer 'evolutionized' his existing concept of 'will'. For him, will is a timeless life force which strives for maximum expression by objectifying itself in a process of evolution.) Chambers's book got a lot of people in Britain talking about evolution, as did the work of a Frenchman, a much better scientist, Jean Baptiste Lamarck.

Lamarck (1744–1829) made perhaps the first serious attempt to discover the laws governing organic evolution. Since Darwin rather defensively dismissed his theories as nonsense, Lamarck has received rather a bad press among English-speaking evolutionists. His starting point, however, that evolution proceeds by an animal making a choice to move into a new region or adopt a new mode of life, was a very fertile idea, as we saw in chapter 4. Its new habits gave rise to new needs (*besoins*). Lamarck went on to say that new needs will result in slight modifications to an animal's structure. He suggested that these useful characteristics, acquired during an animal's lifetime, could be inherited by its own offspring, and thus gradually spread through the species. The characteristics were acquired, he thought, by the animal's internal drive to fulfil its needs more effectively. The Great Chain of Being was reversed. Animals' minds can determine sustained changes in their form; so perfect need *not* precede less perfect. His famous example is the neck of the giraffe. Lamarck suggested that a giraffe's neck might stretch if the best leaves were high in the trees, and the stretched length of neck might become normal in subsequent generations: the inheritance of an acquired characteristic.

Similar theories have still not been quite ruled out by biologists, but it is now clear that Lamarck had not discovered the main mechanism of evolution. That had to await the work of Darwin (who, incidentally, accepted the inheritance of acquired characteristics), unless one accepts the prior claims of one or two relative unknowns.

One of these was Edward Blyth (1810–73), who is said by some to have anticipated Darwin in all important essentials.[269] However, he seems to have derived from his theory of 'natural means of selection' exactly the opposite conclusions to Darwin's: he saw the process as leading to the stabilization of species rather than to evolution. In any case, no one noticed Blyth's work for many years, so let us proceed to Charles Darwin himself.

DARWIN'S DISCOVERY

If the idea of evolution goes back at least to Anaximander in the sixth century BCE, why is Charles Darwin remembered as the man who discovered evolution? The answer is that until the blossoming of careful experimental science in the nineteenth century, evolution, when it was not a mere truism, was no more than another philosophical view to be wrangled over. If someone spoke of the 'evolution' of a foetus as it grew in the womb, there need be no dispute, and the term was a truism. The foetus could be seen, from the evidence of premature births and dissection, invariably to pass through a continuous series of developmental stages: an evolution. As for the evolution of the universe, or the planet earth, or life, that was just speculation, since all three seemed stable, even with a lifetime's observation.

By Darwin's time however, the apparent fixity of the earth had been disproved by the geologists. They found that incredibly slow processes, which are still going on, had gradually altered the earth's features. Mountain ranges had been thrown up and worn away again by the weather. Dry land had been flooded by the sea, and material gently settling particle by particle on the sea-bed had accumulated over aeons into great thicknesses of rock. So the earth, it transpired, was changing, evolving. And occasionally, in those sedimentary rocks, geologists found fossil remains of kinds of animals and plants no longer living on earth – organisms similar enough to living forms to seem like their more primitive ancestors. As a result of such discoveries, it was particularly in the field of biology that the evolutionary philosophy was to gain scientific backing.

The young naturalist Charles Darwin (1809–82) knew of the geologists' discoveries when he set off in 1831 on a five-year voyage round the world on the survey ship HMS *Beagle*.[270] In South America and on Pacific Islands he looked at the way species were distributed, and found more and more evidence that certain groups of species must be related through common ancestors. He came home to England quite convinced of the fact of biological evolution. But the contribution that was to make his a name that everybody knows was still to come. It concerned just how and why a new species evolves from a slightly different ancestor.

Darwin found this out by bringing together an observation and a theory. The observation was that new kinds of animals and plants could be artificially produced in captivity by selective breeding. The theory was implied by Thomas Malthus's pessimistic ideas on human over-population: like humans, animals and plants produce more offspring than are needed to maintain a steady population. So with a limited supply of resources, particularly food, a proportion of each generation will not survive to breed. Now, bring this regular mortality together with the facts of selective breeding. Darwin reasoned that, surely, in each generation, organisms less able to deal with obstacles to survival and less able to take advantage of natural resources are those which are least likely to breed successfully.

What breeders had noticed and exploited were the facts of variation and inheritance. Animals and plants vary a lot in each generation – even offspring of the same parents can vary very considerably, in all sorts of characteristics. On the other hand, there is a tendency in the other direction too – animals or plants inherit many of the charac-teristics of their parents, and are more similar to them than to unrelated members of the same species. So the breeder can *select* a sheep, say, which happens to have extra long wool (as a result of natural variation), breed from it, and confidently expect some of the offspring to have extra long wool, too.

Darwin saw that nature could do the same – in a cold climate, sheep with long wool would tend to survive and breed better than those with short wool, and so long wool would become more and more common in the whole population. (Had Lamarck considered the *besoins* of populations instead of individuals, he would have come close to much of modern neo-Darwinism.) Darwin called his idea 'natural selection', and after years of cautiously amassing evidence, he at last announced the idea to the public. He was, in fact, prompted to publish his theory of evolution sooner than he had hoped to, as another British biologist, A.R. Wallace (1823–1913), had independently arrived at the same the-ory. Their joint paper was read to the Linnaean Society in 1858, and Darwin's famous book, *The Origin of Species by Means of Natural Selec-tion*, was published in 1859.

EVOLUTION'S CHALLENGE TO FIXED VIEWS

The new theory of biological evolution caught the imagination of the Victorian intelligentsia, some attracted by its explanatory powers, some by its elevation of competition into a natural law (which was taken as providing a moral licence for cut-throat capitalism), and some by the ammunition it provided against Church dogmas. Whether applied to nature or to humanity, evolution encourages an understanding of the past in terms of processes of historical development, and it sees the future in terms of trends and possibilities. Consequently, rigid frameworks of dogma or theory are difficult (though not impossible) to reconcile with an evolutionary perspective. It emerges as a middle way between the more extreme forms of science and religion which were so influential in the century before Darwin.

On the one hand was mechanistic science, which described the world as if it were an intricate construction of levers and cogs, or a chaotic swarm of blind particles, following their inevitable but pointless courses. There was no room for life or mind as meaningful aspects of reality in the mechanical view, not even in its account of human society or psychology. Existence had no meaning, no one event or quality could be valued more highly than any other, and those who ascribed true purposes to their actions were vain and deluded. On the other hand, moralists within the Church (and outside it) insisted upon stern and static hierarchies of worth and value. An unapproachable deity commanded the summit of existence, with each thing, being, quality, and idea fixed in its unquestioned place below him.

Both reductionism and teleology frequently represent attempts to escape the discomfort and uncertainty of confronting a changing world in which one has some personal responsibility for the future. The first does so by reducing all phenomena to their lowest common denominators, denying relevance to higher values or ideas of progression. Effectively, it says that minds are not a real aspect of the universe. The second does not deny higher and lower, but says that what is 'lower' can never of itself give rise to what is 'higher', and so an unchangeable 'highest' must have been present from the beginning, toying with its creations. (How 'higher' *can* come from 'lower' is a genuine philosophical difficulty, but perhaps a more satisfactory solution can be found by questioning the absolute validity of the distinction between lower and higher as concepts.) Mind is not denied, but all individual minds are subjected to one supreme ruler mind, or to the abstract deity 'progress'.

Reductionist science and teleological religion, in their more dogmatic forms, are both seeking a reliable and changeless basic reality as far removed as possible from the unstable world of ordinary subjective experience. They seek certainty at opposing poles, however, and thus have tended to see each other as natural opponents. Science starts from those sensory experiences which are least dependent upon people's states of mind: absolute identities or differences of appearance and location, and quantitative measurements of ratios. Science then abstracts from these observations to postulate invisible fundamentally 'real' entities and laws. Religion also tends to arrive at invisible entities and laws, though quite different ones. It follows a subjective, non-sensory path, and abstracts supreme or universal consciousness from the characteristics of human consciousness, including the vaguely emerging contents of the unconscious mind.

Despite their antagonism, science and conventional religion have each rendered great service to mankind, the first by extending the reach of the senses to new domains, detecting beautiful symmetries in nature, and generating technologies that can reduce the hardships of bodily life; the second by providing mythologies and ceremonies that can promote mental well-being and social stability. Both have also done great harm when used thoughtlessly or maliciously. I need not give examples here. It would seem important to avoid the extreme, dogmatically fixed forms of religion and science which deny human values and human choice. A fluid, evolutionary view can be both scientific and religious in the best senses of these words.

EVOLUTIONARY IDEAS SINCE DARWIN

In late nineteenth-century Europe and America, increasing numbers of influential thinkers saw the advantage of the evolutionary view. The idea spread rapidly from biology into other disciplines, largely through the eloquence of a number of enthusiastic champions of the cause. In England, there were the science-writer Thomas Henry Huxley (1825–95, 'Darwin's Bulldog'), and the philosopher Herbert Spencer (1820–1903). The latter elevated evolution to a cosmic law of the unstoppable movement from homogeneity (formlessness) to heterogeneity (the arising of more and more distinct features). 'Evolution' was not Darwin's term; it was suggested by Spencer, as was 'the struggle for existence'.[271] Spencer was particularly interested in the great law of evolution as applied to human races and society, and was not at all afraid to pronounce on what was more highly evolved and what was primitive or degenerate.

In Germany, Darwin's champion was Ernst Haeckel (1834–1919), the originator of the now largely rejected theory that an embryo has to pass through stages resembling all its evolutionary ancestors as it develops. In the United States it was Chauncey Wright who popularized Darwin, and he speculated about the evolution of the human mind. He tried to show how human self-reflective consciousness developed from more elementary conscious processes common to animals.

Soon, the idea of evolution was common currency, and writers on all subjects jumped on the band-wagon. They included many whose interests were not in the areas to which 'hard' science had so far restricted itself, and some found in evolution a world view which offered positive and optimistic conclusions on the development of humanity. On the other hand, evolutionary views had already been used to justify economic exploitation. Around the turn of the century, they were also used to support doctrines of racial superiority. Naturally, the particular race or nation of each doctrine's founder was firmly fixed at the top.

In the sphere of religion and the 'occult', Mme H.P. Blavatsky, founder of the Theosophy movement, eagerly incorporated evolutionary ideas into her massive system of esoteric philosophy.[272] (The uses she put his ideas to would have made the good-natured but matter-of-fact Charles Darwin extremely uncomfortable.)

By combining Darwinian evolution with Eastern religious teachings on the development of consciousness, the Theosophists were able to talk about a further evolution, which extended beyond the ordinary human level to divine reaches of consciousness. Benign Masters, hidden in the fastnesses of the Himalayas, were, said the Theosophists, directing the future course of human evolution.

From Theosophy, an evolutionary approach to religion spread to India – it suited Eastern doctrines of process far better than the fixed hierarchical relationships of the Western monotheistic religions (notwithstanding the success of a few Christians, notably the Jesuit paleontologist Pierre Teilhard de Chardin, in producing evolutionary versions of Christianity).[273] Thus we find the Hindu sage Sri Aurobindo using an evolutionary theme in his book *The Life Divine*.

Many other thinkers of the present century have followed, wittingly or unwittingly, the lead of the Theosophists in considering the evolution of consciousness, though they have not usually felt the need to bring in the Masters in their mountain retreats. The first Buddhist to speak of the Dharma in evolutionary terms was Allan Bennett. He was the first Englishman to be ordained as a Buddhist monk, given the name Ananda Metteya. His book *The Wisdom of the Aryas* was published in 1923, the year of his death. It talked of the Dharma (in its widest sense) as being the source of all evolutionary advancement, as well as of spiritual development.[274]

ESCALATOR EVOLUTIONISM

Evolution has been interpreted to give support to teleological world views of divinely ordained fixed hierarchies. The teleological view usually envisages a divine plan, worked out by the successive manifestation of a hierarchy of preordained forms of life and mind. In some forms of teleology, everything that appears in evolution is seen as having existed in a hidden, germinal form right from the beginning, in the same way that physicians once taught that a perfectly formed homunculus already existed in the egg or sperm. The Christian socialist Gilbert Cope, for example, wrote: 'Biological evolution, the class conflict succession, the action of the Holy Spirit – all three are characterized by a definite motion towards an end. That motion may be deflected or hindered for a time by deliberate human action, but its gathering momentum cannot be dissipated.'[275]

The fixed teleological view of evolution has been held by a surprisingly large number of scientists, though not always in its god-directed form. The philosopher Mary Midgeley, in her very sensible book *Evolution as a Religion*, calls such notions 'escalator' evolutionism: 'The idea of a vast escalator, proceeding steadily upwards from lifeless matter through plants and animals to man, and inevitably on to higher things.'[276] The inevitable 'higher things' sometimes culminate in the submergence of every individual in a universal, collective superconsciousness, as in the works of Pierre Teilhard de Chardin.[277] More often, they refer simply to the automatic development of a utopian society run by a new, super-intelligent breed of men, usually scientists.[278]

To be fair, the escalator evolutionists do not always see evolutionary 'advance' as being completely inevitable, but their predictions are based very definitely on where they think the future ought to go. Such ideas shade dangerously into advocating the genetic manipulation of the population by a technocratic state, which in turn is not far from the race-hierarchies of the Nazis. So the fixed teleological versions of evolution, just like the fixed hierarchies of medieval theologians, can easily become a rationalization for claims of superiority by certain groups, and the oppression or even destruction by them of groups thought of as inferior.

The levels to which the escalator takes its occupants are an evolutionary sophistication of the Great Chain of Being. The 'more perfect' future is attracting the 'less perfect' present to it; like the medieval theologians, the escalator evolutionists assume that the 'higher' can *not* emerge from the 'lower'. Scientists, as we have seen, tend to take a quite different view, at least in public. With the young Darwin, they remind themselves: 'never use the words higher and lower'. What in the world is conventionally regarded as highest is no more than one among a million products of a mechanical evolution, one picked out because we possess it, and we like to believe we are life's crowning achievement. All they will admit is, yes, the earlier does indeed give rise to the later, with no divine creation, and no teleological back-causation.

The Buddhist view does not lie between the two, but it is a middle way. Every mind, by virtue of being a mind, has a faculty by which it can break out of the habitual cycles set by its past. It can transcend itself. A being, someone with mind, reaching beyond himself or herself, is not mechanically compelled to do so, nor (except in metaphorical terms) drawn forward by what is to come. It, we, may or may not respond to our glimpse of a next step. When we do, we are evolving.

THANKS AND DEDICATION

Quite a number of people read and commented on drafts of *The Evolving Mind*, and I am very grateful to them, as I am to everyone involved in the production of the book. Its main ideas came from my *kalyana mitra*, the venerable Sangharakshita, as well as from his predecessors in the noble lineages of the Buddha, and from the newer lineages of science.

Whatever value you have found in these pages, please direct it to everybody's welfare: to an advance in mental clarity and an easing of frustrations in all who might take part in the evolutionary journey.

Robin Cooper (Ratnaprabha)
Cambridge
February 1996

NOTES AND REFERENCES

INTRODUCTION

1 H. Melville, *Moby Dick*, quoted in introduction to Penguin edition, 13.

2 'Higher evolution' was originally a Theosophical term. It is used in passing by H.P. Blavatsky in her eccentric *Isis Unveiled* and also in *The Secret Doctrine*. W.Y. Evans-Wentz, who was both a Theosophist and a keen student of Buddhism before the Second World War, uses the term in his *Tibetan Yoga and Secret Doctrines*, 12. Sangharakshita took up the term for a lecture given in 1950, and used it as the basis for a lecture course delivered in 1968 entitled 'The Higher Evolution of Man'.

3 Goudge, *The Ascent of Life*, 178.

4 The diagram shows human evolution, and evolution leading to the human level. For correlation with the Buddhist orders of conditionality, see note 182. Perhaps 'biological' evolution is a slight misnomer; this dimension refers to the evolution of the structure of living things. Aspects of mental and cultural evolution are also of interest to biologists.

5 Hardy, *Darwin and the Spirit of Man*, 145–50.

6 Waddington, *The Nature of Life*, 87.

7 Conn, quoted Hardy, *The Living Stream*, 179.

CHAPTER 1

8 Examples of self-transcendence in animals are infrequent and individual, so we have to make cautious use of anecdote, rather than controlled experiments or statistical observations.

9 Marais, *The Soul of the Ape*, 63–5.

10 McFarland, *Oxford Companion to Animal Behaviour*, 113.

11 Sangharakshita, *The Three Jewels*, 8.

12 Plato (see quote at beginning of chapter).

13 Huxley, 'The Evolutionary Vision', 257 and 261.

14 Huxley, introduction to Teilhard, *The Phenomenon of Man*, 13.

15 Using the word truth in a common sense way, virtually everyone who has studied biology will agree that it is clearly true to assert that animals and plants have ancestors who were different from themselves; it is true that the changes have come about in continuous and causal ways; it is true that organisms improve their adaptations to their environments over the generations; and it is true that the overall process reveals a trend of increasing mental capacity. Similarly, they will agree that it is false to claim that the presently-known species all appeared exactly as they are now, and have remained unchanged since; and that it is also false to say that they have changed in haphazard ways.

16 P.A. Sorokin, quoted Dobzhansky, *The Biology of Ultimate Concern*, 35.

17 Kennedy, *The Buddhist Vision*, 32–150; Pallis, *A Buddhist Spectrum*, 1–6, 145–7; Govinda, *Foundations of Tibetan Mysticism*, 236–47.

18 See Simpson, *The Meaning of Evolution*, 122.

19 This may be influenced by personality type, extraverts plumping for unity and empathy, introverts for individual growth. Anthony Storr discusses this issue in his *Solitude*, 86–90.

20 Snell, *The Discovery of the Mind*, 29, 159.

21 Mo Tzu, in Wing Tsit Chan (trans.), *A Source Book in Chinese Philosophy*, 213–4.

22 Some recent scholarship puts the Buddha's dates a little later (see Gombrich, *Theravada Buddhism*, 32); some scholars don't (see Schumann, *The Historical Buddha*).

23 Sangharakshita (trans.), *Dhammapada*, verses 276 and 280.

CHAPTER 2

24 Charles Darwin, *Origin of Species*, 169–70.

25 ibid, 81–9.

26 See Maynard Smith, 'The Status of Neo–Darwinism', in his *On Evolution*, 83–4.

27 Exceptions have been claimed, but are only well attested in bacteria, e.g. New Scientist, 13 September 1990, 'Science' section.

28 Dobzhansky, *Genetics of the Evolutionary Process*, 216.

29 Eiseley, *The Firmament of Time*, 8.

30 Although sexual reproduction surely speeds up evolution, it is still not clear why it should not be adaptive for individual females to produce only female young, without sexual fertilization. See Maynard Smith, 'The origin and maintenance of sex', in his *On Evolution*, 115–125. The answer may be that 'virgin birth' offspring will be almost identical, but in an unpredictable

environment a female producing diverse young is less likely to lose all of them in some calamity.

31 Hominids, as I define them, are, at the time of writing, sometimes being called 'hominines'.

32 Owen Lovejoy, quoted in Leakey, *The Making of Mankind*, 52.

33 Quoted by Flew, *Darwinian Evolution*, 123.

34 Gordon Childe, *Man Makes Himself*, 9–10.

35 Simpson, *The Meaning of Evolution*, 110.

36 Thoday, *Natural Selection and Biological Progress*, 316–7.

37 Huxley, *Evolution, the Modern Synthesis*, 559–62.

38 Huxley, *Evolution in Action*, 81.

39 This point is made by J. Maynard Smith in his 'The Status of Neo-Darwinism', *On Evolution*, 89–90.

40 Simpson, op cit, 121. I have never seen the fact of the growing-tip increase in mental capacity challenged, yet denigrators of progress in evolution fail to mention it unaccountably often!

41 This account of the trends suggested by biologists has necessarily been brief: the historian of biology Robert Reid describes a wider range of such ideas in his *Evolutionary Theory* (especially 7, 194ff, 228, 237, 295, 326, 339, 352). Also see Simpson, op cit, 110–119.

CHAPTER 3

42 Agar, quoted Thorpe, *Purpose in a World of Chance*, 112.

43 See text following, plus Walker, *Animal Thought*, Stenhouse, *The Evolution of Intelligence*, Crook, *The Evolution of Human Consciousness*, Herrick, *The Evolution of Human Nature*, Jerison, 'On the Evolution of Mind', Griffin, *The Question of Animal Awareness*.

44 See Klopfer, *An Introduction to Animal Behaviour*, 71.

45 Rensch, *Homo Sapiens*, 72.

46 Using the familiar term 'image' here aids one in imagining the likely nature of rudimentary mental processes, so long as only the most general associations of the word are permitted to cling to it. The image is much the same as what used to be called, in psychological jargon, a 'percept'.

47 Some authors make sensation a distinct mental process (e.g. R. Herrick, *The Evolution of Human Nature*, 300.) I mean by sensation just the physical stimulation of a sense organ. Goldfish: Walker, *Animal Thought*, 265. Butterflies and frogs: Ornstein, *The Psychology of Consciousness*, 22–3; Crook, *The Evolution of Human Consciousness*, 311.

48 Crook, *The Evolution of Human Consciousness*, 123, 155. The large brain size and impressive behavioural abilities of mammals and birds lead most commentators to treat them separately from other animals.

49 This was proposed (originally by Halstead) as a vital factor in intelligence: the 'P-factor' (Stenhouse, *The Evolution of Intelligence*, 80ff).

50 Walker, op cit, 257. See also Dunbar, 'Common Ground for Thought', 48.

51 Walker, op cit, 252. Such an idea could conceivably be innate, but the experiments that Walker describes demonstrate that pigeons can learn new ideas.

52 See also several papers in Oakley, *Brain and Mind,* especially 5, 32, 44–6, 73, 99, 124, 133–6. It may be that even some reptiles have 'mental maps' (Oakley, 136). Networks of associated images, or something roughly equivalent, have been designated in various ways. See S. Walker, *Animal Thought,* 252–3.

53 Rensch, *Homo Sapiens,* 76–7. Alfred Russell Wallace had a similar idea, suggesting that human mental powers were well in excess of biological needs (Eiseley, *The Unexpected Universe,* 83–4).

54 Walker, *Animal Thought,* 208, Walker's italics. See also 194–208, 235, and McFarland, *The Oxford Companion to Animal Behaviour,* 315. The alternative theory is that the ancestors of intelligent animals (chimpanzees in particular) did not have it so easy as their living descendants, and experienced selection pressures towards intelligence, which is thus an anomalous remnant of lost life-styles.

55 Rensch, *Homo Sapiens,* 86. For a discussion of cognitive abilities in monkeys and apes, see Walker, *Animal Thought,* 339–352.

56 Oakley, *Brain and Mind,* 114–5.

57 Bucke, *Cosmic Consciousness,* 18.

58 See Taylor, *The Natural History of the Mind,* 109; Rensch, *Homo Sapiens,* 74.

59 Koehler, 'Nonverbal thinking', 352.

60 James, *Psychology,* 326–7.

61 For an interesting comparative discussion of communication or 'language' in animals, see Thorpe, *Purpose in a World of Chance,* 54–74.

62 There is some suggestion that dolphins can pass on simple information vocally, but this is much disputed (McFarland, *The Oxford Companion to Animal Behaviour,* 90; Bateson, *Steps to an Ecology of Mind,* 334–8).

63 Herrick, *The Evolution of Human Nature,* 240–53; Young, *An Introduction to the Study of Man,* 485–98; Jerison, 'On the Evolution of Mind', 26; Walker, *Animal Thought,* 145–191, 319–337.

64 Crutchfield et al, 'Chaos', 48.

65 Jerison, op cit, 17–22.

66 See, for example, Valera Thompson and Rosch, *The Embodied Mind;* N Humphrey, *A History of the Mind.*

67 S.J. Gould, *Wonderful Life,* 233.

CHAPTER 4

68 Lewontin, 'Adaptation', 159.

69 See Eldridge, *Time Frames,* passim.

70 There is a third factor, which most biologists think plays only a minor role in evolution. It is called random drift, and is not dealt with here. Dobzhansky, *Genetics of the Evolutionary Process,* 230ff.

71 Odling-Smee, 'Niche-Constructing Phenotypes', 73–110.

72 Patterson, *Evolution,* 93–4.

73 Quoted in Taylor, *The Great Evolution Mystery,* 222.

74 Hammond, 'The origin and development of reproductive barriers', 50; McFarland, *The Oxford Companion to Animal Behaviour,* 320–5.

75 A similar example was given by H.W. Conn in 1900, quoted by Hardy, *The Living Stream*, 179.

76 Reid, *Evolutionary Theory*, 244; Bateson, 'The Active Role of Behaviour in Evolution', p6 of preprint. But John Maynard Smith (*The Birth of Sociobiology*, 50) doubts that the behaviours themselves would become genetically fixed.

77 Behaviour-led selection is a specific form of the 'organic selection' independently proposed by C. Lloyd Morgan in Britain and J. Mark Baldwin and H.F. Osborne in America. The history and status of the idea of organic selection is reviewed by Reid, *Evolutionary Theory*, (239–247). It is also discussed by (among others) the following biologists: Julian Huxley (*Evolution, the Modern Synthesis*, 523), G. Simpson ('The Baldwin Effect', 110–117), E. Mayr (*Animal Species and Evolution*, 95, 106–7,604–5), A. Hardy (*The Living Stream*, 154–5, 162–207. Hardy gives a number of other references to writing on organic selection in *The Living Stream* and *Darwin and the Spirit of Man*), C.H. Waddington (*The Evolution of an Evolutionist*, 89, 279–281), J. Piaget (*Behaviour and Evolution*, xiv–xv, 15–45, 134–145), Patrick Bateson, ('The Active Role of Behaviour in Evolution', passim). The philosopher of science Karl Popper is an enthusiastic proponent of behaviour-led selection as the source of direction in evolution. (*Objective Knowledge*, Chapter 7, and *Unended Quest*, 173–80.) Interestingly, standard university textbooks on biology or evolution rarely mention organic selection or the Baldwin Effect (as it is also known), and negligible experimental work has been done on its behavioural aspect.

78 Waddington, 'Evolutionary Systems, Animal and Human'. Waddington included the selection of niches by behaviour in his 'exploitive system' ('Evolutionary Adaptation').

79 Popper, *Unended Quest*, 180 (Popper's emphasis).

80 Lumsden and Wilson (*Genes, Mind and Culture*, 263) argue for a genetically-based innovative capacity. See also Roe, *Behaviour and Evolution*, 354. On the source of innovation, Gregory Bateson (*Mind and Nature*, 200) writes: '*Creative thought must always contain a random component. The exploratory process – the endless trial and error of mental progress – can achieve the new only by embarking upon pathways randomly presented, some of which when tried are somehow selected for something like survival.*' He does not explain why the possible pathways need to be 'random', however.

81 e.g. J.Z. Young, in Gregory, *Oxford Companion to the Mind*, 147. Waddington was already writing of animal choice in 1960 ('Evolutionary Adaptation').

82 Taylor, *The Natural History of the Mind*, 14; McFarland, *The Oxford Companion to Animal Behaviour*, 159.

83 Bateson, *Mind and Nature*, 124.

84 In a sense, asserting that mental factors can act to drive evolution in a particular direction is a form of 'vitalism', using the term rather loosely. Vitalistic theories of evolution ascribe the driving principle of evolution to a mysterious 'life force', the '*élan vital*' of the French philosopher Henri Bergson (1859–1941) (*Creative Evolution*, 92–102), popularized in Britain by Bernard Shaw. For an account of the development of vitalist ideas, see Reid, *Evolutionary Theory*, 84–104, and Rainer, Schubert, and Soldern, *Mechanism and Vitalism*. To say that evolution is sometimes directed by behaviour, which of course originates in

consciousness, is not to postulate any external life force. But one could argue that any exploratory or innovative drive felt by an animal is a sort of internal life force, a 'vital' factor influencing evolution in addition to the merely mechanical factor of natural selection.

85 Waddington, *The Evolution of an Evolutionist*, 89; R. Ewer quoted Hardy (*The Living Stream*, 187); Reid, *Evolutionary Theory*, 24.

86 Mayr, *The Growth of Biological Thought*, 612.

87 Hardy, *Darwin and the Spirit of Man*, 150.

88 e.g. Monod, *Chance and Necessity*.

89 McFarland, *The Oxford Companion to Animal Behaviour*, 299, with other examples of innovations. Some instances of behavioural changes likely to lead to structural changes are given by Taylor, *The Great Evolution Mystery*, 217–9.

90 Dobzhansky, *The Genetics of the Evolutionary Process*, 211; Maynard Smith, *The Theory of Evolution*, 305–7. See Birch, *The Liberation of Life*, 56–7, for examples of the genetic assimilation of behaviours.

91 Quoted Hardy, *The Living Stream*, 188.

92 Bonner, *The Evolution of Culture in Animals*, passim; McFarland, *The Oxford Companion to Animal Behaviour*, 112–4; Gale, 'Social transmission of acquired behaviour', 77–100.

93 Bonner, op cit, 172–5.

94 In his otherwise excellent *The Evolution of Culture in Animals*, John Tyler Bonner defines culture as 'the transfer of information by behavioural means' (p10), a definition so broad that it would include one animal mating with, or even eating, another!

The term culture is here being transferred from its normal human context to an animal context, and in the process needs to keep its principal connotations if it is to be of value. Animal behaviour, like human, can have a learnt cultural basis in the sense of transmitted behaviour patterns.

95 Bonner, op cit, 179, 185.

96 Thorpe, *Purpose in a World of Chance*, 50–1.

97 Bonner, op cit, 176–7. Bonner believes that the shyness was culturally, not genetically, transmitted; I have not checked his evidence.

98 Plotkin, *The Role of Behaviour in Evolution*, 159–60.

99 A. C. Wilson, quoted in Plotkin (op cit, 145–7). Evolutionary rate is measured by testing how fast species diverge from each other, by comparing various morphological traits. There is also a good correlation between brain size (relative to body weight) and rate of evolution (loc cit).

100 Mental carriers of culture are called memes by Dawkins (*The Selfish Gene*) and Bonner (op cit).

CHAPTER 5

101 James, *Psychology*, 146ff; Oakley, *Brain and Mind*, 132; Herrick, *The Evolution of Human Nature*, 289.

102 Introspection cannot be dispensed with in coming to understand the human mind, if only because terms such as consciousness, experience, awareness, the self, and so on, all assume a reference to one's own mental processes, and

to. The behaviourist psychologists of earlier in this century who attempted to model human psychology without any reference to internal states are now considered to have failed in this aim, and there is a renewed respect for the honest attempts of William James and his followers to communicate what their minds actually felt like, and what went on in them.

103 See Teilhard, *The Phenomenon of Man*, 165; also Crook, *The Evolution of Human Consciousness*, 315.

104 Crook, op cit, 252.

105 By psychologists including H.S. Terrace, 'who trained his own ape, Nim Chimpsky (named in honour of [the American linguist] Noam Chomsky) to converse in American Sign Language, but later, after methodically reviewing videotapes of Nim's performance, Terrace ruefully concluded that Nim's utterances were the result of "pure drill" and of cues unconsciously given by his trainers.... trained apes do not create new grammatical sentences of their own but only repeat fortuitous combinations of symbols they have used that resulted in reward.' (Hunt, *The Universe Within*, 213. See also Gardner, *Science, Good, Bad, and Bogus*, 393–7).

106 Crook, *The Evolution of Human Consciousness*, 73–87; Humphrey, *Consciousness Regained*, 20.

107 Humphrey, op cit, 6, 35ff, 52f.

108 ibid, 186.

109 Crook, op cit, 314–5.

110 Ken Wilber surveys current thinking on child mental development very well in his books, showing how each stage transcends the previous one, e.g. see *Eye to Eye*, 87–90. I have also used Atkinson, Atkinson, and Hilgard (*Introduction to Psychology*, p70): they say that a mental image of people and situations may be formed by eight months.

111 Fromm, quoted Dobzhansky, *The Biology of Ultimate Concern*, 68.

112 Some modern cognitive philosophers ascribe intentionality to non-self-aware states, and even to machines, but only by changing the meaning of the term.

113 Reverence for, and indeed fear of, unseen beings is presumably modelled on similar emotions originally felt for actual people, combined with wonder or awe at natural phenomena, including other animals.

114 The German philosopher G.W.F. Hegel went to great lengths to establish that human history is primarily a development of self-awareness. (*The Philosophy of History*, 321 and passim, and introduction by C.J. Friedrich (no page number).)

115 Neumann, *The Origins and History of Consciousness*, passim.

116 Wilber, *Up from Eden*, passim.

117 The table is based on a number of sources, including Leakey, Toth, Collins, Darlington, and Bowle. A number of quite important breakthroughs and discoveries have not been included in the table, either because so little seems to be known about them, or because they do not seem so closely connected with the development of self-reflective consciousness. In the biological sphere, there is the loss of oestrus (going on heat) in women. In the social sphere, they include the sexual division of labour, warfare, and the first cities. In the technical sphere: shelters, clothes, musical instruments, water transport,

spinning and weaving, the use of metals, pottery, wheeled transport, irrigation, and the plough.

Chapter 6

118 Toynbee, *Study of History*, 48–50.

119 ibid, 49.

120 Paul (*Nature into History*, 59–61) asserts (attacking Toynbee) that such myths refer to the beginnings of humanity, not of civilization. But perhaps they refer to both – to all breakthroughs.

121 Toynbee, op cit, 68.

122 Popper, *The Poverty of Historicism*, 110ff, and *The Open Society and its Enemies*, vol I, 231–2n.

123 Evans (in Bowle, *Concise Encyclopedia of World History*), 20. Roberts (*Pelican History of the World*, 63) supports the drought theory, adding that migrations forced by drought may have led to creative encounters between different cultures, resulting in a potential for civilizing ideas.

124 Quoted Daniel, *The First Civilizations*, 82.

125 Evans, op cit, 32–3.

126 Wheeler in Piggott (ed), *The Dawn of Civilization*, 248. Wheeler's emphasis.

127 Toynbee, *Study of History*, 75–6.

128 Toynbee, *Mankind and Mother Earth*, 148; and *Study of History*, 75.

129 Many of the earliest texts can be found in English translation in McNeil and Sedlar, *The Origins of Civilization*.

130 Wilber, *Up from Eden*, 104ff.

131 Jaynes, *The Origin of Consciousness…*, 211.

132 Jaspers, *The Origin and Goal of History*, 2. On Jaspers's axial age, also see ibid, 1–21, 51–2, 262–3, and his *The Way to Wisdom*, 98–102.

133 Hegel originated the idea (*The Philosophy of History*, 319), but, as a Christian, placed the axis at the time of Christ. (Jaspers was also a Christian, but stressed the need for an axis to history which would be empirically demonstrable and meaningful to people of all beliefs. *The Origin and Goal of History*, 1.) The period coincides with Jaspers's dating in two nineteenth-century sources that he cites: Viktor von Strauss and Lasaulx (ibid, 8). Jaspers was writing in 1949; before him, authorities describing the same period in similar terms include L.L. Whyte (*The Next Development in Man* (1944 edition), 10–11); Gerald Heard (*The Emergence of Man* (1931), 140–2); and T.W. Rhys Davids (*Buddhist India* (1903), 239–40). Since Jaspers's time, Ken Wilber (*Up from Eden*, 241ff) and Julian Jaynes (285–6) both come to the same conclusions, but do not credit Jaspers. Toynbee (*Mankind and Mother Earth*, 176–183) and other historians also emphasize the axial age.

134 Toynbee, *Mankind and Mother Earth*, 97–9, 109–10. Modern scholars are sceptical about this theory. See Hart, *A Dictionary of Egyptian Gods and Goddesses*, 45.

135 Ling, *The Buddha*, 94; see also 43–63.

136 Jaspers, *The Origin and Goal of History*, 51.

137 Toynbee, *Mankind and Mother Earth*, 179.

138 James, *Psychology*, 197; James's italics. More recent psychologists have called James's 'me' a person's 'identity'.

139 Whyte, *The Next Development in Man*, 59.

140 'Jataka Commentary', translated in Jennings, *The Vedantic Buddhism of the Buddha*, 8–9; and 'Middle Length Sayings', No 36, translated Nanamoli, *The Life of the Buddha*, 21.

141 *Anguttara Nikaya* III, 38, translated in Nanamoli, op cit, 9. Translation condensed.

142 Jaynes (*The Origin of Consciousness…*, 225–35, 312–3) associates this with the increasing silence of the voices of 'gods' as self-reflective consciousness intensified. Karl Popper calls it the 'strain of civilization', felt as the old, closed tribal society broke down (*The Open Society and its Enemies*, 176). Erich Fromm calls it 'the fear of freedom' (*The Fear of Freedom*, 27–9).

CHAPTER 7

143 Wilber gives some examples in exposing the confusion between 'pre subject–object' and 'post subject–object' (*Up From Eden*, 24n–25, 211; *Eye to Eye*, 215–261).

144 Wilber, *Up From Eden*, 130. William Blake's myths incorporate this pull as the 'female will' (Damon, *A Blake Dictionary*, 447–8, Frye, *Fearful Symmetry*, 75), and Jaspers speaks of the 'gravitational pull' (*The Origin and Goal of History*, 47).

145 Neumann, *The Origins and History of Consciousness*, 213–9.

146 Wilber, *Up From Eden*, 198.

147 Jaspers, *The Way to Wisdom*, 101.

148 Apparently Pythagoras founded an Order inculcating a programme of individual self-mastery, and introduced new ideas into Hellenic culture, probably including reincarnation. Gorman, *Pythagoras, a Life*, 113–31.

149 Characteristics of the emerging individual approximately as given by Erich Fromm (*Fear of Freedom*, 29) and by Sangharakshita ('The Axial Age …'). Referring to the new individual as 'him' does not imply that all were male, a point discussed in note 151.

150 Wilber, *Up From Eden*, 175. Gerald Heard has a similar hypothesis (*The Ascent of Humanity*, 67ff).

151 The predominance of men as contributors to axial age advances may of course be due to social barriers to this sort of achievement by women, or to the subsequent suppression of their work. The only ones I can think of in addition to Sappho are some of the Buddha's disciples, particularly Dhammadinna (see chapter 8), and, if she existed, Socrates' brilliant teacher Diotima. (See Plato, *The Symposium*, introduction by W. Hamilton, 19–20.) None of the biblical women seems to fit the bill.

152 Snell, *The Origins of Mind*, 60–66.

153 ibid, 66.

154 Whitehead, quoted (and challenged) by Antony Flew, *Introduction to Western Philosophy*, 41.

155 Jaspers, *The Origin and Goal of History*, 2.

156 On the distinction between ethnic and universal religions, see Geering, *Faith's New Age*, 35, 44. He calls universal religions 'post-Axial religions'. Leo Tolstoy makes a very similar distinction in *The Kingdom of God is Within You*, 105–6. Toynbee uses the term 'universal religion' occasionally, e.g. *Mankind and Mother Earth*, 295, as does Paul Johnson (*A History of Christianity*, 14). There is a great deal of overlap between the idea of a universal religion and that of a 'higher' religion (e.g. Toynbee, *An Historian's Approach to Religion*, 17 etc, and *A Study of History*, 563; Maslow, 'The "Core Religious" or "Transcendent" Experience'), a 'World' religion (e.g. Jaspers, *The Way to Wisdom*, 100), and to some extent the idea of 'personal religion' (James, *The Varieties of Religious Experience*, 29).

157 Geering, *Faith's New Age*, 35.

158 Evans-Pritchard, *Witchcraft, Oracles and Magic among the Azande*.

159 Smart, *The Religious Experience of Mankind*, 229.

160 Revealing examples are provided by Christianity in the Roman Empire (Johnson, *History of Christianity*, 67–103, 126) and Buddhism in China (Wright, *Buddhism in Chinese History*, passim).

161 See Smart, *The Religious Experience of Mankind*.

162 Lao Tsu (*sic*), *Tao Te Ching*, chapter 28.

163 e.g. Mark 3:31–5, 10:29–30; Matthew 5:19–28, 10:36, 12:46–50, 19:21–4; Luke 12:49–53, 14:25–7, 17:34–7, 18:28–30; John 2:4; I Corinthians, 7:8; etc. William Blake provides an excellent impression of Jesus' anti-ethnic stance, in 'The Everlasting Gospel'. See also his 'Annotations to Watson'; and Tolstoy's *My Religion*. For the universal character of Christianity, see Johnson, *History of Christianity*, 28, 34, 36.

CHAPTER 8

164 See Govinda, 'Consciousness Expansion and Disintegration', 77–81.

165 Simpson, *The Meaning of Evolution*, 168.

166 Davids, *Sakya*, 41–3.

167 A seeming paradox to newcomers to the study of Buddhism is how a man with such a distinct and powerful personality could teach the 'extinction' – or even illusion – of individuality. The problem is a false one, ascribable to misleading translations of Indian texts. It is true that the Buddha taught that there is no eternal soul, no core of unchanging ego behind a person's experience; yet he was certainly a 'true individual' and taught a path for the individual, though not a path of selfish individualism.

The German scholar Lama Govinda explains: 'Individuality is different from the illusion of egohood: the latter results in a mental and emotional imbalance and is the cause of suffering and unhappiness. Similarly the Buddha's individuality was not annihilated in the process of Enlightenment or by the experience of his universality. He did not "merge into the infinite" or "dissolve into the All", but led an active life for another forty years.' (Govinda, *Creative Meditation*, 40.)

The term 'true individuality' is used by the Buddhist scholar Edward Conze (*Buddhism*, 14), and in the writings of Sangharakshita.

168 Nanamoli, *The Life of the Buddha*, 18–19. The traditions concerning the Buddha's life as preserved in the Theravadin School are collected in Nanamoli's *The Life of the Buddha*. Two traditional Mahayana accounts, which contain beautiful poetry, and myth of great symbolic value, are the *Lalitavistara* (Gwendolyn Bays (trans.), *The Voice of the Buddha*), and Ashvaghosha's *Buddhacarita* (part in Conze's *Buddhist Scriptures*, 34–68). A good and concise modern introduction to Buddhism (chiefly from the Theravada angle) using the Buddha's life as its framework is Michael Carrithers's *The Buddha*.

169 'Buddhacarita', in Conze, *Buddhist Scriptures*, 50–1.

170 Nanamoli, op cit, 10.

171 *Udana*, Woodward's trans. (*Minor Anthologies*), 1.

172 For meanings of 'Dharma', see Conze, *Buddhist Thought in India*, 92–4.

173 Nanamoli, *The Life of the Buddha*, 37.

174 Woodward, *Some Sayings of the Buddha*, 221.

175 Nanamoli, op cit, 38. The text represents 'the god of a thousand worlds' (considered by Buddhists to be inferior to someone who has gained enlightenment) as entreating the Buddha to teach, upon which he contemplated the world as a lotus pool.

176 See Rhys Davids, *Sakya*, 18.

177 Woodward, *Some Sayings of the Buddha*, 25–6.

178 Nanamoli, *The Life of the Buddha*, 52, completed from Rhys Davids, *Sakya*, 293.

179 'Conditioned co-production' is Edward Conze's rendering of the Sanskrit *pratitya-samutpada* (Conze, *Buddhist Thought in India*, 156).

180 Von Glasenapp, quoted in Govinda, *Creative Meditation*, 8.

181 See Conze, op cit, 144–158.

182 Orders of conditionality (Pali *niyamas*): (1) the physical order (*utu-niyama*); (2) the biological order (*bija-niyama*); (3) the mental order (*mano-niyama* or *chitta-niyama*), corresponding to both mental and cultural evolution, (4) and (5) the karmic and transcendental orders (*kamma-niyama* and *dhamma-niyama*), corresponding to higher evolution (Narada Thera, *A Manual of Buddhism*, 87).

183 Barua, 'Buddhism as Buddha's Personal Religion' in *Ceylon Lectures*, 157. The source is in Horner (trans.), *Middle Length Sayings*, I, 367. Dhammadinna does not explain the difference in detail there.

184 ibid, 158. For traditional similes illustrating that enlightenment is not outside the conditioned process, see Conze (trans.), *The Perfection of Wisdom in Eight Thousand Lines*, 43.

185 See Appendix: 'Evolutionary ideas since Darwin'.

186 Criticisms of Heraclitus based on Popper, *The Open Society and its Enemies*, 14–17.

187 Condensed by Rahula (*What the Buddha Taught*, 11) from Horner, *Middle Length Sayings of the Pali Canon* (vol. I, 260–1). The teachings on *shunyata* (emptiness) provide the same sort of safeguard.

CHAPTER 9

188 Toynbee, *Mankind and Mother Earth*, 413.

189 Stutley, *Dictionary of Hinduism*, 178. See also Kempers, *Ageless Borobudur*, 177–180.

190 Govinda, *Psycho-Cosmic Symbolism in the Buddhist Stupa*, 66. They are enumerated in Roth, 'Symbolism of the Buddhist Stupa', 187–90.

191 'Satipatthana Sutta', in Nyanaponika Thera, *The Heart of Buddhist Meditation*, 117ff; see also p191; and Kato et al, *Threefold Lotus Sutra*, 64.

192 Govinda, *Psycho-Cosmic Symbolism in the Buddhist Stupa*, 63; also *The Psychological Attitude of Early Buddhist Philosophy*, 70.

193 Govinda, *Psycho-Cosmic Symbolism in the Buddhist Stupa*, 63. Soni (*The Only Way to Deliverance*, 71–3) also sees the path of ethics, meditation, and wisdom as a spiral, as does Sangharakshita (*Guide to the Buddhist Path*, 94ff).

194 Reid, *Evolutionary Theory*, 356. Others likening evolution to a spiral include Gerald Heard (*The Ascent of Humanity*, pp.xii and 18); Dobzhansky, (*The Biology of Ultimate Concern*, 24); and Neumann (*The Origins and History of Consciousness*, 18).

195 *The Anapanasati Sutta*, translated by Nanamoli, *Mindfulness of Breathing*, 10–13. I have removed some of the repetition.

196 Amadeo Solé-Leris, *Tranquillity and Insight*, 121; see also Nyanaponika, *The Vision of Dhamma*, 198–9.

197 e.g. Nyanaponika Thera, *Heart of Buddhist Meditation*.

198 Teilhard de Chardin, *The Phenomenon of Man*, 165.

199 e.g. Jaynes, *The Origin of Consciousness* ..., 27, 42. Mindfulness and alienated watching: see Sangharakshita, *A Guide to the Buddhist Path* (170–3). A similar distinction is made in Govinda, *Creative Meditation* ..., 125–130.

200 Integrated awareness is very similar to the 'flow' experience in M. Csikszent-mihalyi's studies of leisure etc. Crook, *The Evolution of Human Consciousness* 318–326).

201 Teitsaro Suzuki (trans.), *The Awakening of Faith* ..., 75–8. Suzuki translates *manas* as ego, *alaya vijnana* as all-conserving mind, and *manaskara* as attention. The word 'unconsciously' in the penultimate sentence is absent in other translations. *The Awakening of Faith* is ascribed to the first century master Ashvaghosha, but is probably a Chinese work of the sixth century or before. This is a work of the Yogacharin School. For more information on their view of the evolution of mind, see Sangharakshita, *A Survey of Buddhism*, 392ff, and Suzuki, *Outlines of Mahayana Buddhism*, 128f. For another Buddhist account of the importance of 'awareness of being aware', see Conze, *Buddhist Thought in India*, 268.

202 There is a common misunderstanding that the Buddha's denial of the reality of the *atman* (a permanent, self-existent, separate ego-entity) means that Buddhism denies everybody's experience of themselves, the 'empirical self'. It does not. See note 167, and Puliganbha, *Fundamentals of Indian Philosophy*, 65–7; Sangharakshita, *Progress and Religion*, 9–18.

203 The Buddha provides a clear explanation of this in F.L. Woodward (trans.), *Kindred Sayings*, V, 53; and in Horner (trans.), *Middle Length Sayings*, II, 87–90. Sometimes neutral mental states are referred to as well.

204 For a fuller treatment of karma, see Govinda, *The Psychological Attitude of Early Buddhist Philosophy*, 53–9.

205 These ways of applying energy are the 'four right efforts'. See Guenther, *Philosophy and Psychology in the Abhidharma*, 237; and Rhys Davids (trans.), *Dialogues of the Buddha*, III, 215.

206 William Blake, 'Auguries of Innocence'.

207 Walshe (trans.), *Thus Have I Heard*, 111.

208 See Lati Rinboche et al, *Meditative States in Tibetan Buddhism*, 53–73, 173–4. The authors say it can be physical as well as mental, but they seem to conflate tranquillity with rapture (p74).

209 Sanskrit *rupa-loka*. The higher reaches of the meditative sphere are termed 'formless' (*arupa-loka*) – see note 217.

210 *Visuddhi Magga*, quoted Solé-Leris, *Tranquillity and Insight*, 31. J.M. Reynolds comments: '[The] Buddha was quite familiar with the experience of Cosmic Consciousness, of merging one's individual finite consciousness for a time in the totality of nature or the infinity of space ... but nowhere does he say that such transpersonal experiences are the ultimate goal of human evolution, as some current writers on transpersonal psychology would have us believe.' (*Self-Liberation...*, 100.)

211 The equanimity of the absorptions is of a more limited character than equanimity as a Factor of Enlightenment, which has a transcendental significance.

212 Chang (trans.), *The Hundred Thousand Songs of Milarepa*, I, 128.

213 *Anguttara*, I, 102, quoted Johansson, *The Dynamic Psychology of Early Buddhism*, 199.

214 Sangharakshita, *Mind – Reactive and Creative*, 19–20.

215 Sangharakshita, *A Survey of Buddhism*, 135–40.

216 Conze, *Buddhist Thought in India*, 89.

217 A further four absorptions are listed, called 'formless', sometimes regarded as higher levels than those of the level of pure form. Other texts treat of them as levels within the fourth absorption of pure form, and yet others seem to imply that they represent a separate way of describing higher states of consciousness. Meditating on equanimity is said to lead to the third formless absorption, 'no-thing-ness'. (Woodward (trans.), *Kindred Sayings* V, 101).

218 That the Factors of Enlightenment culminate in transcendental insight is indicated in several suttas of the *Kindred Sayings* V, e.g. 57, 108–9, 114–5. See also Solé-Leris, *Tranquillity and Insight*, 120–1.

CHAPTER 10

219 Milton, *Paradise Lost*, iii, 51–5.

220 The traditional teaching is of the five *indriyas*, or spiritual faculties: *shraddha* (see text), energy, mindfulness, meditation (samadhi), and wisdom. See Conze, *The Way to Wisdom*.

221 The inner 'eye' which opens in deep meditation is traditionally called the *divya-chakshus*, or divine eye.

222 As a new visionary 'sense' organ, wisdom is termed the *dharma-chakshus*, or eye of truth. The commonest Buddhist term for it is *prajna*, or more specifically *bhavana-mayi-prajna* or *prajnaparamita*. Another important term referring to this faculty, usually translated as insight, is *vipashyana*. (All Sanskrit).

223 Buddhist tradition includes other types of living beings, in addition to humans and animals, in its system of levels of consciousness.

224 Guenther, *Mind in Buddhist Psychology*, 38–42.

225 'Abhidharmasamuccaya', quoted ibid, 38.

226 Suzuki, *Outlines of Mahayana Buddhism*, 303–6.

227 Suzuki (trans.), *The Awakening of Faith*, 112–3.

228 e.g. *The Gandavyuha Sutra*, passim (Cleary's translation: Entering the Realm of Reality).

229 Chang (trans.), *The Hundred Thousand Songs of Milarepa*, I, 128–9. The bodhi-heart (Sanskrit *bodhichitta*) is the will to enlightenment. For the path to wisdom, see also Conze, *The Way to Wisdom*, 21–2.

230 Quoted in Suzuki, *Essays in Zen Buddhism*, first series, 254–5. Ganto was a famous Chinese Zen master, the story of whose tragic death had greatly troubled Hakuin. It is important to note that every description of an insight experience is quite unique, and that the flavour of such accounts varies from school to school. In Zen Buddhism, the experiences of *satori* and *kensho* are arguably equivalent to insight (see Kapleau, *The Three Pillars of Zen*, 336, 344).

231 E. Conze, *Buddhist Thought in India*, 166.

232 This is an idea found in the so-called 'Lesser Vehicle' texts, including those preserved in Pali by the Theravadin School, where one who has reached the point of no return is called a 'stream entrant' (Sanskrit *shrotapanna*). Those texts which treat of the attainment of the transcendental level in terms of the arising of the will to enlightenment sometimes state that it is possible to suffer a setback in spiritual progress even after this point, by losing touch with the altruistic will to enlightenment and falling on to a 'lower path' of spiritual individualism.

233 Davids (trans.), *The Psalms of the Sisters*, 72–3.

234 The traditional Eightfold Path, Three Trainings, and Six Perfections (see Conze, *Buddhist thought in India*, 215) are all sometimes described as being traversed twice, as mundane and transcendental paths.

235 Sangharakshita, *The Taste of Freedom*, 13–17. The Sanskrit terms are (1) *satkaya-drishti*, (2) *vichikitsa*, and (3) *shilavrata-paramarsha*.

236 See Har Dayal, *The Bodhisattva doctrine in Buddhist Sanskrit Literature*, 9; Conze, *Selected Sayings from the Perfection of Wisdom*, 35–7.

237 The term 'bodhisattva' is also sometimes applied to those who have taken a series of formal bodhisattva vows, possibly incorporated in a 'bodhisattva ordination'. They are called novice bodhisattvas, although the will to enlight-enment may still be dormant. Bodhisattvas can also be the male and female forms representing aspects of enlightenment, which are objects of devotion, and of visualization in certain meditation practices. (Sangharakshita, 'The Bodhisattva Hierarchy', 11–21; Dayal, *The Bodhisattva Doctrine*, 9.)

238 See Conze, *Buddhist Thought in India*, 160.

239 *Tathagataguhya Sutra*, quoted by Shantideva, *Shiksa-Samuccaya* (Bendall and Ruse translation), 8. Bodhichitta is translated in this reference as 'thought of Enlightenment'.

240 Shantideva, ibid, 173; Suzuki, *Outlines ...*, 297–302.

For eulogies of the will to enlightenment, see Shantideva, *A Guide to the*

Bodhisattva's Way of Life, 33–4, and the *Gandavyuha Sutra*, e.g. the section quoted by Shantideva in Bendall and Ruse, op. cit, 5–6.

241 Saint Exupéry, *Wind, Sand and Stars*, 37.

242 See Sangharakshita, *The Bodhisattva Principle*.

Conclusion

243 Hughes, *A High Wind in Jamaica*, 94–6.

244 Quoted in Lu K'uan Yu's *Ch'an and Zen Teachings*, First Series, 67.

245 Hakuin, in Suzuki, *Manual of Zen Buddhism*, 151.

246 Tsongkhapa, *The Principal Teachings of Buddhism*, 118.

247 Xu Yun: see Luk, *Empty Cloud*; Shinran: see Ueda (ed.), *Letters of Shinran*; Yeshe Tsogyal, see Dowman, *Sky Dancer*; Dharmapala: see Sangharakshita, *Flame in Darkness*.

248 Shantideva, *A Guide to the Bodhisattva's Way of Life*, 89. (The first stanza roughly quotes a text ascribed to the Buddha, who lists a whole range of animals: dogs, vultures, crows etc, as well as insects; ibid, 182n.)

Appendix

249 Bulfinch's *Mythology*, p15.

250 Wiener, *Dictionary of the History of Ideas*. Taoism: Needham, *Science and Civilization in China*, II, 79–80.

251 Reese. Plato's nephew, Speusippus, is said to have been an ardent evolutionist (Findlay, *Plato: the Written and Unwritten Doctrines*).

252 Lovejoy, *The Great Chain of Being*.

253 Radhakrishnan, pp181–3, 198.

254 Sangharakshita, *A Survey of Buddhism*, 27–29.

255 Gombrich (*Theravada Buddhism*, 85) supports this view, as does T.W. Rhys Davids (*Dialogues of the Buddha*, Part 1, 107).

256 Pali *samvatta* and *vivatta*; alternatively 'contraction and expansion': (Walshe (trans.), *Thus Have I Heard*, 74).

257 ibid, 411.

258 From five versions: Walshe, op cit, 409–14; Jones (trans.), *Mahavastu*, vol. I, 285–294; Buddhaghosha, *Visuddhi Magga*, in Warren, *Buddhism in Translations*, 324–7; the Sanskrit *Ekottara*, from a Chinese translation in Conze *et al* (ed.), *Buddhist Texts Through the Ages*, 283–5; *Crystal Mirror*, 1984, 13–14. The last source seems to derive from the Sarvastivadin Vinaya. The *Mahavastu* account confirms that the radiant beings were reborn in this world in order to work towards nirvana (p285).

259 Walshe, op cit, 399–403.

260 e.g. ibid, 381.

261 Davids, *Stories of the Buddha*, xix. The bodhisattva is never represented as female in the birth stories (Jones, *Tales and Teachings of the Buddha*, 20).

262 Rhys Davids, *Stories of the Buddha*, 149–53. It is interesting that the Buddha told this story, tradition says, when discussing the value of seeking the welfare of one's kin. Now, feats of courage and self-sacrifice in defence of the troop are well known among the macaque group of monkeys (an early illustration of

this birth story from the Bharat Stupa shows monkeys of this type), and are ascribed to kin-selection. The idea is that it is genetically worth while to risk your life if you save the lives of close relatives, since they carry similar genes to yours. However, despite the naturalistic observation of much of this two-thousand-year-old story, it is important as a moral fable, and not for its portrayal of animal behaviour.

263 Olschak and Wangyal, *Mystic Art of Ancient Tibet*, 108–9.

264 Hyde-Chambers, *Tibetan Folk Tales*, 1–2.

265 From Wangyal, *The Door of Liberation*, 33–4, Dharma Publishing's *Ancient Tibet*, 102–4, and Tarthang, 'A History of the Buddhist Dharma', 132.

266 These points are supported by the scholar David Snellgrove (*Indo-Tibetan Buddhism*, 521–2).

267 Koestler, *The Act of Creation*, 132.

268 *Origin of Species*, 55. 'Dr Darwin' is Erasmus, Charles Darwin's grandfather, who wrote his chief treatise (*The Botanic Garden*: for which William Blake provided some engravings) in rhymed heroic couplets!

269 Hoyle, *Evolution from Space*, 170ff; Hitching, *The Neck of the Giraffe*, 231–2.

270 Coleman, 72.

271 The term 'evolution', in its modern biological sense, was first used by the geologist Charles Lyell in 1832, when discussing Lamarck's views.

272 See note 2.

273 Pierre Teilhard de Chardin, *The Phenomenon of Man*.

274 Bennett, *The Wisdom of the Aryas*, 112–4.

275 Cope, *Christians in the Class Struggle*, quoted Popper, *The Open Society and its Enemies*, 203n.

276 Midgeley, *Evolution as a Religion*, 34.

277 See Pierre Teilhard de Chardin, *The Phenomenon of Man*.

278 e.g. Herbert Spencer, *First Principles*; Bernal, *The World, the Flesh and the Devil* (1929), etc; see Midgeley, 34–40, 60–63.

BIBLIOGRAPHY

Books are published in London unless another town is given.

Atkinson, R.L., R.C. Atkinson, and E.R. Hildegard, *Introduction to Psychology* (8th edn), Harcourt, New York 1983

Aurobindo, Sri, *The Life Divine*, India Library Society, New York 1965 (1st edn 1949)

Barua, B.M., *Ceylon Lectures*, Bharati Mahavidyalaya, Calcutta 1945

Bateson, G., *Mind and Nature: A Necessary Unity*, Wildwood House 1979

Bateson, G., *Steps to an Ecology of Mind*, Granada 1973

Bateson, P., 'The Active Role of Behaviour in Evolution' in M.-W. Ho and S.W. Fox, *Evolutionary Processes and Metaphors*, 191–207, Wiley 1988

Bays, G. (trans), *The Voice of the Buddha*, Dharma, Berkeley 1983

Bendall, C. and W.H.P. Ruse (trans), *Shiksa-Samuccaya of Shantideva*, Motilal, Delhi 1974 (1st edn 1922)

Bennett, A., *The Wisdom of the Aryas*, Kegan Paul 1923

Bergson, H., *Creative Evolution*, Macmillan 1911

Bernal, J.D., *The World, the Flesh and the Devil*, Cape 1970 (1st edn 1929)

Birch, C. and J.B. Cobb, *The Liberation of Life*, Cambridge University Press, Cambridge 1981

Blake, W., *Complete Writings*, (ed Geoffrey Keynes), Oxford University Press 1966

Blavatsky, H.P., *Isis Unveiled*, Theosophical University Press 1960 (1st edn 1877)

Blavatsky, H.P., *The Secret Doctrine* (2 vols), Theosophical University Press 1963 (1st edn 1888–97) (1938 edn of Theosophical Publishing House, Adyar, also used)

Bonner, J.T., *The Evolution of Culture in Animals*, Princeton University Press, Princeton 1980

Bowle, J., *The Concise Encyclopedia of World History*, Hutchinson 1971 (1st edn 1958)

Bucke, R.M., *Cosmic Consciousness: A Study in the Evolution of the Human Mind*, Olympia Press 1972 (1st edn c.1900)

Bulfinch, T., *Mythology*, Dill, New York 1959

Carrithers, M., *The Buddha*, Oxford University Press, Oxford 1983

Cavalli-Sforza, L.L., and M.W. Feldon, *Cultural Transmission and Evolution*, Princeton University Press, Princeton 1981

Chang, G.C.C. (trans), *The Hundred Thousand Songs of Milarepa*, Shambhala, Boulder 1977

Childe, C. G., *Man Makes Himself*, Watts 1941 (1st edn 1936)

Cleary, T. (trans), *Entry into the Realm of Reality*, Shambhala, Boston 1987

Coleman, W., *Biology in the Nineteenth Century: Problems of Form, Function and Transformation*, Wiley 1971

Collins, D., *The Human Revolution from Ape to Artist*, Phaidon, Oxford 1976

Conze, E., *Buddhist Texts Through the Ages*, Shambhala, Boston 1990

Conze, E., *Buddhist Scriptures*, Penguin, Harmondsworth 1959

Conze, E., *The Way to Wisdom*, Wheel, Buddhist Publication Society, Kandy 1980

Conze, E., *Buddhist Thought in India*, Allen & Unwin 1962

Conze, E. (trans), *The Perfection of Wisdom in 8,000 Lines*, Four Seasons Foundation, San Francisco 1973

Crook, J.H., *The Evolution of Human Consciousness*, Oxford University Press, Oxford 1980

Crutchfield, J.P., Farmer, Packard and Shaw, 'Chaos' in *Scientific American*, December 1986

Damon, S.F., *A Blake Dictionary*, Thames & Hudson 1973

Daniel, G., *The First Civilizations: The Archaeology of Their Origins*, Thames & Hudson 1968

Darlington, C.D., *The Evolution of Man and Society*, Allen & Unwin 1969

Darwin, C., *The Origin of Species by Means of Natural Selection*, Penguin 1968 (1st edn 1859)

Davids, C.R. (trans), *Psalms of the Sisters*, Pali Text Society/Luzac 1980 (1st edn 1909)

Davids, C.R. (trans), *Stories of the Buddha*, Dover, New York 1989 (1st edn 1929)

Davids, C.R., *Sakya, or Buddhist Origins*, Oriental Books Reprint Corp., New Delhi 1978 (1st edn 1928)

Davids, T.W.R., *Buddhist India*, Motilal Banarsidass, Delhi 1971 (1st edn c.1903)

Davids, T.W.R. (trans), *Dialogues of the Buddha*, vol I, Pali Text Society/Routledge 1899

Davids, T.W.R. and C.A.F.R. (trans), *Dialogues of the Buddha*, vol III, Pali Text Society/Luzac 1957

Dawkins, R., *The Selfish Gene*, Granada 1978

Dayal, H., *The Bodhisattva Doctrine in Buddhist Sanskrit Literature*, Motilal, Delhi 1932

Dharma Publishing (no author), *Ancient Tibet*, Dharma Publishing, California 1986

Dobzhansky, T., *The Biology of Ultimate Concern*, Collins 1971 (1st edn 1967)

Dobzhansky, T., *The Genetics of the Evolutionary Process*, Columbia University Press 1970

Dowman, K. (trans), *Sky Dancer*, Routledge & Kegan Paul 1984

Dunbar, R., 'Common Ground for Thought' in *New Scientist*, 7 January 1989, 48–50

Durrell, L., *Clea*, Faber 1960

Eiseley, L., *The Unexpected Universe*, Penguin, Harmondsworth 1973 (1st edn 1964)

Eldridge, N., *Time Frames*, Simon & Schuster, New York 1984

Eliot, G., *Daniel Deronda*, Panther 1970 (lst edn 1876)

Evans-Pritchard, E.E., *Witchcraft, Oracles and Magic Among the Azande*, Clarendon, Oxford 1937

Evans-Wentz, E., *Tibetan Yoga and Secret Doctrines*, Oxford University Press 1958 (1st edn 1935)

Findlay, J.N., *Plato: the Written and Unwritten Doctrines*, Routledge & Kegan Paul 1974

Flew, A., *Darwinian Evolution*, Granada 1984

Flew, A., *An Introduction to Western Philosophy*, Thames & Hudson 1971

Fromm, E., *The Fear of Freedom*, Kegan Paul 1942

Frye, N., *Fearful Symmetry*, Princeton University Press, Princeton 1969 (1st edn 1947)

Galef, B.G., 'Social Transmission of Acquired Behaviour' in *Advances in the Study of Behaviour*, vol 6, 77–100, New York 1976

Gardner, M., *Science, Good, Bad and Bogus*, Oxford University Press, Oxford 1981

Geering, L., *Faith's New Age*, Collins 1980

Gombrich, R., *Theravada Buddhism*, Routledge & Kegan Paul 1990

Gorman, P., *Pythagoras, A Life*, Routledge & Kegan Paul 1979

Goudge, T.A., *The Ascent of Life: A Philosophical Study of the Theory of Evolution*, Allen & Unwin 1961

Gould, S.J., *Wonderful Life*, Penguin, Harmondsworth 1991

Govinda, Lama, *Foundations of Tibetan Mysticism*, Rider 1960

Govinda, Lama, *Creative Meditation and Multi-Dimensional Consciousness*, Unwin 1976

Govinda, Lama, *The Psychological Attitude of Early Buddhist Philosophy*, Rider 1961

Govinda, Lama, 'Consciousness Expansion and Disintegration vs. Concentration and Spiritual Regeneration' in *Middle Way*, xlvi (2), 77–81 (August 1971)

Govinda, Lama, *Psycho-Cosmic Symbolism of the Buddhist Stupa*, Dharma, Emeryville 1976 (1st edn 1935 (part))

Gregory, R.L. (ed), *The Oxford Companion to the Mind*, Oxford University Press 1987

Griffin, D.R., *The Question of Animal Awareness*, Rockefeller University Press 1976

Guenther, H., *Philosophy and Psychology of the Abhidharma*, Shambhala, Berkeley 1976

Guenther, H., *Mind in Buddhist Psychology*, Dharma, Emeryville 1975

Hammond, P.M., 'The Origin and Development of Reproductive Barriers' in Forey, P. (ed), *The Evolving Biosphere*, Cambridge University Press 1981

Hardy, A., *The Living Stream*, Collins 1965

Hardy, A., *Darwin and the Spirit of Man*, Collins 1984

Hardy, A., *The Spiritual Nature of Man*, Oxford University Press, Oxford 1979

Hart, G., *A Dictionary of Egyptian Gods and Goddesses*, Routledge & Kegan Paul 1988

Heard, G., *The Emergence of Man*, Cape 1931

Heard, G., *The Ascent of Humanity*, Cape 1929

Herrick, C.J., *The Evolution of Human Nature*, Harper, New York 1961 (1st edn 1956)

Hitching, F., *The Neck of the Giraffe: or Where Darwin Went Wrong*, Pan 1982

Horner, I.B. (trans), *Middle Length Sayings*, vols I & II, (Pali Text Society/Luzac) 1954 and 1957

Hoyle, F. and C. Wickramasinghe, *Evolution from Space*, Granada 1981

Hughes, R., *A High Wind in Jamaica*, Penguin 1971 (1st edn 1929)

Humphrey, N., *Consciousness Regained*, Oxford University Press 1984

Humphrey, N., *A History of the Mind*, Simon & Schuster, New York 1992

Hunt, M., *The Universe Within: A New Science Explores the Human Mind*, Corgi 1984 (1st edn 1982)

Huxley, J., *Evolution in Action*, Scientific Book Club, undated (1st edn 1953)

Huxley, J., 'The Evolutionary Vision' in S. Tax (ed), *Evolution After Darwin*, vol III, 249–61

Huxley, J., *Evolution, the Modern Synthesis*, Allen & Unwin 1942

Hyde-Chambers, F. and A., *Tibetan Folk Tales*, Shambhala, Boston 1981

James, W., *Psychology: The Briefer Course*, Premier, Fawcett Publ, NY/University of Notre Dame Press, Indiana 1985, 1963 (1st edn 1892)

James, W., *The Varieties of Religious Experience*, Longmans 1952 (1st edn 1902)

Jaspers, K., *The Origin and Goal of History*, Routledge & Kegan Paul 1953 (1st edn 1949)

Jaspers, K., *Way to Wisdom: An Introduction to Philosophy*, Yale University Press 1954

Jaynes, J., *The Origin of Consciousness in the Breakdown of the Bicameral Mind*, Penguin 1982 (1st edn 1976)

Jennings, I., *The Vedantic Buddhism of the Buddha*, Motilal, Delhi 1947

Jerison, H.J., 'On the Evolution of Mind' in D.A. Oakley (ed), *Brain and Mind*, Methuen 1985

Johansson, R.E.A., *The Dynamic Psychology of Early Buddhism*, Curzon Press, Oxford 1979

Johnson, P., *A History of Christianity*, Penguin 1980 (1st edn 1976)

Jones, J.G., *Tales and Teachings of the Buddha: The Jataka Tales in Relation to the Pali Canon*, Allen & Unwin 1986

Jones, J.J. (trans), *The Mahavastu*, vol I, Luzac 1949

Jung, C.G., *Jung: Selected Writings*, (ed A. Storr), Collins 1983

Kapleau, P., *The Three Pillars of Zen*, Beacon Press, Boston 1965

Kato, B. *et al* (trans), *The Threefold Lotus Sutra*, Weatherhill, New York 1975

Kaufmann, W., *Nietzsche*, Princeton University Press, Princeton N.J. 1974

Kempers, A.J. Bernet, *Ageless Borobudur*, Servire/Wassenaar 1976

Kennedy, A., *The Buddhist Vision*, Rider 1985

Kloetzli, R., *Buddhist Cosmology*, Motilal, Delhi 1983

Klopfer, P.H. and J.P. Hailman, *An Introduction to Animal Behaviour: Ethology's First Century*, Prentice Hall, Englewood Cliffs 1967

Koehler, O., 'Nonverbal Thinking' in B. Grzimek (ed), *Grzimek's Encyclopedia of Ethology*, Van Nostrand, New York 1977

Koestler, A., *The Ghost in the Machine*, Macmillan 1967

Lao Tsu, *Tao Te Ching*, trans. G.-F. Feng and J. English, Wildwood House 1972

Lawrence, D.H., *Phoenix*, Heinemann 1936

Leakey, R.E., *The Making of Mankind*, Michael Joseph 1981

Lewin, R., 'The Great Brain Race' in *New Scientist* (supplement), 5 December 1992

Lewontin, R.C., 'Adaptation' in *Scientific American*, September 1978

Ling, T., *The Buddha*, Penguin, Harmondsworth 1976 (1st edn 1973)

Lovejoy, A.O., *The Great Chain of Being*, Harvard University Press, London 1964 (1st edn 1936)

Lu K.Y., *Ch'an and Zen Teaching*, First Series, Century 1987 (1st edn 1960)

Luk, C., *Empty Cloud*, Element 1988

Lumsden, C. and E.O. Wilson, *Genes, Mind and Culture: The Coevolutionary Process*, Harvard University Press 1981

Marais, E., *The Soul of the Ape*, Penguin 1973 (1st edn 1969)

Maslow, A., 'The "Core-Religious" or "Transcendent" Experience' in White, J., *The Highest State of Consciousness*, Anchor, Doubleday, New York 1972

Mayr, E., *Animal Species and Evolution*, Harvard University Press 1963

Mayr, E., *The Growth of Biological Thought*, Harvard University Press, Cambridge 1982

McFarland, D. (ed), *The Oxford Companion to Animal Behaviour*, Oxford University Press, Oxford 1987

McNeill, W.H. and J.W. Sedlar, *The Origins of Civilization*, Oxford University Press, Oxford 1968

Melville, H., *Moby Dick*, Penguin, Harmondsworth 1972 (1st edn 1851)

Midgeley, M., *Evolution as a Religion*, Methuen 1985

Milton, J., *Paradise Lost*, Penguin 1989 (1st edn 1667)

Monod, J., *Chance and Necessity*, Collins 1974 (1st edn 1970)

Nanamoli, Ven., *Mindfulness of Breathing*, Buddhist Publication Society, Kandy 1964 (2nd edn)

Nanamoli, Ven., *The Life of the Buddha*, Buddhist Publication Society, Kandy 1972

Narada Thera, *A Manual of Buddhism* (4th edn), Associated Newspapers of Ceylon, Colombo 1953

Needham, J., *Science and Civilization in China*, vol II, Cambridge University Press 1962

Neumann, E., *The Origins and History of Consciousness*, Princeton University Press, Princeton 1970 (1st German edn 1949)

Nyanaponika Thera, *The Heart of Buddhist Meditation*, Rider 1962

Nyanaponika Thera, *Vision of Dharma*, Rider 1962

Oakley, D.A. (ed), *Brain and Mind*, Methuen 1985

Odling-Smee, F.J., 'Niche-Constructing Phenotypes' in Plotkin, H.C., *The Role of Behaviour in Evolution*, MIT Press, Cambridge, Mass. 1988

Olschak, B.S. and T. Wangyal, *Mystic Art of Ancient Tibet*, Allen & Unwin 1973

Ornstein, R.E., *The Psychology of Consciousness*, Freeman, San Francisco 1972

Pallis, M., *A Buddhist Spectrum*, Allen & Unwin 1980

Patterson, C., *Evolution*, Routledge & Kegan Paul 1978

Paul, L., *Nature Into History*, Faber & Faber 1957

Perry, R.B., *Thought and Character of William James*, publisher unknown 1935

Piaget, J., *Behaviour and Evolution*, Routledge & Kegan Paul 1979 (1st edn 1976)

Plato, *The Symposium*, Penguin 1951

Plotkin, H.C., *The Role of Behaviour in Evolution*, MIT Press, Cambridge, Mass. 1988

Popper, K., *The Poverty of Historicism*, Routledge & Kegan Paul 1961 (1st edn 1957)

Popper, K., *Unended Quest*, Collins 1976

Popper, K., *Objective Knowledge*, Clarendon, Oxford 1972

Popper, K.R., *The Open Society and Its Enemies*, Routledge & Kegan Paul 1966 (1st edn 1945)

Puliganbha, R., *Fundamentals of Indian Philosophy*, Abingdon Press, New York 1975

Radhakrishnan, S., *Indian Philosophy* (vol I), Allen & Unwin 1929 (1st edn 1923)

Rahula, W., *What the Buddha Taught*, Grove Press, New York 1974 (1st edn 1959)

Ratnaprabha (J.R. Cooper), 'A Re-Emergence of Buddhism' in P. Clarke, *The New Evangelists*, Ethnographia 1987

Reese, W.C., *Dictionary of Philosophy and Religion*, Harvester 1980

Reid, R.G.B., *Evolutionary Theory: The Unfinished Synthesis*, Croom Helm 1985

Rensch, B., *Homo Sapiens: From Man to Demigod*, Methuen 1972

Reynolds, J.M. (trans), *Self-Liberation Through Seeing With Naked Awareness*, Station Hill, New York 1989

Ridley, M., *The Problems of Evolution*, Oxford University Press 1985

Rinboche, Lati *et al*, *Meditative States in Tibetan Buddhism*, Wisdom 1983

Roberts, J.M., *The Pelican History of the World*, Penguin, Harmondsworth 1980

Roe, A. and G.G. Simpson (eds), *Behavior and Evolution*, Yale University Press, London 1958

Roth, G., 'Symbolism of the Buddhist Stupa' in A.L. Dallapiccola (ed), *The Stupa*, Wiesbaden 1980

St Exupéry, A. de, *Wind, Sand and Stars*, Penguin 1966

St Exupéry, A. de, *Wisdom of the Sands*, Hollis & Carter 1952

Sangharakshita, 'The Axial Age and the Emergence of the New Man' (taped lecture), Dharmachakra Tapes, Cambridge 1969

Sangharakshita, 'The Bodhisattva Hierarchy' in *Mitrata* no.38, October 1987

Sangharakshita, 'The Bodhisattva Principle' in *The Priceless Jewel*, Windhorse, Glasgow 1983

Sangharakshita (trans), *The Dhammapada* (some chapters), privately circulated

Sangharakshita, 'Evolution, Lower and Higher' (taped lecture), Dharmachakra Tapes, Cambridge 1969

Sangharakshita, *Flame in Darkness: the Life and Sayings of Anagarika Dharmapala*, Triratna Grantha Mala, Pune 1980

Sangharakshita, *A Guide to the Buddhist Path*, 170–3, Windhorse, Glasgow 1990

Sangharakshita, *Mind – Reactive and Creative*, Windhorse, Birmingham 1995

Sangharakshita, *Progress and Religion*, Triratna Grantha Mala, Pune 1985

Sangharakshita, *A Survey of Buddhism*, Windhorse, Glasgow 1993 (1st edn 1957)

Sangharakshita, *The Taste of Freedom*, Windhorse, Glasgow 1990 (1st edn 1985)

Sangharakshita, *The Three Jewels*, Windhorse, Glasgow 1991 (1st edn 1967)

Schubert-Soldern, R., *Mechanism and Vitalism*, University of Notre Dame Press 1962

Schumann, K.W., *The Historical Buddha*, Penguin 1989

Shantideva, *A Guide to the Bodhisattva's Way of Life* (trans S. Batchelor), Library of Tibetan Works and Archives, Dharamsala 1979

Simpson, G.G., 'The Baldwin Effect' in *Evolution*, vol 7 (1953), 110–117

Simpson, G.G., *The Meaning of Evolution*, New American Library, Mentor 1951 (1st edn 1949)

Smart, N., *The Religious Experience of Mankind*, Collins, Glasgow 1971

Smith, J.M., *The Theory of Evolution*, Penguin 1975 (1st edn 1958)

Smith, J.M., *On Evolution*, Edinburgh University Press 1972

Smith, J.M., 'The Birth of Sociobiology' in *New Scientist* 26 September 1985, 48–50

Snell, B., *The Discovery of the Mind in Greek Philosophy and Literature*, Harper New York 1960 (1st edn 1948, trans 1953)

Snellgrove, D., *Indo-Tibetan Buddhism*, Serindia 1987

Solé-Leris, A., *Tranquillity and Insight*, Rider 1986

Soni, R.L., *The Only Way to Deliverance*, Prajna, Boulder 1980

Spencer, H., *First Principles*, Watts 1937 (1st edn 1862)

Stenhouse, D., *The Evolution of Intelligence*, Allen & Unwin 1974

Storr, A., *Solitude*, Collins 1989

Stutley, J. and M., *A Dictionary of Hinduism: Its Mythology, Folklore and Development, 1500BC–AD 1500*, Routledge & Kegan Paul 1977

Suzuki, D.T., *Manual of Zen Buddhism*, Rider 1950

Suzuki, D.T., *Essays in Zen Buddhism*, I, Rider 1970 (1st edn 1949)

Suzuki, D.T., *Outlines of Mahayana Buddhism*, Schoken, New York 1963 (1st edn 1907)

Suzuki, D.T. (trans), *The Awakening of Faith in the Mahayana*, Open Court, Chicago 1900

Tarthang Tulku, 'A History of the Buddhist Dharma' in *Crystal Mirror V*, Dharma, Emeryville 1977

Taylor, G.R., *The Natural History of the Mind*, Secker & Warburg 1979

Taylor, G.R., *The Great Evolution Mystery*, Sphere 1984 (1st edn 1983)

Teilhard de Chardin, P., *The Phenomenon of Man*, Collins 1959 (1st edn 1955)

Thoday, J.M., 'Natural Selection and Biological Progress' in S.A. Barrett (ed), *A Century of Darwin*, Heinemann 1958

Thorpe, W.H., *Purpose in a World of Chance*, Oxford University Press, Oxford 1978

Tolstoy, L., *The Kingdom of God is Within You*, Oxford 1936 (1st edn 1894)

Tolstoy, L., *My Religion*, (vol.16 of *Complete Works*), Dent 1904 (1st edn 1884)

Toth, N., 'The First Technology' in *Scientific American*, April 1987, 104

Toynbee, A., *Mankind and Mother Earth*, Oxford University Press 1976

Toynbee, A., *A Study of History* (abridgement of parts I–IV), Oxford University Press 1946

Toynbee, A., *An Historian's Approach to Religion*, Oxford University Press 1956

Tsong Kha Pa, *The Principal Teachings of Buddhism* (trans Geshe L. Tharchin with M. Roach), Mahayana Sutra and Tantra Press, Hewell, N.J. 1988

Ueda, Y. (ed), *Letters of Shinran*, Honganji International Centre, Kyoto 1978

Varela, F.J., E. Thompson, and E. Rosch *The Embodied Mind*, MIT Press, Cambridge, Mass. 1991

Waddington, C.H., *The Evolution of an Evolutionist*, Edinburgh University Press, Edinburgh 1975

Waddington, C.H., *The Nature of Life*, Unwin 1963 (1st edn 1961)

Waddington, C.H., 'Evolutionary Systems, Animal and Human' in *Nature*, vol 183, 1634–8

Waddington, C.H., 'Evolutionary Adaptation' in S. Tax (ed), *The Evolution of Life* (Chicago 1960)

Walker, S., *Animal Thought*, Routledge & Kegan Paul 1983

Walshe, M., *Thus Have I Heard: The Long Discourses of the Buddha*, Wisdom 1987

Wangyal, Geshe, *The Door of Liberation*, Lotsawa, New York 1978

Warren, H.C., *Buddhism in Translations*, Harvard University Press, Cambridge, Mass. 1909

Wheeler R.E.M., in S.Piggott (ed), *The Dawn of Civilization*, Thames & Hudson, 1961

White, J. (ed), *The Highest State of Consciousness*, Anchor, Doubleday, New York 1972

Whyte, L.L., *The Next Development in Man*, New American Library, Mentor, New York 1950 (1st edn 1944)

Wiener, P.P. (ed), *Dictionary of the History of Ideas* (vol II), Scribners, New York 1973

Wilber, K., *Eye to Eye*, Shambhala, Boston 1990 (1st edn 1987)

Wilber, K., *Up from Eden: A Transpersonal View of Human Evolution*, Routledge & Kegan Paul 1983 (1st edn 1981)

Wing Tsit Chan (trans), *A Sourcebook in Chinese Philosophy*, Princeton University Press, Princeton 1963

Woodward, F.L. (trans), *Minor Anthologies of the Pali Canon*, Oxford University Press, London 1948

Woodward, F.L. (trans), *Kindred Sayings*, vol V, Pali Text Society 1979 (1st edn 1930)

Woodward, F.L. (trans), *Some Sayings of the Buddha*, Buddhist Society, Oxford University Press, London 1973

Wright, A.F., *Buddhism in Chinese History*, Stanford University Press, Stanford 1959

Young, J.Z., *An Introduction to the Study of Man*, Oxford University Press, Oxford 1971

INDEX

The Windhorse symbolizes the energy of the enlightened mind carrying the Three Jewels – the Buddha, the Dharma, and the Sangha – to all sentient beings.

Buddhism is one of the fastest growing spiritual traditions in the Western world. Throughout its 2,500-year history, it has always succeeded in adapting its mode of expression to suit whatever culture it has encountered. Windhorse Publications aims to continue this tradition as Buddhism comes to the West. Today's Westerners are heirs to the entire Buddhist tradition, free to draw instruction and inspiration from all the many schools and branches. Windhorse publishes works by authors who not only understand the Buddhist tradition but are also familiar with Western culture and the Western mind.

For orders and catalogues contact

WINDHORSE PUBLICATIONS
UNIT 1-316 THE CUSTARD FACTORY
GIBB STREET
BIRMINGHAM
B9 4AA
UK

WINDHORSE PUBLICATIONS (USA)
14 HEARTWOOD CIRCLE
NEWMARKET
NEW HAMPSHIRE
NH 03857
USA

Windhorse Publications is an arm of the Friends of the Western Buddhist Order, which has more than sixty centres on four continents. Through these centres, members of the Western Buddhist Order offer regular programmes of events for the general public and for more experienced students. These include meditation classes, public talks, study on Buddhist themes and texts, and 'bodywork' classes such as t'ai chi, yoga, and massage. The FWBO also runs several retreat centres and the Karuna Trust, a fundraising charity that supports social welfare projects in the slums and villages of India.

Many FWBO centres have residential spiritual communities and ethical businesses associated with them. Arts activities are encouraged too, as is the development of strong bonds of friendship between people who share the same ideals. In this way the FWBO is developing a unique approach to Buddhism, not simply as a set of techniques, less still as an exotic cultural interest, but as a creatively directed way of life for people living in the modern world.

If you would like more information about the FWBO please write to

LONDON BUDDHIST CENTRE
51 ROMAN ROAD
LONDON
E2 OHU
UK

ARYALOKA
HEARTWOOD CIRCLE
NEWMARKET
NEW HAMPSHIRE
NH 03857
USA

ALSO FROM WINDHORSE

SUBHUTI

SANGHARAKSHITA: A NEW VOICE IN THE BUDDHIST TRADITION

Today Buddhism is a growing force in Western life, sowing the seeds of a spiritual, cultural, philosophical, artistic, and even economic revolution. Among the personalities at the heart of this development is a remarkable Englishman: Sangharakshita.

Sangharakshita was one of the first Westerners to make the journey to the East and to don the monk's yellow robe. In India he gained unique experience in the main traditions of Buddhist teaching and practice. His involvement with the 'mass conversion' of ex-Untouchable Hindus to Buddhism exposed him to a revolutionary new experiment in social transformation. More recently he founded one of the most successful Buddhist movements in the modern world—pioneering a 'living Buddhism' that seems ideally suited to our times.

Highly respected as an outspoken writer and commentator, he has never been afraid to communicate his insights and views, even if they challenge venerated elements of Buddhist tradition.

But what are those insights and views? How have they arisen and developed? Here one of Sangharakshita's leading disciples offers an account of his evolution as a thinker and teacher.

328 pages, Index
ISBN 0 904766 68 3
£9.99, $19.95

KAMALASHILA

MEDITATION: THE BUDDHIST WAY OF TRANQUILLITY AND INSIGHT

A comprehensive guide to the methods and theory of Buddhist meditation,
written in an informal, accessible style. It provides a complete introduction
to the basic techniques, as well as detailed advice for more experienced
meditators seeking to deepen their practice.
The author is a long-standing member of the Western Buddhist Order, and
has been teaching meditation for over twenty years. In 1979 he helped to
establish a semi-monastic community in North Wales, which has now grown
into a public retreat centre. For more than a decade he and his colleagues
have been developing approaches to meditation that are firmly grounded in
Buddhist tradition but readily accessible to people with a modern Western
background. Their experience – as meditators, as students of the traditional
texts, and as teachers – is distilled in this book.
288 pages, 244 x 175, with charts and illustrations
ISBN 0 904766 56 X
Paperback £11.99/$22.99

SANGHARAKSHITA

WHO IS THE BUDDHA?

Who is the Buddha? What does it mean to be a Buddhist?
Here a leading Western Buddhist looks at these questions from several
angles. We see the Buddha in historical context, as the Indian warrior prince
who went forth in search of the truth. We see him in the context of the
evolution of the human race, in the context of karma and rebirth, in the
context of time and in the context of eternity.
Above all, we meet the Buddha as a man who struggled to understand the
mysteries of life, suffering and death. He won that understanding by
transcending human life altogether and becoming a Buddha – 'one who
knows, who is awake'. For thousands of years people in the East have been
following his path. Now it is the turn of the West.
176 pages, black and white line drawings, index
ISBN 0 904766 24 1
£6.99/$11.95

ANDREW SKILTON

A CONCISE HISTORY OF BUDDHISM

How and when did the many schools and sub-sects of Buddhism emerge?
How do the ardent devotion of the Pure Land schools, the magical ritual of
the Tantra, or the paradoxical negations of the Perfection of Wisdom
literature, relate to the direct, down to earth teachings of Gautama the
'historical' Buddha? Did Buddhism modify the cultures to which it was
introduced, or did they modify Buddhism?

Here is a narrative that decribes and correlates the diverse manifestations of
Buddhism – in its homeland of India, and in its spread across Asia, from
Mongolia to Sri Lanka, from Japan to the Middle East. Drawing on the latest
historical and literary research, Andrew Skilton explains the basic concepts
of Buddhism from all periods of its development, and places them in a
historical framework.

272 pages, maps, index, extensive bibliography
ISBN 0 904766 66 7 Paperback £9.99/$19.95

Orders and catalogues from
Windhorse Publications
Unit 1-316 The Custard Factory
Gibb Street
Birmingham
B9 4AA